# THE PAST TIMES BOOK OF
# NAVAL BLUNDERS

### GEOFFREY REGAN

*For David Coltman*

Published in Great Britain by
Guinness Publishing Ltd
338 Euston Road, London NW1 3BD

"Guinness" is a registered trademark of
Guinness Publishing Ltd.

First published 1993, Reprinted 1994 (three times), 1995 (twice), 1996 (twice), 1997 (twice), 1998

ISBN 0–85112–713–4 (Guinness Publishing)
ISBN 0–85112–076–8 (The Past Times)

A catalogue record for this book is available from the
British Library

Designed by Cathy Shilling

Picture Research by Image Select

Typeset by Ace Filmsetting Ltd, Frome, Somerset

Printed and bound in Great Britain by
The Bath Press, Bath

Front cover illustration:
The Battle of Lissa, 1866, by C.F. Sorenson (Heeregeschichtliches
    Museum, Wien)
The illustrations on pages 10 and 133 both depict the sinking of HMS *Victoria*, 1893

### Picture Acknowledgements
The Publishers wish to thank the following for permission to reproduce pictures
in this book: Archiv für Kunst und Geschichte; Image Select; Imperial War
Museum; Mary Evans Picture Library; National Maritime Museum; Peter Newark's
Military Pictures; Popperfoto.

# CONTENTS

# INTRODUCTION

Naval blunders generally have a finality that is not achieved on land. The captain who drives his ship onto rocks or into collision with other vessels is clearly to blame for the damage or loss that ensues. The fact that the elements – in the shape of storms or fogs – have made his task almost impossible, is rarely enough to save him from court-martial and disgrace. If he is a popular commander – like Sir Clowdesley Shovell – and has the wit to go down with his ship, as Shovel did in the *Association*, wrecked in the Scilly Isles – the public may overlook his errors and cloud them in a romantic aura of hopeless struggle against a relentless Nature and worthy self-sacrifice. If, however, like Sir Hovenden Walker at Louisburg in 1711, the victim is unpopular and returns like a 'half-drown'd rat' to tell the tale then neither their lordships of the Admiralty nor the great British public are likely to be merciful.

The history of war at sea is full of personal disasters, suffered by individual captains or admirals, and I have attempted to give this aspect of the subject a full coverage in this book. Peopling its pages are 19th-century eccentrics like 'Pompo' Heneage and Prothero the Bad, the redoubtable Lord Belly-Cloth and the crazy French admiral Pierre, in whom was little harm and even less ability. There are also naval 'villains' like Sir John Byng, who failed to relieve Minorca; Sir Ernest Troubridge, who failed to intercept the German battlecruiser *Goeben*; Admiral Persano, who allowed himself to be surprised and defeated at Lissa; and Vice-Admiral Richard Lestock, who refused to come to the aid of Admiral Matthews at Toulon in 1744. Cowards – surprisingly – have always found it easier to find somewhere to hide at sea than on land. In the days of sail, Benbow's villainous captains simply had to 'fight shy' of the action rather than literally run away. Others, like Admiral Albini at Lissa, had only to misunderstand or misinterpret orders. In the book there are bunglers too, like Ralph Seymour, whose signals robbed Admiral Beatty of victory at the battle of the Dogger Bank in 1915, and Admiral Plumridge who spent much of his time, like some latter-day Viking, destroying British property by mistake.

Yet personal or individual failure at sea were often merely reflections of the inefficiency of the Admiralty, which sent fleets into action undermanned, underfed, armed with inadequate weapons, on 'wild-goose-chases' or even suicide missions. In such cases the commanders and their men were victims of bureaucratic muddle or political interference. Sometimes the wrong man was appointed for the job – like Admiral Price at Petropavlovsk, Tom Phillips at Singapore or the pugnacious Codrington at Navarino. Sometimes the wrong ship was selected for the task – the choice of the *Hood* to face the *Bismarck* has to be the worst error of this kind. Most ridiculous of all, sometimes the wrong task is set for the ships available. In this category Duckworth's struggle through the Dardanelles in 1807 was only a forerunner of the much more disastrous operation in 1915, which still failed to convince naval opinion that ships come out second best when fighting forts. Sometimes the 'price of Admiralty' was no more than a Gilbertian farce – like 'Operation Menace' sent to Dakar in 1940 – but more often it was tragic, like the scattering of Convoy PQ17, the failure to rescue the crew of the stricken *Indianapolis* or the squandering of many young lives in the *Aboukir*, *Hogue* and *Cressy* on the Broad Fourteens in 1914. Nor have Admiralty designers been free from responsibility for naval disasters. Faulty ship design – comical in the French battleship *Hoche* and the Russian circular ironclads – was tragic in the British battlecruisers sent into action at Jutland in 1916 as little more than floating coffins.

Life at sea has never been easy; a life on the ocean wave was not for the weak or the squeamish. Yet much of the suffering was unnecessary and imposed by ignorant and sadistic tyrants. As on land, disease was always a bigger killer than enemy action. Yet little effort was made to improve living conditions, quality of food or shore leave. Venereal disease, scurvy, yellow fever and typhus were the scourge of sailors well into the 19th century. Even though it was well known that to maintain fleets for any length of time in the Caribbean was little less than a death sentence for their crews, Britain continued to squander thousands of lives there both at sea and ashore during the 17th and 18th centuries. Admiral Hosier's grim story speaks volumes for the ignorance of the Admiralty administrators. Nor can the famous and triumphant circumnavigation by Anson remain gilt-edged in history books, when its cost in human suffering is set in the balance. Those sailors who did not die from disease or the appalling food and rum, suffered such ill-treatment at the hands of officers responsible for maintaining discipline in the Royal Navy that it would have made Oriental potentates – no strangers themselves to brutality – sick in the stomach. Britain – cradle of democracy and parliamentary government – continued to treat its sailors worse than Brazilian slave owners or Arab slave traders treated their victims, well into the 19th century. In the War of 1812 between Britain and the United States, it is ironic to note how many British sailors deserted His Majesty's ships to serve in the navy of the new United States of America, where conditions were fairer. And it was these men who provided the stiffening that enabled American crews to beat their British opponents on so many occasions. Such men did not see themselves as traitors so much as liberated slaves, unwilling to labour under the lash.

In the present century the submarine and the development of naval air power have produced a revolution in naval warfare. In both world wars Britain's failure to come to terms with the threat from beneath the waves brought her close to defeat. Yet though the opponents of the submarine blundered by failing to appreciate its threat, all did not go smoothly for the submariners. Sometimes it was the fault of the submarine – as in the case of the incredible British 'K' ships – and sometimes it was their weaponry, as with the appallingly inefficient German torpedoes in 1939 and 1940. Properly equipped, the U-boats might have crippled the British capacity to continue the war after the evacuation from Dunkirk.

All ship losses are tragic yet history has recorded a number of incidents which have earned special notoriety. Sometimes the fault lay with the captain or crew – as with King Henry I's White Ship or the *Royal George*. On other occasions the ship's loss was due to faulty design, as with the *Vasa* or the *Mary Rose*. Collisions as well as the elements have added to the toll of shipping losses. There have been few more remarkable collisions in naval history than that between the *Victoria* and the *Camperdown*. In this case, an admiral of impeccable qualities made an error so basic that it would have been astonishing had it been made by a midshipman. Admiral Tryon's blunder is proof, if proof be needed, that no man is immune from error. Tryon had not been promoted beyond his level of competence like so many commanders in this book. He was worthy of his rank as few men had been before him. Yet obedience to orders was bred into Tryon, and into his second-in-command, Rear-Admiral Markham, as into all naval officers at that time. It would have taken a Nelson, a Blake, a Hood, or a Rodney to have disobeyed orders to win a victory or avoid a disaster. Markham was not in the Nelson mould – and neither was Tryon. Tryon was God-like in his efficiency but he was also unloved because he was unlovable. So far above his men did he seem that they feared to question him. He had created no 'band of brothers' like Nelson; instead he had surrounded himself with unquestioning acolytes. It was not what he had sought but it was what he got. And so a disaster took place not because an officer was incapable but because he seemed too capable.

In the first part of the book I have been concerned with themes of naval incompetence, while in the second I have dealt with a number of famous battles or naval disasters which illustrate the many forms that naval blunders can take. Some are amusing, some poignant, some tragic, but all are – I hope – instructive. And all of them remind us that war – on sea or on land – is a complex activity in which the human ability is stretched to breaking point as in no other activity in which humans have indulged.

## THE VOYAGE OF THE DAMNED (1905)

The 18,000-mile voyage of the Russian Baltic Fleet to face the Japanese at Tsushima in 1905 is one of the epics of naval warfare. However, for much of the journey it was only the strength and determination of its commander, Admiral Rozhestvensky, that prevented it from dissolving into farce. It was as if Rozhestvensky was cast as the Flying Dutchman in Wagner's opera, condemned to sail the oceans of the world, while the other parts were played by the Marx brothers. There was even a comic subplot provided by the fleet repair ship, *Kamchatka*, which could be relied upon for a laugh even at the most serious moments.

The Russo-Japanese War had broken out when, without any formal declaration of war, Japan made a pre-emptive strike against the Russian Far East Fleet. On the night of 8 February 1904, the Japanese torpedoed two battleships and a cruiser at Port Arthur. From that moment onwards Japan kept a tight grip on the seas which the Russians were never able to break. When they did try to break out of port in August, they suffered a resounding defeat at the battle of the Yellow Sea. Rather than convincing the Russian government that the war was lost, this setback only seemed to make them more determined, and they reached the extraordinary decision that their Baltic Fleet – to be renamed the Second Pacific Squadron – should sail most of the way round the world to meet an enemy who had already defeated a naval squadron stronger than itself. To make matters worse, between the Gulf of Finland and Port Arthur there were no Russian bases, and the ports of neutral nations and even those of Russia's ally, France, would be closed to them. To supply the immense amounts of coal needed by the fleet – half a million tons – Admiral Rozhestvensky had to rely on prearranged meetings at sea with 60 colliers of the German Hamburg–Amerika line, and the length of the journey would mean that his 40 warships would need to recoal on as many as 30 occasions, each time in the open sea, subject to wild weather and heavy waves. Yet, making light of every obstacle, the Russian government sent Rozhestvensky forth on his odyssey.

For all the impressive appearance of Rozhestvensky's quartet of battleships – *Kniaz Suvoroff*, *Borodino*, *Alexander III* and *Oryol* – the strength of the Russian fleet was more apparent than real. Like many battleships built at this time they were top heavy – 1,500 tons above specification – the result of their long gestation period during which every new gadget and device was added to their superstructure regardless of its effect on stability. One of the results was that in heavy seas the secondary armament could not be used, another that the main armour

A group of Russian naval officers during the Russo-Japanese War. Their hopes of regaining mastery of the seas from the Japanese were to be crushed with the sinking of two-thirds of the Russian fleet in the Straits of Tsushima.

belt was actually below the water line and thus no defence against enemy shells. The *Oryol* had actually sunk at anchor in Kronstadt Harbour a year before because of a mechanical fault, and had to be refloated. So top heavy, indeed, were these ships that the admiral was warned not even to raise flag signals – and definitely not celebratory bunting. Not that there would be much to celebrate.

If the ships looked better than they were, the crews did not even look good in the first place. Few were drawn from the coastal, seafaring parts of Russia; most of the sailors were simply untutored peasants, who received little training at sea as the Baltic was iced over for half the year. With the greater technical demands of modern sea warfare the lack of education of the Russian sailors was a particular drawback. During one training exercise Rozhestvensky sprang a surprise alarm – 'defence against torpedo attack'. He waited on the bridge of his flagship but nothing happened – no men took up their posts – for everyone, officers and men, was fast asleep. One British sailor described the Russians he met as 'odorous, rough, coarse but a happy lot'. An officer aboard the *Suvoroff* complained about his gunners: 'One half have to be taught everything because they know nothing; the other half because they have forgotten everything;

but if they do remember anything, then it is obsolete.' What nobody could have guessed at the outset was that some of the seamen were revolutionaries, who tried to foment unrest among the crews. It was not a happy situation for any commander. Nor was Rozhestvensky very happy about his senior officers, describing the obese Rear-Admiral Fölkersam, his second-in-command, as 'a manure sack', and Rear-Admiral Enkvist, who commanded the cruisers, as 'a vast empty space'.

As the fleet left the Russian Baltic port of Libau on 16 October, the flagship set the pattern for the entire journey by running aground, and a cruiser lost her anchor, wasting hours trying to locate it. While this was going on a destroyer rammed the battleship *Oslyaba* and had to return to Reval for repairs. But once these wrinkles had been smoothed out the fleet moved peacefully into the narrow waters between Denmark and Sweden. Here reports that the Japanese had torpedo boats stationed along the Danish coast meant that the Russians were continually on the lookout for spies, saboteurs or indeed Japanese warships disguised as trawlers or yachts. Their paranoia helps to explain the events of the next few days. The Russian government had paid its agents huge sums of money to prevent any more Japanese surprise attacks. A certain Captain Hartling had been sent to organize counter-espionage in Copenhagen, where he inhabited a fantasy world of spies and secret weapons, and from which he transmitted daily to the fleet. Everyone, it seemed, was against them and the seas were awash with Japanese mines, submarines and especially torpedo boats. The mass hallucinations on the part of the Russian crews are more suitable as the subject of a psychological study than military history. Against this background Rozhestvensky ordered that 'no vessel of any sort whatever must be allowed to get in amongst the fleet'. When two fishermen were sent out by a Russian consular official to deliver a telegram to the flagship they were nearly blown out of the water by the trigger-happy Russians. In fact, the telegram informed Rozhestvensky that he had been promoted to Vice-Admiral by Tsar Nicholas. Other terrors for the Russians were two silvery balloons seen in the distance but never traced afterwards, which convinced the fleet that the Japanese were observing their every move. As if to lighten the gloom the *Kamchatka* – self-appointed fleet comedian – reported that she was under attack by torpedo boats. When Rozhestvensky asked how many, the vessel replied, 'About eight. From all directions.' Naturally it was a false alarm – but fleet comedians are like that.

Once in the North Sea Rozhestvensky almost brought about a war between Russia and Great Britain. Identifying the Hull trawler fleet as Japanese torpedo boats, the Russians let fly with everything they had. Pandemonium broke loose. The trawlers, known as the Gamecock Fleet, were tiny 100-ton vessels out of Hull, carrying a crew of eight and fishing on the Dogger Bank. How the Russians could have identified them as Japanese warships is beyond comprehension. Some Russian ships claimed they had actually been hit by torpedoes though in the light of dawn there were no signs of any damage. It was another case of mass hysteria. Some sailors on the battleship *Borodino* actually donned lifebelts and jumped overboard; others lay prone on the decks with their hands over their ears. Some even ran around the decks wielding cutlasses and shouting that the Japanese were boarding them. Meanwhile, the big guns of the battleships kept firing at the trawlers, damaging four and sinking one, as well as inflicting hits on each other – the cruiser *Aurora* had four hits below the waterline and the ship's chaplain was cut in half by a shell. As soon as he realized his mistake Rozhestvensky was like a man possessed, throwing overboard one of his own gunners who was continuing to fire at a damaged trawler. The truth dawned with the coming light. It had been a night of madness, with seven battleships in line firing at the cruisers *Aurora* and *Donskoy*. Fortunately the gunnery had been deplorable – the *Oryol* fired over 500 shells without scoring a hit. But how would the British react to this unprovoked assault on their fishermen? The British press worked itself into a fury of jingoistic hatred for Russia and demanded war, while the German newspaper *Berliner Tageblatt* wrote that the Russian commander must have lost his mind.

Although the Russian government made an official apology Britain was slow to forgive. Twenty-eight British battleships raised steam and prepared for action, while swarms of British cruisers shadowed Rozhestvensky's fleet as it moved fearfully across the Bay of Biscay and down the coast of Portugal. The diplomatic storm caught up with Rozhestvensky at Vigo, where he was ordered to leave behind those of his officers who had been responsible for the attack on the trawlers. The admiral took the opportunity of leaving behind his most bitter enemy, Captain Klado. As Klado left the *Suvoroff,* another officer was heard to say, 'I see the rats are leaving the sinking ship.' But Klado was to get his revenge on Rozhestvensky when he returned to St Petersburg to organize reinforcements for the Second Pacific Squadron. Anything would do, however unfit and derelict it might be. After all, it would increase the number of targets the Japanese would have to fire at. Klado knew that Rozhestvensky had previously condemned these 'old tubs' as worthless and nothing more than a millstone, which would hold back the rest of the fleet. Jokingly he had called them the 'sink-by-themselves' squadron. But, like it or not, he was going to get them.

When the fleet reached Tangier the *Kamchatka*, which had been detached for some days, caught up and excitedly reported to Rozhestvensky that she had survived the battle in the North Sea, having fired 300 shells in a tussle with three Japanese ships, and vehemently denying that these had in fact been a Swedish merchantman, a German trawler and a French schooner. Before leaving Tangier one of the Russian vessels fouled the underwater telegraph cable with her anchor and cut off communication between the city and Europe for four days.

At Dakar, in West Africa, ten German colliers awaited Rozhestvensky's fleet. Double loads of coal were taken on board each ship; this had to be stored on the decks and the dust spread everywhere. In the heat of the Equator, life became hell for the crews of the Russian ships. The atmosphere resembled a mine shaft and men died, choking in the filthy air. During a storm off the coast of Angola, presumably to keep up the spirits of the fleet, the *Kamchatka* signalled to the flagship, 'Do you see torpedo boats?' A general alarm was sounded throughout the fleet until the repair ship admitted it had used the wrong code and had simply meant, 'We are all right now.'

At Cape Town Rozhestvensky received news that Klado was sending the 'sink-by-themselves' squadron to join him and so he decided to do everything in his power to avoid a rendezvous with them. He was furious: 'If they are so old that they can't steam then they may go to the devil. We have no use for rubbish here.' Meanwhile, discipline among the men of the squadron reached an all-time low. Certain by now that they were sailing to destruction, the Russian sailors tried to take their minds off the future by indulging in all kinds of exotic pursuits, most popular of which was bringing pets back with them from shore visits. Unfortunately some of the pets were unsuited to long sea voyages – like the crocodile brought back aboard one battleship, and the poisonous snake which bit and nearly killed one of the engineers. On another ship monkeys and dogs, first primed with champagne, were set to fight each other. The whole fleet resounded to a curious babel of farmyard noises, as pigs, cows, sheep – not to mention the parrots, porcupines, chameleons, frogs and so forth – rushed around the decks, squealing, mooing, barking and squawking, turning the Second Pacific Squadron into a floating zoo. One pet goat lived only on paper, with a predilection for visiting cards. On a shore visit it refused an offer of hay and instead ate a Frenchman's newspaper.

Rotting meat had to be thrown overboard when the refrigeration ship *Espérance* broke

The Russian battleship *Oryol* prior to her epic seven-month voyage to Tsushima. The *Oryol* and her sister ships were poorly constructed and were no match for the Japanese Admiral Togo's British-made flagship *Mikasa*.

down, with the result that the fleet was surrounded by swarms of sharks. For two weeks at Madagascar Admiral Rozhestvensky stayed in his cabin suffering from acute neuralgia, while his Chief of Staff had a brain haemorrhage and was partly paralyzed. Nobody really commanded the fleet and the Russians spent increasing amounts of time ashore at a makeshift city – known as Hellville – which sprang up to cater for their needs. Saloons, gambling houses and brothels flourished. Meanwhile, barnacles smothered the hulls of the ships and their speed was cut by the sea grass which grew there and trailed behind them as they sailed.

Disease was rife in the fleet. Malaria, dysentery and typhoid took their toll and funeral services were a daily event. The *Kamchatka* did what she could to relieve the gloom of these occasions. A shell she fired to honour one of her dead turned out to be live and ricocheted off the unfortunate and long-suffering cruiser *Aurora*, which seemed to be the butt of all the fleet's jokes. Lunatics abounded, overcome by the long period at sea. Some men roamed the decks in a kind of religious fervour, believing they saw the Day of Judgment at hand; others merely muttering things like 'Do you fear death?' A young officer wrote to his wife in Russia, 'If, by God's grace, I ever see you again, I shall have things to tell you past belief or imagining.' The worst cases – along with mutineers and revolutionaries from the *Admiral Nakhimov* – were sent back to Russia on the *Malay*.

Rozhestvensky's greatest problem was to maintain the fleet in tip-top fighting condition. Yet his officers were frequently drunk or drugged. One who had bought 2,000 cigarettes in Nossi-Bé found that they were filled with opium. The admiral needed to be resupplied with shells because so many had been expended in the battle with the trawlers. Expectations were high, therefore, when the supply ship *Irtysh* arrived, supposedly carrying shells from the battleships' main armaments. In the sweltering African heat the sailors had to unload the cargo which turned out to be 12,000 pairs of fur-lined boots and a similar number of Russian winter coats.

At gunnery practice Rozhestvensky, who had been renowned for his gunnery as a young officer, watched while his destroyers scored not one single hit on a stationary target. When the battleships joined in, his flagship managed just one hit, which was on the ship towing the target. The gunnery hoist of one battleship jammed because there was a cobra wrapped around the rope. A formation of destroyers, ordered to form line abreast, scattered in every direction because they had not been issued with the new code books. The torpedoes were even worse: of seven that were fired, one jammed, while two swung at right angles to port, one at right angles to starboard, two chugged slowly ahead but missed the target, and the last went round in circles causing all the ships to scatter in panic. The *Kamchatka*, robbed of her chance to join in these capers, signalled instead that she was sinking. Further investigation revealed a cracked pipe in the engine room.

Meanwhile, Klado's reinforcements had sailed from Reval under the gentle and frail Admiral Nebogatoff. How this old man felt about his mission is not recorded but his whole performance in the weeks to come breathed a refreshing air of humanity and common sense into the affair. All the Admiralty could tell him was that Rozhestvensky was currently at Madagascar; further than that they knew nothing. They were aware that the commander of the Second Pacific Squadron had no intention of rendezvousing with Nebogatoff's 'archaeo-logical collection of naval architecture'. Few admirals can ever have set sail with such vague instructions as, 'You are to join up with Rozhestvensky, whose route is unknown to us . . .' For Nebogatoff it became an exercise in detective work, in which he had to enquire at neutral ports for news of the main fleet and plot his course accordingly. For Rozhestvensky it was as if nemesis followed him in the shape of these 'ghost ships'.

Rozhestvensky suffered the final insult when he read in a newspaper that St Petersburg had ordered him to destroy the Japanese Fleet, sail on to Vladivostok, and there hand over command to Admiral Biriloff, who was travelling to the Russian Pacific port by the Trans-Siberian Railway. Biriloff, known as 'the fighting Admiral', had never even been in action.

After crossing the Indian Ocean the fleet was met by one of their transports, the *Gortchakoff*, which it was hoped would be bringing letters from home. The mood aboard the Russian ships lifted at the thought of hearing from their loved ones. But it was soon dashed when it was found the transport was still carrying the letters the sailors had sent home from Madagascar a month before. This was too much. The Russians felt completely abandoned and nobody more than their commander. But help was coming – even though it was as unwelcome as an attack by Japanese torpedo boats – the Third Pacific Squadron, the floating dead, were about to join them. On 11 May, off the coast of Indo-China, the two fleets met. Although Rozhestvensky did not welcome the new arrivals, at least they brought news from home: of unrest, mutiny and revolution.

Rozhestvensky was nearing the end of his voyage. In many ways he had achieved a miracle in getting this far and it was not his fault that the ships and crews that were being sent against the Japanese were not adequate to their task. He had known this from early on but had stuck at his job like an admiral going down with his ship. In a sense the whole voyage resembled a protracted sinking, and only through his iron personality had the Russian commander managed to stave off the final cataclysm. But the stress of command had worn away his health, and by the time he met the ebullient and immensely confident Japanese Admiral Togo at Tsushima – the island aptly named the 'Donkey's Ears' – he had accepted fate's decree that he should be the victim. The destruction of the Russian fleet that followed was a one-sided encounter in which the Japanese achieved one of the most crushing victories in naval history. Rozhestvensky was even denied the chance to perish with his flagship, being plucked wounded from the sea and taken to a Japanese hospital where he was later visited by Togo himself. On his return to Russia he found himself – as he had expected – to be the scapegoat. Witnesses had reported that during the battle Rozhestvensky had been delirious, but he was long past that stage. It was fatalism that commanded the Russian fleet at Tsushima. And fate had not quite finished laughing at Rozhestvensky. While staying at a hotel in St Petersburg in 1908, he received a telegram giving details of a requiem service in his memory to be held in the city. Apparently he was dead – and nobody had bothered to tell him.

# Part I

# CHAPTER 1: LUNATIC ADMIRALS

In the long history of the British Admiralty their Lordships have encountered numerous strange problems and many eccentric officers. But rarely – one might even venture the words 'never before' – had they had to deal with the deification of one of their junior officers. And yet the more one finds out about Lieutenant-Commander Geoffrey B. Spicer-Simpson the more one is left wondering why his deification took so long in coming. In every way Spicer-Simpson was a 'larger than life' character. As surely as Alice had to adapt herself to some strange experiences in 'Wonderland', so the members of the Lake Tanganyika Expedition of 1915 needed to come to terms with the world seen through the eyes of Bwana Chifunga-tumbo, Lord Belly-Cloth.

## Lord Belly-Cloth, D.S.O.

In August 1914 Lake Tanganyika formed a boundary between German East Africa to the east, the Belgian Congo to the west, and the British colony of Northern Rhodesia to the south. When war broke out in Europe, control of the lake became of vital importance for the Germans. They employed two gunboats – the 100-ton *Hedwig von Wissermann* and the smaller *Kingani* – to sweep all Belgian shipping from the lake. Even worse, and unknown to the British, they were nearing completion of the 800-ton *Graf von Götzen*. While Britannia might be said to 'rule the waves' there could be no doubt that on the waters of Lake Tanganyika *Deutschland* was definitely *über alles*.

Although a distant field of conflict, the war in East Africa was conducted with great energy by the British and with great skill by the Germans, led by Paul von Lettow-Vorbeck. The danger, from the Allied point of view, was that by controlling Lake Tanganyika the Germans might be able to foment unrest amongst the natives of the weakly governed Belgian Congo. To remove this threat a big-game hunter by the name of John Lee presented the Admiralty with an amazing plan to gain control of the lake by transporting a large motorboat by sea, road and rail across Africa to within 120 miles of its shores. After this, the boat could be dragged by oxen-trains over hills and mountains and then refloated on the Belgian shores of Lake Tanganyika. The First Sea Lord Sir Henry Jackson resisted his first reaction (which was to have Lee thrown out in the street), and decided that he liked the idea. Sir Henry felt that it might just work, and that 'it is both the duty and the tradition of the Royal Navy to engage the enemy wherever there is water to float a ship'. The plan was now taken up by Admiral Sir David Gamble, who added a second boat to the expedition. Lee was given the rank of lieutenant-commander in the Royal Naval Volunteer Reserve, but Gamble insisted that there must be a real naval officer in charge of the expedition. With every worthwhile officer serving at sea where could the Admiralty find a man suitable to lead such a 'madcap venture'? Then someone thought of Lieutenant-Commander Geoffrey B. Spicer-Simpson, at that moment pushing a pen in a dusty corner of the Intelligence Department. It was scraping the barrel, Gamble agreed, but Spicer-Simpson seemed keen to go.

Paul von Lettow-Vorbeck (second from right), shown here in relaxed frame of mind in a pre-war photograph, was to lead a brilliant German guerrilla campaign in East Africa during the First World War. It was to break his control of Lake Tanganyika that Lieutenant-Commander Spicer-Simpson led an expedition to Africa in 1915.

The future Lord Belly-Cloth had not enjoyed a very distinguished naval career up to that moment. He had once commanded a destroyer but had been removed for ramming another vessel, after which he was given the soul-destroying task of dockside security. As the oldest lieutenant-commander in the navy he was well aware that his career was going nowhere until, with the outbreak of war, he was given another chance and sent to command a flotilla of two gunboats and six armed tugs. However, within two weeks he had been sacked again for anchoring his vessels where he had been advised not to and having one of his gunboats torpedoed while he was ashore in a hotel with a woman. His future looked black indeed but he was not a man to stay depressed for long. He was always certain that something would 'turn up' – and it did.

Yet Spicer-Simpson was not the kind of eccentric beloved of a long line of English humorists from Laurence Sterne to Evelyn Waugh. Apparently it was far more pleasant to read of his antics, or hear of them from others, than to meet the man in the flesh. For Spicer-Simpson – a huge, muscular man with a pointed beard, who loved browbeating waiters and people from a lower class than himself – was a self-seeker, a liar and a sadist, whose eccentricity bordered on insanity. His sense of humour was very individual. When presented with his two launches

– requisitioned from the Greek Air Force – Admiral Jackson asked him to name them as they only had numbers and were 'not convicts'. Spicer-Simpson was not amused and called them 'Dog' and 'Cat'. The First Sea Lord was disappointed at this – presumably expecting them to be dubbed something more appropriate like 'Thunderer' or 'Conqueror' – and asked the expedition commander to come up with something better. 'Mimi' and 'Toutou' was Spicer-Simpson's next effort; the Admiralty gave up and the names were adopted. Both *Mimi* and *Toutou* were to carry a single 3-pounder gun and would have a top speed of 15 knots.

Once the expedition reached Cape Town some of Spicer-Simpson's less pleasant characteristics began to surface. The big-game hunter Lee had gone ahead to survey the route and Spicer-Simpson had sent one of his cronies, Sub-Lieutenant Douglas Hope, with him to help. In fact, Hope was there to spy on Lee and in due course he reported back to Spicer-Simpson that Lee had been arrested when drunk, had given away details of the expedition and had insulted the Belgian authorities. None of this was true but it was all that Spicer-Simpson needed to wire the Admiralty that he had been forced to dismiss Lee and replace him with Hope. With Lee gone Spicer-Simpson seemed very much relieved. Everywhere the expedition went the commander embarrassed his men by singing aloud and telling outrageous stories of his strength and his achievements as a big-game hunter. Once in Belgian territory he began boasting that as a destroyer captain he had once sunk a German cruiser. At this stage his behaviour was more boorish than dangerous but on arriving at the lake his eccentricity increased dangerously. First he began flying the flag of a vice-admiral, to which he said he was entitled, and then he started wearing skirts which he claimed he had designed for himself and had his wife make. The Belgians laughingly called him *'le commandant à la jupe'*, to which Spicer-Simpson took great offence, insisting, for some reason, that they call him *'mon colonel'*. When the British sailors tried to celebrate Christmas and hung up decorations, Spicer-Simpson exploded, 'What's this? A whorehouse? Take all that down and burn it.'

The Germans, meanwhile, had heard rumours that there were English ships on the lake. At first they could not believe that it was possible for the ships to have been hauled over the Mitumba Range of mountains but when the gunboat *Kingani* came too close to the port of Lukuga, where *Mimi* and *Toutou* were based, they were astounded when the two vessels came roaring out at full speed with their white ensigns flying. The first battle of Lake Tanganyika was about to take place.

Spicer-Simpson in *Mimi* attacked from one side and Lieutenant Arthur Dudley, commanding *Toutou*, from the other. The German boat was larger than either of the British launches and its 6-pounder gun could have blown them out of the water, but the British closed in to point-blank range and scored a decisive hit on the *Kingani*'s wheelhouse, blowing the German captain and several of his crew to pieces. Soon a white cloth was being waved to indicate that the *Kingani* wished to surrender. Unfortunately, *Mimi* was being steered by an ex-army lance-corporal whose navigational skills were rather basic. As Spicer-Simpson closed in to accept the German surrender, *Mimi* rammed into the *Kingani* to the great amusement of the watching Belgians, who thought it an unorthodox way of taking a prize at sea. On board the German vessel there were scenes of terrible carnage as well as one unexpected prisoner – a tethered goat, which was adopted by the British as a mascot. A young naval petty officer, scorning the incompetence of the lance-corporal, took over the *Kingani* and steered her towards the shore. Unfortunately he ran her aground and promptly fainted. It had been a hard day.

In spite of the doubts that had been expressed by many people before the action Spicer-Simpson had triumphed: the first part of his task had been achieved and he celebrated by cutting off the German commander's ring finger, wearing the ring and keeping the finger in a bottle.

When the news of victory reached the Admiralty in London there was first astonishment and then a smug feeling that such triumphs were only to be expected of a British naval officer. Spicer-Simpson was confirmed in his rank of commander, dated from the day of his triumph on the lake, and Dudley was made a full lieutenant. But this was only the first round: two far bigger German ships awaited the tiny British flotilla.

Spicer-Simpson's success seemed to have impressed the native Ba-HoloHolo people as much as it did the British Admiralty. Having seen him triumph in battle and slaughter his fellow white men they began to exhibit every sign of worshipping him as a god. Spicer-Simpson encouraged them and took to bathing in public, smoking and drinking vermouth while his African servant poured water down his body. What made this white man even more astounding in native eyes was that he seemed to be adorned from head to foot with tattoos of snakes, birds, flowers and insects. When it was bath-time he would arrive with a towel around his waist and entertain the Ba-HoloHolo by flexing his biceps and making the snakes on them wriggle. While his men watched in embarrassed silence – and a Belgian missionary accused him of 'demoralizing Africa' – Spicer-Simpson performed wonders for his adherents, who thereupon named him Lord Belly-Cloth because of his bath-towel.

Meanwhile, British and Belgian engineers had rebuilt the damaged *Kingani* and equipped her with the 12-pounder gun she would need if she was to meet either of the powerful German vessels on the lake. No sooner had she been completed than the second German contestant entered the ring – the *Hedwig von Wissmann* – armed with two 6-pounder guns. At once the *Kingani* – renamed *Fifi* by the ever resourceful Spicer-Simpson – steamed out to battle, accompanied on this occasion just by *Mimi*. But the second battle of Lake Tanganyika was a very different affair from the first. For a start Spicer-Simpson in *Fifi* could not keep pace with the German vessel as it fled from the British flotilla and when Sub-Lieutenant Wainwright, commanding *Mimi*, kept up the chase, leaving Spicer-Simpson behind, Lord Belly-Cloth was furious and ordered him back. But Wainwright simply ignored the commander and kept after the German, at last managing to hit her with his 3-pounder and slow her down. This enabled *Fifi* to catch up. Unfortunately Spicer-Simpson had used up all but three of his shells for his 12-pounder in trying futile long shots. The commander knew that he had just three shots with which to achieve an even greater triumph than before. But his next shot misfired and everyone had to wait a nerve-jangling 20 minutes before they dared to remove the unexploded shell from the breech. Loading the penultimate shell, and taking careful aim, the *Fifi*'s gunner sent the shot straight into the engine room of the *Hedwig von Wissmann*, ripping her open and sinking her in minutes.

Naturally the question of Wainwright's insubordination was overlooked and Spicer-Simpson took all the credit for this new triumph. In London Sir Henry Jackson was beside himself with joy: 'I doubt whether any one tactical operation of such miniature proportions has exercised so important an influence on enemy operations.' But Spicer-Simpson was now betraying a marked tendency to rest on his laurels. He had done well so far, far better if the truth be told than even he could have imagined. Now the biggest challenge of all – the 800-ton *Graf von Götzen* – needed to be faced and he felt uneasy for the first time. When Lieutenant Dudley urged him to take his chance and attack the German vessel, Spicer-Simpson found eminently good reasons to withdraw from the lake. Morale in the British party began to drop as the truth dawned on them: Spicer-Simpson might be a god to the natives but he had feet of clay to them.

Next the British commander decided that he must leave the port of Lukuga, and travel 1,600 miles down the River Congo on the pretext of checking on other vessels which might join his flotilla. It was a thin excuse while the *Graf von Götzen* continued to dominate the lake. He did not return for three months and when he did arrive back at Lukuga it was only just in time to prevent a combined Anglo–Belgian attack on the *Graf von Götzen*. He refused to cooperate with any further Belgian operations and took *Mimi*, *Fifi* and *Toutou* to the south of the lake where he insisted he was needed to assist a British thrust from Northern Rhodesia towards Bismarckburg (now Kasanga). As his flotilla travelled south the British sailors, who had achieved so much with such limited resources, knew that they were sailing away from the real target for which they had come to Africa. If they could sink the *Graf von Götzen* they would have won complete control of Lake Tanganyika. Anything else was a mere sideshow. But their commander's nerve had failed him at the moment of victory and he feared to lose the reputation he had so surprisingly gained.

If Spicer-Simpson had expected to be welcomed by the Rhodesian forces under Lieutenant Colonel Ronald 'Kaffir' Murray he was in for a disappointment. Murray could not see how the naval flotilla could be of any use to him and regarded the tattooed and skirted British naval officer as faintly disgusting. Eventually he asked Spicer-Simpson if he would cover the German escape route from Bismarckburg, which Lord Belly-Cloth agreed to do. He found the attitude of the Rhodesians – who shouted things at him like 'Kiss me, Gertie' and 'Chase me Charlie' – disconcerting for someone of his exalted reputation.

Spicer-Simpson and Dudley took the flotilla up to Bismarcksburg, where the Germans kept a collection of dhows and canoes for transporting troops. In the event of Murray capturing the town these boats might be used by the Germans to effect their escape. Dudley implored Spicer-Simpson to sink these vessels but he refused to risk the fire from the German guns and sailed back to his base at Kituta without firing a shot. He stayed there overnight but by the time he returned to Bismarckburg he found that the fort was in British hands and the German garrison had escaped – in their dhows and canoes. The Rhodesian rank and file ridiculed the navy men, calling 'Where the hell were you navy chaps last night?' But Colonel Murray was far from amused and tore into Spicer-Simpson to such effect that the latter took to his bed and handed over command to Dudley and Wainwright. He was plainly in decline and, on the excuse of suffering from malaria and dysentery, he returned to England.

Back at the Admiralty their lordships listened in rapture to the revelations of their one-time desk clerk. With nobody to question his version of events Spicer-Simpson had a field day, even convincing everyone that his failure to take on the *Graf von Götzen* was only because the Germans had refused to come out and fight. Decorations were lavished on the whole naval expedition when it returned – Spicer-Simpson himself receiving the D.S.O. and the Belgian *Croix de Guerre* with three palms. But there was soon to be a reckoning and as reports came into the Admiralty from other sources – Belgian and Rhodesian included – it became obvious that Spicer-Simpson's part in affairs had been far less laudable than they had been led to believe. His three months' absence without leave, his dereliction of duty at Bismarckburg and his tactless behaviour with Britain's Belgian allies soon tarnished the medals on his broad chest. His fall was massive and immediate. From a god to the Ba-HoloHolo people he became an office-clerk once again, in a dusty, gloomy room at the base of the mighty structure which, only months before, had echoed with his praises. In the final analysis he had failed to free Lake Tanganyika, and the mighty *Graf von Götzen* remained supreme on the lake until its guns were removed by Lettow-Vorbeck for use by his *Schutztruppen*. Yet few men leave so much of themselves behind them and the legend of Lord Belly-Cloth ensured Spicer-Simpson a kind of immortality – if not with the British Admiralty, at least with the Ba-HoloHolo people of the former Belgian Congo.

# Admiral Pierre and the Case of the Drugged Wine

The mental health, or otherwise, of leading naval figures has long been a matter for discussion. Where it takes the form of eccentricity unaccompanied by incapacity – as in the notable case of 'Pompo', Admiral Sir Algernon Charles Fiesché Heneage – it can be a source of some entertainment. But where it drives an individual to imperil peaceful relations between Britain and France, as over Madagascar in 1883, one is compelled to take a more serious view. Thus the mysterious case of Rear-Admiral Pierre and the 'Drugged Wine' earns its place in the annals of naval incompetence.

In April 1883 a powerful French naval squadron under the command of Rear-Admiral Pierre, flying his flag in the cruiser *La Flore* and asserting national rights under a treaty dating from the time of Richelieu, began a bombardment of coastal towns in Madagascar. On 31 May Pierre arrived off the capital, Tamatave, and issued an ultimatum to the Hova government there. If they failed to surrender all of Madagascar north of the 16th parallel, Pierre warned, he would open fire on their defenceless capital. The British consul in Tamatave, Mr Pakenham – who was seriously ill at the time – tried to remonstrate with the French but was curtly told to mind his own business. Captain Johnstone of the British sloop *Dryad*, which happened to be in harbour at the time, ordered the British nationals in Tamatave to take refuge on board his vessel. But Pakenham was not prepared to be driven from his consulate in this way and he asked Johnstone to send 20 British sailors from the *Dryad* to guard the consulate building. The French admiral was furious at this British 'invasion' and demanded that Johnstone remove the *Dryad* from the harbour. Johnstone bowed to the French pressure and anchored a little further away. When the ultimatum expired without the Hova giving in to Pierre's demands, the French began their bombardment. It was a curious affair since there were no Hova troops to fire at, and the French concentrated on the empty fort at Tamatave, which had no guns and did not even fly the Madagascan flag. For two hours six large French warships battered the fort with shells before shifting to the now deserted town. The native houses were built of straw and thatched with leaves so, not surprisingly, fires broke out in all directions. On *La Flore* Pierre insisted that these fires were the work of Hova incendiaries helped by the sailors guarding the British consulate. While the French gunners stopped for breakfast, some of the British residents who were still on shore took the chance to see what damage had been done. In fact, there were holes everywhere and many fires – but no injured or dead Hova. At 11.30 am the bombardment began again and continued for the rest of the day, ending at nightfall. The result was the same – fires, holes and lots of noise. The inferno started by the French shells was undiscriminating enough to set fire to some houses belonging to the French community. Only the onset of rain put an end to Admiral Pierre's conflagration.

The next morning Pierre sent scouts ashore to see if it was safe to land troops. He warned everyone that the Hova had laid traps, mines and hidden dangers for the unwary, but no one discovered any and the local people, encouraged to return to Tamatave now the bombardment had ceased, walked about confidently. Pierre's troops – 600 strong – poured ashore and occupied the empty Hova fort. He declared Tamatave to be under a state of siege and instructed the British consul that the town was now under martial law. But where was the enemy? He must have an 'enemy' or how could he justify his actions to Paris?

Meanwhile, Mr Shaw, a British missionary, was trying to rebuild his property which had been damaged by French shells. His house contained a dispensary with a large collection of medicines in bottles and the French placed a picket on the building to prevent looting. The next morning Shaw found that his dispensary had been broken into, some medicines stolen, and some of his best bottles of claret removed from another part of the house. The French pickets had gone and so Shaw set out to find them.

The stress of the French occupation was proving too much for Consul Pakenham's health and he now succumbed to a serious kidney ailment. While he lay dying, Captain Johnstone of the *Dryad* appointed himself 'acting consul' and tried to represent British interests in Tamatave. At once he was called into action. When Missionary Shaw arrived at the old Hova fort to complain about the break-in, he was promptly arrested by the French commandant and taken aboard the cruiser *La Niève*. Admiral Pierre had found his enemy at last. He now presented the dying British consul with the extraordinary ultimatum that he must leave Tamatave within 24 hours. Pakenham, in fact, left this life a mere 12 hours later.

On board the French warship Shaw found that he was under suspicion of attempting to poison French soldiers with drugged wine. According to the charge, Mr Shaw – whom the French believed was in the pay of the Hova – had asked pickets to guard his house but 'when they came to take up their quarters they found in the garden bottles of wine, evidently set out to tempt them. Those who tasted [the wine] suddenly fell into a state of lethargic intoxication. The officer in command at once broke the bottles and poured out the liquid, keeping a bottle as a specimen, which is at present at Réunion undergoing chemical analysis.' In spite of every effort from Captain Johnstone, Shaw was kept under close arrest for ten days. When his wife asked Admiral Pierre for permission to see him she was refused.

Admiral Pierre's state of mind was getting worse all the time. Even his officers began to suspect that he was going mad. On 26 June he ordered his men to stop and search the British steamer *Taymouth Castle* and demanded that the captain hand over the mail from Tamatave. Next he ordered Captain Johnstone of the *Dryad* to send his despatches to the Admiralty via the French flagship. If the stopping of the British steamer was an act of piracy, Pierre's interference with the *Dryad* was an act of war. Johnstone smuggled his despatches to the *Taymouth Castle* and then put his tiny vessel at action stations ready to resist the French if it should come to fighting.

Fortunately the British consul at Zanzibar had got hold of the story and telegraphed London, indicating that Pierre – who was clearly 'off his head' – had cut off communications with Madagascar and forced the foreign residents to lower their national flags. Soon the wires between London and Paris were red hot with accusations and counter-accusations. The outcome was that the French Foreign Ministry was forced to admit its complete mystification over the admiral's behaviour, particularly about the missionary and the drugged wine. On 7 August – after Shaw had been in prison for nearly two months – orders from Paris forced Pierre to release the missionary in the absence of 'sufficient evidence'. Pierre was invalided home but died shortly afterwards, his insanity probably the product of a malignant tumour of the brain. To support Captain Johnstone, who had so stoutly maintained the British flag against overwhelming odds for nearly two months, Admiral Sir W. Hewitt arrived off Madagascar with a squadron strong enough to cope with the French if hostilities did break out.

Shaw – the villain or hero of the piece, depending on one's viewpoint – returned to a great reception in England. Through the good offices of Lord Granville the French government was encouraged to make him an indemnity payment of £1,000 to cover his 54-day detention on a French warship. And so the Tamatave incident was brought to a peaceful conclusion. Yet it had been a close thing. Had firing taken place between the *Dryad* and the much more powerful French squadron there could only have been one result – the destruction of the courageous Johnstone and his tiny vessel. And the consequences for Anglo-French relations of Admiral Pierre's extraordinary behaviour would have been severe indeed.

# The Loss of the *Northumberland*, 1744

On 8 May 1744 the 70-gun *Northumberland* was detached by Vice-Admiral Charles Hardy to pursue an unidentified craft off the coast of Portugal. Her captain, Thomas Watson, had a previously unblemished record and had served well at Cartagena under Admiral Vernon. Nothing from his past gave reason to cast doubt on his capability, unless it was the fact that on a previous expedition he had fractured his skull so that 'a small matter of liquor rendered him quite out of order, which was his unhappy fate that day'. Clearly he was no longer fit to command a ship at sea, yet in the absence of regular medical examinations, once an officer reached the rank of captain little short of death or dishonour could remove him. As a result Watson continued in his command, although he was on occasions little better than a raving lunatic.

As Watson pursued the fleeing vessel the weather became stormy and Hardy signalled for him to return. For some reason Watson ignored the signal and kept up the chase. Suddenly three ships could be made out to leeward and, without a second thought, Watson set off in pursuit as if he were chasing a fox with hounds. The new adversaries turned out to be two French two-deckers and a frigate. Although the odds were still in his favour Watson handled his vessel miserably, ignoring the good advice to call up support from the rest of the fleet, and not even preparing his ship for battle. The decks of the *Northumberland* were littered with hammocks and nothing was cleared away before the fighting began. Rather than engaging the French ships separately Watson decided to fight them all at once. Even so, the French gunnery was so bad that he would still have got away with it if he had been in his right senses, instead of roaring drunk.

Early in the action Captain Watson was killed by a cannon ball. None of his lieutenants dared to take up the command which fell by default to Dixon, the Master. Overwhelmed by the responsibility, Dixon promptly struck his colours and surrendered to the French, even though the *Northumberland* had suffered little damage and few casualties. It was probably the most shameful surrender of one of His Majesty's ships of the 18th century.

The *Northumberland* was taken into Brest and for 50 years the trophy name of *Northumberland* appeared in the lists of French ships. When the officers and crew were released and returned to England a court-martial was inevitable. The main culprit – Thomas Watson – was dead, though the court recorded its view 'that Captain Watson had behaved very rashly and inconsiderately, to which was owing chiefly the loss of her'. But the scapegoat – in the absence of Watson – was Dixon, who had surrendered the ship. Even though the cowardly officers were honourably acquitted, Dixon, the man who had 'bitten the bullet', was sentenced to life imprisonment in the Marshalsea Prison.

# Price at Petropavlovsk

Although Britain's war with Russia, which began in 1854, has become known to history as the Crimean War, this should not mislead people into thinking that military operations were confined to the Black Sea. In fact, Britain and France conducted not only a major naval campaign in the Baltic, but also lesser-known operations in the White Sea and the Pacific. Unfortunately, the same problems that undermined military performance in the main theatre of war were present elsewhere (see p. 25).

In the China Sea the British had a squadron of five ships, commanded by Rear-Admiral David Price, flying his flag in the 50-gun *President*. With him was a French flotilla under Rear-Admiral Febvrier-Despointes – a sick old man – flying his flag in the *Forte*. Against this combined strength of nine ships and 282 guns, the Russian commander, Rear-Admiral Poutiatin, felt himself helpless. He sent two of his ships to reinforce the settlement of Petropavlovsk, in Kamchatka, which he guessed Price was hoping to take by surprise. When the Allies reached the Russian port they were therefore disappointed to find it well defended, with the Russian warship *Aurora* stationed behind a sandbank so that it could fire a broadside against any ship that approached.

For Admiral Price – a Welshman – this was his first command at the age of 64. In a naval career of 53 years he had spent just four afloat, four employed ashore and the rest on half pay and unemployed. During the years of his prime – 25 to 44 – he had seen no service at all. Yet at the age of 64 he was suddenly put in command of a squadron at war. Unable to cope with his responsibilities, he took the easy way out by retiring to his cabin and shooting himself in the heart. However, the bullet missed his heart and lodged in his lungs, leaving him to die slowly and painfully. He was in great agony, calling on the surgeon to 'Kill me at once'. But no one obliged. His officers came to see him one by one and he explained why he had done the dreadful deed: 'He could not bear the thought of taking so many noble and gallant fellows into action.' As Chaplain Holme, an eyewitness, recounted, 'The poor old man was always weak and vacillating in everything he did.' Before he died he apologized to everyone for his 'crime', including the French admiral, who came to visit him. The chaplain was aware of the implications of what Price had done, saying: 'And what all will say at home of an English [sic] Admiral deserting his post at such a moment we cannot conceive.' What people said then is not what we would say now. Clearly Price was psychologically unfit for command. He was prey to his own fears, both for himself and for the men for whom he felt responsible. He knew he was not up to his job and looked for any way out of a situation he could not resolve. Price was suffering from depression in an age which had no name for it but dereliction of duty.

Command now devolved on Captain Sir Frederick William Erskine Nicolson, who ordered an attack on the Russian settlement the next day, with allied landing parties sent to spike the guns being driven off by a large force from the *Aurora*. Meanwhile, three American seamen – apparently deserters from a whaler – gave the British and French vital information about the best way to attack Petropavlovsk. Whether they were treacherous or genuinely misinformed we will never know. But their information turned out to be disastrous for the allies. On 4 September a combined British and French force of 700 men landed at the base of a wooded hill. The landing party drove back the few Russians who held the hill, but as they advanced through the bushes and brambles, led by one of the Americans, they walked into an ambush. The Russians poured deadly fire into the startled sailors who fled back to their boats, having suffered over 200 casualties. It later transpired that the place where the landing had taken place was just about the worst possible. Depressed by both the suicide of Admiral Price and their disastrous reverse, the two squadrons withdrew from Petropavlovsk, well and truly beaten.

# The Man Who Walked on Water

It is given to few men in any human activity to so dominate their profession that in a sense they seem 'larger than life' to their peers. Yet this was the case with Vice-Admiral Sir George

Vice-Admiral Sir George Tryon, K.C.B. An overwhelming personality, he was regarded with such awe by his subordinates that they felt unable to question any of his orders, even when the latter were fatally flawed.

Tryon, commander of Her Majesty's Mediterranean Fleet, in 1891. Tryon was in every way an overwhelming person – tall, massive-chested and with a huge black beard; his sharp, incisive mind was constantly at work seeking ways to improve the performance of his ships and his men. In the words of one observer, 'He conducted his work so skilfully as to prove every admiral arrayed against him his inferior.' And therein lay the problem. None of his officers, however senior they might have been, dared to question the orders of such a man, a man who seemed to 'walk on water'.

Tryon had risen to the top through ability. His intellect had enabled him to dominate all around him and, as one of his colleagues wrote, 'Most people felt no use arguing with George Tryon, and that it was better to acquiesce quietly.' But this very quality was to bring ruin on him. Tryon was dissatisfied with the lack of initiative that he found among the majority of officers in the navy and he made it his task to instil initiative in his juniors. But so powerful was Tryon's personality and so successful had been his career hitherto that most of the officers who served with him wanted only to be given orders by him. While Tryon sought to test them and develop their own skills, they were afraid to display their inadequacies and longed for the certainty which came when Tryon 'told' them what to do. And the officer who most felt this way was none other than Rear-Admiral Sir Hastings Markham, Tryon's second-in-command, a man 'anxious, conforming, hidebound, conventionalist, dedicated to staying out of trouble and not displeasing his superiors'.

On taking up command of the Mediterranean Fleet Tryon set about introducing new ideas and challenging existing systems. Inevitably he met not opposition but inertia. Accepted methods had been comfortable; Tryon was never comfortable. Sir Geoffrey Phipps Hornby observed that under Tryon, 'there appears to have been an absence of the friendly banter that used to characterise the Mediterranean in years gone by'. Part of the problem was Tryon's own 'TA' system, which he was keen to introduce to his new command. In his own words the 'TA' system involved less a system of signalling than of 'follow my leader'. 'I have been long impressed with the importance of exercising a fleet from the point where the drill books leave off . . . It is apparent to me that a fleet that can be rapidly manoeuvred without having to wait for a series of signal repetitions will be at a great advantage.' This was not very reassuring for his subordinates who would now be confronted with a series of fleet manoeuvres without signals. The idea was that Tryon would raise the signal 'TA' and the rest of the fleet would then conform with the movements of the flagship. What would happen if, in action, the flagship was disabled, Tryon does not seem to have considered. *The Times* reported the new system as 'Unsound in theory and perilous in practice', but with Tryon around to defend his new scheme nobody dared to tell him that he was wrong. And Rear-Admiral Markham was far from being the sort of man who would express doubts about his superiors. His thirteen months' serving with Tryon were little less than a nightmare, relieved only by his visits to historical sites in the Middle East. On manoeuvres Markham showed himself quite incapable of dealing with the constant tests set by Tryon to keep the fleet on its toes. Nor was Tryon slow to express criticism of his second-in-command, much of it in public. If Tryon was no bully, he did not suffer fools gladly.

On 22 June 1893, the eleven ironclads of the Mediterranean Fleet left harbour at Beirut and put to sea on manoeuvres. The sea was as calm as a millpond and the heat was oppressive. Tryon was feeling lethargic after a heavy lunch and the officers and men aboard the flagship *Victoria* went about their duties as if the five days' leave they had spent in the souks of Beirut needed to be cleared from their systems by a short, sharp shock. The *Victoria* was a brand new battleship – just three months old – and in design one of the worst in the history of the Royal Navy. Her low forecastle often disappeared completely in a heavy sea and she wallowed badly. Her massive guns – which supposedly made her the most powerful ship afloat – were feared more by her own crew than the enemy. When they fired her main armament the blast often buckled the deck and damaged the bridge, as well as playing havoc with the paintwork. In many respects the *Victoria* and her sister, the *Sans Pareil*, were regarded as blunders, even by their own crews.

None of this was passing through Admiral Tryon's mind that lazy summer's afternoon. Instead he was thinking of setting the captains and crews of his fleet a real brain-teaser. 'I shall form the fleet into columns of two divisions, six cables apart, and reverse the course by turning inwards,' he suddenly announced to Staff Commander Thomas Hawkins-Smith. Hawkins-Smith immediately felt uneasy: six cables was just 1,200 yards, and if the two columns were to turn inwards that would surely be too close for comfort. Plucking up courage he replied to Tryon, 'It will require at least eight cables for that, sir.' Tryon thought for a moment and then agreed, 'Yes, it shall be eight cables.' But when Lord Gillford, Tryon's flag-lieutenant, came into his cabin Tryon told him, 'Will you make a signal to form columns of divisions line ahead, columns disposed abeam to port. And make the columns six cables apart.' To confirm this he handed Gillford a scrap of paper containing the single figure 'six'. The flag-lieutenant left without questioning the order and prepared the signal. Within minutes the flags were fluttering and had been acknowledged by the other battleships of the fleet. Looking up from his work in the fore-bridge Hawkins-Smith experienced a moment's uncertainty – that was the wrong signal. He hurried over to Gillford. 'Haven't you made a mistake? The admiral said the columns were to be eight cables.' Gillford showed him the scribbled figure on the paper, but Hawkins-Smith was still not satisfied and sent Gillford back to see Tryon himself. The admiral was not pleased to be cross-examined on his orders and told Gillford brusquely, 'Leave it at six cables.'

Gillford was now thoroughly alarmed. He knew that the combined turning circles of ships like the *Victoria* and the *Camperdown* – the flagship of Rear-Admiral Markham, leading the other column – was eight cables or 1,600 yards. Tryon must have made a mistake – probably confusing the radius of the turning circle with its diameter. The manoeuvre was surely impossible, and at least two other officers – Hawkins-Smith and the *Victoria*'s commander, Captain Archibald Maurice Bourke – shared his view. Yet, as Bourke remarked, 'open criticism of one's superior is not consonant with true discipline', and so there was nothing anyone could do but to grit their teeth and pray.

The fleet was now travelling at about nine knots towards the coast of Syria and a turn of some sort was necessary before the battleships ran aground. Tryon was furious; why had *Camperdown* not begun to turn yet? Markham was holding up the entire manoeuvre. Tryon ordered a signal made to *Camperdown*, 'What are you waiting for?' It was a public rebuke and Markham would have to obey whatever the consequences. He clearly thought that Tryon intended his column to turn first but this was not so and the two flagships turned inwards simultaneously. Trying to conceal his anxiety Bourke remarked to the admiral, 'We had better do something, sir, we shall be too close to [the *Camperdown*].' But Tryon ignored him, absorbed in the awesome potential of his own geometry. Bourke, his voice rising slightly, 'We are getting too close, sir! We must do something, sir! May I go astern?' Tryon's voice was no more than a whisper, 'Yes, go astern.' 'Full speed astern both screws,' bellowed Bourke, but it was far too late now – a collision was inevitable. Bourke ordered the watertight doors closed – at least it might do something to save the ship. As the *Camperdown* bore down on the *Victoria*, Tryon and Markham were within hailing distance for a few moments and Tryon shouted through cupped hands,

'Go astern – go astern', a spit in the wind as the *Camperdown*'s huge ram ripped nine feet into the *Victoria*'s side, forcing her 70 feet sideways and wounding her fatally.

Ironically at the moment of impact a yeoman passed a signal to Tryon from the *Camperdown*. It was Markham's reply to his signal demanding to know why *Camperdown* had not begun her turn. It was simple and in context quite ridiculous: 'Because I did not quite understand your signal.' Less than 50 yards away Markham and his officers were gazing in horror from their bridge at the damage they had just inflicted on the fleet flagship. Tryon bellowed across, 'Go astern, go astern. Why didn't you . . . ?' There was really nothing more to say but Tryon found words, pitiful and tragic to a man like him. 'It is all my fault,' he was heard to mutter.

The other battleships of the fleet had begun lowering boats to begin rescuing Tryon's crew but the admiral was not giving up his ship as easily as that. Angrily he ordered them to cancel sending boats – in his opinion, the *Victoria* had not been struck in a vital spot. But he was wrong. The disastrously low forecastle was already under water and the sea was pouring into the ship through every open porthole and door. The *Victoria* was heeling to starboard and water was gushing through the turret apertures. Within five minutes of impact the bows had sunk some fifteen feet. Everything was happening so quickly. Now Tryon was faced with the consequences of his own error in rejecting the offers of help. Four more minutes and the *Victoria* began to go under (see also pages 10 and 133). The men in the boiler rooms had received no order to abandon their stations and stop engines – and they were drowned to a man. Lucky to survive was John Jellicoe – then a lieutenant but later commander-in-chief of the Grand Fleet in the First World War – who had been in sick bay on the *Victoria* with Malta fever and had escaped in his pyjamas, helped by young Midshipman Philip Roberts-West.

The last moments of Admiral Tryon's flagship, *Victoria*, seen from the battleship *Collingwood*. To the left the battleship *Nile* stands by to pick up survivors.

Tryon made no attempt to save himself. With the loss of the flagship his whole world had crashed down about his ears. He had blundered and he would not outlive the disgrace. It was better this way. In the words of Hawkins-Smith, who saw him standing 'perfectly calm and collected to the last', Tryon 'died as he had lived, a brave man'.

Yet so large a persona could not be extinguished without the hint of legend and so it was with Admiral Sir George Tryon. At the moment of his death, it is claimed, he was clearly identified by a number of guests on the stairway of his wife's house in Eaton Square, London, during one of her grand 'at homes'. Along with Tryon, 357 officers and men died as the result of an inexplicable disaster on a sea as calm as glass and in visibility as perfect as any seaman had ever experienced. After holding a sombre funeral ceremony at sea, Markham ordered the fleet to return to Malta. As each battleship entered Grand Harbour there was a noticeable atmosphere of solemn mourning. That is, until the *Camperdown* herself arrived, down at the bows but with her band playing lively airs on the quarterdeck. Admiral Sir Charles Dundas, observing Markham's return, remarked, 'I remember thinking that on such a pathetic occasion it would have shown better taste if there had been less demonstration.' Yet *Camperdown* had little to regret; she had done what she had been built to do, rammed and killed one of her own kind.

The British press soon took up the question of why the *Victoria* had sunk in a flat calm and from a blow so far forward, and gone under in just ten minutes. Were there serious design faults in Britain's ironclad fleet which foreign navies – notably the French – could exploit? The London *Standard* wrote, 'There is the most painful suspicion that the principles of shipbuilding which have prevailed in the Royal Navy for so many years may, after all, turn out to be unsound.' The fact was that the *Victoria*'s design was similar to that of all other British battleships of the time. The implications for Britain's supremacy at sea were considerable.

The court-martial – inevitable in such a case – was held at Malta and reached the decision that Sir George Tryon had been responsible for the disaster but also regretted that Markham had not questioned the fatal order more effectively before beginning the turn which led to the collision. This did not go down well in military circles. The Duke of Cambridge complained that 'A good deal has been said of late as to freedom being given to inferiors to question and disobey the orders of a superior officer. Discipline must be the law, and must prevail. It is better to go wrong according to orders than to go wrong in opposition to orders.' Yet Tryon would have hated such an epitaph for himself. He had been trying to prove to his fleet captains that they should show more initiative. He would never have accepted the idea that Markham – his second-in-command – should be a slave to his orders. It has been suggested that Tryon's order was misinterpreted by his officers and that what he was attempting was for the *Camperdown* to move outside him, while the *Victoria* moved inside Markham's ship. Be that as it may, Tryon was asking more of officers trained to obey orders without question than they could possibly offer. Markham never held another important command and the Admiralty made it clear that they felt the *Camperdown* had been ineptly handled during the crisis. But none of this helped to restore the reputation of Sir George Tryon. His one mistake had been enough to destroy a career of unparalleled achievement. Command is a lonely business. Nobody will ever know what was in Tryon's mind when he gave the order for the manoeuvre which killed him. We can only agree with Admiral Kerr who said, 'Sir George Tryon was not a person who was agreeable on being asked questions or cross examined.'

# Admiral Plumridge Scores an Own Goal

On 29 March 1854 – at the outbreak of the Crimean War – the Secretary of State for War, the Duke of Newcastle, wrote to the Admiralty:

> It is Her Majesty's anxious desire that the interests of humanity should be regarded in the war upon which Great Britain has now entered, to the fullest extent which its operations will admit; and I am to request your Lordships to give positive orders to Sir Charles Napier to respect private property wherever it can be spared, without a sacrifice of the objects of the war, and on no account to attack defenceless places and open towns . . .'

Unfortunately it does not appear that the British commander-in-chief, Sir Charles Napier, communicated this sentiment clearly to Rear-Admiral James Hanway Plumridge, commander of a squadron of paddle-steamers, who was ordered to reconnoitre the Aland Islands and blockade the coastal towns of Bothnia. During a five-week period, from 5 May to 10 June, Plumridge in the *Leopard* carried out an 'orgy of destruction' which prompted the King of Sweden to describe his actions as 'barbarous and unworthy of our time'. Plumridge, a somewhat diffident character who allowed himself to be influenced by the 'gung-ho' Captain Giffard of the *Leopard*, undertook to 'take, burn and destroy' in the style of a latter-day Viking. Had it been enemy property that he took, burned and destroyed there might have been some excuse for it. But Plumridge unwittingly waged economic warfare on Britain herself.

Failing at the outset to reconnoitre the Aland Islands as the fog was too thick and the floating ice too dangerous, Plumridge instead began seizing the vessels of the coastal farmers, plundering their equipment, hoisting their sails and setting fire to them. Leaning heavily on Giffard for advice, Plumridge next raided the Finnish ports. In his journal Giffard takes an unseemly delight in listing the depradations of the British squadron, without considering for a moment that the people who were suffering were not Russians at all but Finns. Moreover, many of the products the British were destroying – notably timber and pine tar – were destined for Britain. Before the war Britain had imported annually 56,500 barrels of tar from Finland – 35 per cent of the total. Now the vital tar trade was devastated. Nobody seemed to have told Plumridge or Giffard that the local population was pro-British and vital trading partners. It was often British produce – paid for in advance by British companies – which went up in flames to the delight of Giffard and his desperadoes. All they were achieving was to damage British trade, ruin poor farming folk, and drive the whole population into the arms of the Russians. Significantly, as time passed, the villagers began calling in Russian troops to help them defend their farms and villages from the marauding British squadron. But none of this seemed to bother Plumridge and Giffard. At Uleaborg they threatened a group of villagers, who were holding up a flag of truce, that they would bombard their church if there was any resistance. And when the Finns did fight back Giffard described their action as 'treachery'.

Sir Charles Napier, meanwhile, was quite out of touch with the real damage that was being done. On 18 June he proudly reported to the Admiralty that Plumridge had 'destroyed 46 vessels afloat and on the stocks . . . from 40,000 to 50,000 barrels of pitch and tar . . . a great number of stacks of timber, spars, plank and deal, sails, rope and various kinds of naval stores to the amount of from £300,000 to £400,000, without the loss of a single man'. But their Lordships were unimpressed. In London, British trading houses were receiving news of the destruction of their property from their trading partners in Finland, such as the house of Hackmann in Viborg. Rew, Prescott and Co demanded compensation from the government for these 'unnecessary and barbaric' raids. *The Times* was quick to respond, condemning the

British ships in the Baltic during the Crimean War. By the beginning of the 1850s naval warfare had
made some dramatic advances: the advent of steam made warships independent of wind and tide, while
the introduction of rifling and shellfire greatly enhanced their destructive capabilities.

British raids against a friendly trading partner. To make matters worse, the raids led to a wave
of anti-British feeling in neutral Sweden. Admiral Plumridge was described as an arsonist and
the British fleet as no better than Vikings. As one Finnish writer has observed, 'These opening
moves in the Crimean War stirred up real hatred of Britain, and at the same time caused loyalty
to the [Russian] Emperor to become more pronounced. In their crisis the Finns looked to him
for protection.'

Plumridge's expedition had not just been a blunder, it had been a catastrophic mistake. The
rest of the fleet knew that it would only serve to make the Finns join the Russians in resisting
them. At Gamla Carleby, on 9 June, the villagers, stiffened by a few Russian troops, drove off
a British raiding party, killing 50 of the crew of the paddle-steamer *Vulture*. In London, Sir
James Graham tried to distance the government from Plumridge's excesses, reminding
Parliament of the Duke of Newcastle's instruction, issued even before the fleet had sailed.

# 'The Duckworth Touch'

In an age of naval heroes Admiral Sir John Duckworth was up with the best of them. His victory
over the French at Santo Domingo in 1806 was the greatest the Royal Navy won after
Trafalgar, yet it brought him little of the recognition he deserved. His second and third-in-
command were both knighted for their parts in the battle, yet he received nothing for the five
French battleships he destroyed. The problem was that Duckworth was something of a rogue.
He behaved more like a privateer than a British admiral, and their Lordships felt that he had

already amply rewarded himself for his victory. Nevertheless, he was a fine seaman and an inspiring leader, keen, like so many naval officers of the time, to show that Nelson was not the only man who had the 'touch' that brings success.

In February 1807 Duckworth found himself with the delicate task of disarming or seizing the Turkish fleet, to prevent it attacking Britain's ally Russia. To accomplish this he would need to navigate the Dardanelles and reach Constantinople, where his fleet of seven battleships and two frigates would need to outface – or outfight – a stronger Turkish force of twelve battleships and nine frigates. It was a job which might have appealed to Nelson. And so, eager to emulate Britain's greatest hero, Duckworth set out without waiting for any help from a Russian force with whom he was supposed to cooperate in the venture. Accompanied by a band of officers as daring and desperate as himself – notably Sir Sidney Smith in the *Pompée* and Thomas Louis (reputedly a descendant of Louis XIV) in the *Canopus* – Duckworth sailed majestically into the Dardanelles, flying his flag in the mighty 100-gun *Royal George*. At first all went well. Some Turkish forts opened a desultory fire which Duckworth treated with the contempt it deserved, and a few Turkish vessels were simply brushed aside. Sir Sidney Smith, pleased to be in action once again, could not resist capturing some Turkish ships and driving others aground. He then sent a landing party ashore to spike the Turkish batteries, reporting back to Duckworth after his seven-hour 'rough-and-tumble', having suffered 72 casualties.

Duckworth's fleet soon reached Constantinople – relatively unscathed – and anchored prior to accepting a Turkish surrender. Unfortunately, Duckworth soon found that he was no match for the Turks as a diplomat. He had expected the presence of the British fleet to speak for itself, but the Turks just were not listening and refused to be overawed.

Duckworth now applied his 'touch' to negotiating with an oriental potentate – a timeless operation for which the men of action who made up the British fleet were ill equipped. He sent a note to the Sultan demanding the immediate surrender of his fleet. Before setting out Admiral Collingwood had advised Duckworth not to waste time negotiating with the Turks but to offer them just 30 minutes to make up their minds. Duckworth ignored this advice and gave them 36 hours. But the Turks refused to allow his envoy even to land. Round One to the Turks. Duckworth now sent another note, giving them 30 minutes this time. The Turks ignored it and Duckworth fumed. Round Two to the Turks. The admiral, his temperature rising, sent a third note warning them not to try to strengthen their shore batteries. The Turks took no notice and strengthened their batteries, with the assistance of a French officer, Colonel Noy. They knew the British would eventually have to go back and when they did they would regret it. Duckworth, meanwhile, had sent a fourth note, threatening to bombard Constantinople if they did not reply. The Turks did not believe him. Instead they ambushed a boat from one of the British ships, the *Endymion*, and kidnapped a midshipman and four sailors. Duckworth demanded their return, but the Turks took no notice. This was not war as Duckworth understood it. His courage seemed to be draining away all the time he lay in front of Constantinople and he did nothing to enforce his demands.

The Turks were almost ready and when a force of Janissaries – under French supervision – opened fire on the fleet, Duckworth was forced to send some marines ashore to try to stop them. In the fighting the British suffered some 30 casualties and were driven off. This was the end. Duckworth's nerve gave way and he began to imagine that his force would soon be bottled up by the Turks and forced into a humiliating surrender. Retreat was the only option. But it would be no easy task to get back through the Dardanelles as the Turks had been busily strengthening their shore batteries for this very eventuality. It was a visibly chastened Duckworth who ordered his 'band of brothers' to turn back and make an ignominious departure. The Turkish Sultan watched unmoved as another invader found the 'Queen of Cities' impregnable.

Duckworth's retreat soon became a nightmare. The Turks were using guns from a different era, yet their size and destructiveness were truly awesome. As the British battleships fired their heavy 32-pounders at the shore batteries they received in return huge stone balls weighing upwards of 1,000 pounds, the sort of missile which might have crushed the galleys of the 16th century. In fact, they still did a good job on 19th-century wooden-walled vessels. A stone ball seven feet in diameter crashed onto the *Standard*, killing and wounding over 50 sailors, while an 800-pounder smashed into Duckworth's flagship, spoiling her good looks and shaking up an admiral who had very much 'lost his touch'. The wheel of the *Canopus* was reduced to matchsticks by another of the Turkish missiles but, smiling as usual and riding a streak of luck a mile wide, Sidney Smith in the *Pompée* was immune to everything the Turks could throw. By the time Duckworth reached the Mediterranean he had hundreds of casualties and almost every one of his ships bore the marks of the Turkish guns. Ironically, the Russian fleet – with whom he had been supposed to link up – was awaiting his return. The Russian admiral suggested the two fleets should now return to Constantinople and despatch the Turkish ships, but Duckworth was a broken man. He could think of nothing but getting back to Gibraltar to show Collingwood what the Turks had done to his ships. After Duckworth had gone, the Russians succeeded in ambushing the Turkish fleet – as it emerged from the Dardanelles – and recapturing the five British sailors who had been in Turkish hands for four months.

Poor Duckworth had lost his 'touch'; although nobody doubted his physical courage, he had proved that he lacked the moral courage to take a difficult decision. At Copenhagen, in 1801, Nelson had shown how to deal with difficult neutrals – but then, of course, he had 'the Nelson Touch'.

# Chinese Junk

Under the influence of Admiral Ting, the Chinese Navy appeared to be making enormous strides towards modernization in the last years of the 19th century. Unfortunately, appearances were deceptive; the war with Japan which broke out in 1894 exposed severe limitations in the efficiency of the Chinese fleet. Discipline aboard Chinese warships may be judged by the curious form of gambling at pitch and toss which took place, usually involving the sentries. The ships themselves were in a filthy state; the watertight doors were never closed, and the gun barrels were used by the crew as dumps for pickles, rice and chopsticks. One Chinese battleship went into action at the battle of the Yalu River minus one of its heavy guns because Admiral Ting had pawned it. The shells used by the Chinese were sometimes found to have been stuffed with charcoal and the gunpowder sold and replaced by cocoa powder. Chinese officers were so terrified of torpedoes that they fired them at twice the proper range with the result that the torpedoes always sank before they had covered half the distance to their targets.

# A Day in the Life of Captain Vukovic

The record for the shortest period of command in the history of naval warfare must surely belong to the Yugoslav commander-in-chief, Captain Vukovic. What made things worse for Vukovic was that his flagship was sunk by people who were not even at war with him and that he felt it necessary to go down with his ship, having only been aboard for a few hours. It was a thoroughly bad day for the Yugoslav navy, and not much better for the Italians who, having failed through three years of war to even damage the Austrian battleship *Viribus Unitis*, managed to sink her only after she had been transferred to the new and neutral state of Yugoslavia.

The four powerful dreadnoughts of the *Viribus Unitis* class gave the Austrian fleet an important advantage in the naval war in the Adriatic from 1915 to 1918. Not surprisingly they were the targets for numerous attacks by the Italians, who enjoyed no success until the last few months of the war. In June 1918 an Italian anti-submarine motor-boat torpedoed and sank the *Szent Istvan*. Then on the night of 31 October two Italian officers, Major Rossetti and Lieutenant Paolucci (the latter, curiously enough, a naval doctor who should have been a non-belligerent), wearing wetsuits and guiding a two-man submarine named the *Mignatta*, set out to attack the *Viribus Unitis* in harbour at Pola. They managed to place a mine on the battleship's hull but were then captured and taken aboard the very ship they were trying to destroy. As they came up the gangplank they had a shock. The *Viribus Unitis* was no longer flying the Austrian flag, but strips of paper bearing the word 'Jugoslavia'. Unknown to the Italians the Austrian Empire had broken up and the battleship was now the property of the Yugoslav National Committee. The Austrian Admiral Horthy had lowered his flag and departed hours before and the man they were to be presented to was the senior Yugoslav officer, Captain Vukovic. The Austrian flag no longer flew over Pola, which was part of the new state of Yugoslavia, definitely not at war with Italy. The two Italians had no option but to tell Vukovic what they had done and he immediately gave the order to abandon ship. The Italians took him at his word and dived overboard, but were arrested by a different group of sailors and brought back on board again.

The mine exploded in the early hours of 1 November 1918. In the confusion, the Italians climbed down a rope and tried to swim off but were arrested for the third time and interned until the end of the war. Without their Austrian officers the crew of the *Viribus Unitis* panicked completely and made no effort to save the vessel. Within fifteen minutes the battleship capsized, with Vukovic – saluting and standing on the upturned hull – going down with his ship.

# A Paper Tiger

Britain's desire to prevent France taking the Chinese territory of Macao from her Portuguese ally in 1808 provoked a curious incident involving Rear-Admiral O'Brien Drury, the commander-in-chief of Britain's Indian Station. With the two frigates *Dédaigneuse* and *Phaeton*, and a number of transports, Drury sailed to Macao, hoping that his force of a thousand sailors and marines would be enough to deter the local Portuguese from objecting to Britain's heavy-handed takeover. True to form, the Portuguese made no objection when the British flotilla arrived. But then Drury was persuaded by the local East India Company representatives to protect Britain's tea trade at Whampoa, by sailing up river from Macao.

Drury was uneasy at this. He knew that he depended entirely on moral force and that if the Chinese resisted there could be a full-scale battle. To emphasize the prestige of his mission Drury led the British flotilla from his admiral's barge, which was rowed slowly towards an anticipated meeting with the local Chinese commander. However, things did not go according to plan. The local Chinese peasants, infuriated by the presence of the Western barbarians – of whom Drury was taken to be a particularly dangerous specimen – lined the river banks and pelted the admiral and his rowers with rotten fruit, offal, stones and vegetables. Ahead Drury could see that the river was blocked by a line of Chinese war junks, one of which opened fire on him – and missed. Then a Chinese peasant woman threw a stone which hit the head of a British sailor. Blood was drawn. Drury faced a difficult choice – to open fire on this 'strange and almost totally defenceless rabble', or to eat humble pie and retreat. Drury was a brave sailor but he had no wish to perpetrate a massacre, and so he ordered his force to withdraw to Macao.

He later reported that it had been 'the most mysterious, extraordinary and scandalous' affair of his career. The prestige of Britannia – mistress of the world's seas – had been lowered by a Chinese rabble, whose knowledge of the world hardly stretched further than the next village. Perhaps that was the point. The Chinese did not know who they were dealing with and Drury had possessed too much humanity to show them. The Chinese emperor later demanded that the British evacuate Macao as he had leased it to Portugal not to Britain. Drury had no option but to obey. The Royal Navy – a paper tiger in China's view – withdrew chastened. British troops had been defeated by bees at Tanga in 1915, and by crabs on Jamaica in 1654, but perhaps never before by a single stone thrown at them by a woman.

# Typhoon

Pride can be a destructive human failing and where it is linked with national interest its effects can be truly devastating. One example of this in a naval context occurred at the outlying harbour of Apia in Samoa, on 15 March 1889. Seven foreign warships – three German, three American and the British cruiser *Calliope* – were at anchor in the harbour, there to represent the interests of their nations during the political upheavals ashore. So much prestige was involved that each commander felt it necessary to set the very best example possible in order to avoid losing face. The problem was that the ships of the three nations were about to be subjected to a natural catastrophe which paid no attention to national differences.

The harbour at Apia was a 'harbour' in name only, for it was open at its northern end to the full sweep of the Pacific and anyway was far too small to hold seven warships, two of which were large cruisers. That much should have been apparent to the ships' officers, yet presumably nobody was prepared to lose face by anchoring elsewhere. But what was unforgivable for all concerned was that there were very clear signs that the coral island was about to be hit by a typhoon. First it was March, the typhoon month in that part of the world. Second, just three years before a similar typhoon had struck the harbour, destroying everything in its path. And third, the barometer was falling, the clouds were darkening and beginning to scud and the locals were issuing dire warnings. Each of the captains knew that if a typhoon struck them while they were cramped together in that harbour, their anchors would be ripped out and they would be crashed together and destroyed by 100-mile-an-hour winds. Their junior officers pleaded with them to put out to sea to try to ride out the typhoon, but none of the seven commanders was prepared to be the first to go – to flee from the elements – and to remove their national presence. What happened next has been described as 'an error of judgment that will for ever remain a paradox in human psychology'. Facing certain destruction the sea captains refused to take the action they knew was necessary to save them.

In the event, the typhoon struck with staggering force. The American cruisers *Trenton* and *Vandalia* were whirled about and sank, with the loss of over a hundred lives. The German ship *Olga* was tossed onto the beach, while the *Adler* and *Eber* were smashed together and sank with the loss of 96 men. The only ship to survive was the British cruiser *Calliope*, which took the only action possible, which was to steam at full speed against the wind – making less than one knot – into open water, where she rode out the storm. Only the superb condition of the British ship's engines saved her, as well as the seamanship of her commander Captain Kane.

The disaster was an entirely unnecessary one. Experienced seamen risked their ships and the lives of their crews for something intangible – perhaps personal or national pride, or an unwillingness to believe that the elements could master them. Whatever the truth the loss of the six vessels and nearly 200 lives was an avoidable one.

# The Capture of the *Rosario*

The taking of the Spanish galleon *Nuestra Senora del Rosario* by Sir Francis Drake, during the Armada campaign of 1588, was probably the most controversial event of that most fateful of encounters. Whether Drake was indeed endowed with 'valour and felicity so great that Mars and Neptune seemed to attend him', as the Spanish commander Don Pedro de Valdés insisted in trying to justify his surrender to the English vice-admiral, is a moot point. In fact, neither Drake nor Valdés emerges with much credit from the episode, which revealed the former as a pirate and a deserter, and the latter as a coward or at best a faintheart.

On 31 July 1588, while the Armada was off the coast of Devon, the flagship of the Andalusian squadron, the *Nuestra Senora del Rosario*, commanded by Don Pedro de Valdés, collided with the *Santa Catalina*, breaking its bowsprit and mainmast. Valdés, without his mainsail, now fell behind and was apparently abandoned by the Spanish commander-in-chief, the Duke of Medina Sidonia. Why the duke chose to leave such a powerful ship to its fate has been long debated. The *Rosario* was one of the fleet's strongest ships and Valdés a commander of some renown. Moreover, the ship was carrying 50,000 ducats, as well as a mass of gunpowder – 114 quintals – and 2,300 rounds of heavy shot for the rest of the fleet. It would be a prize indeed should the English succeed in taking it. Yet Medina Sidonia did not want to break up his formation and risk his whole mission by turning back to help the *Rosario*. Moreover, neither he nor the man on whose advice he relied, Don Pedro's kinsman, Diego Flores de Valdés, was on good terms with the *Rosario*'s captain, and perhaps this may have influenced the Spanish commander's decision to sail on. Also he would have assumed that Don Pedro would fight to the last drop of his blood and scuttle his vessel before the English could seize its great treasure. But in the event he was wrong.

The English fleet, meanwhile, held the weather gauge and were holding off from fighting until they had determined Spanish intentions. On the night of 31 July, Sir Francis Drake in the *Revenge* was appointed by Lord Howard to lead the English fleet by showing a light from his large poop lantern. The captains astern of Drake were dependent on this light, so one can imagine their consternation when it suddenly disappeared. The English fleet was thrown into confusion by Drake's decision to douse the lamp and sail off, apparently in pursuit of some unknown sails, but in reality to seize the *Rosario*. Some of the English ships shortened sail and were left far behind, while Howard in the *Ark Royal,* Lord Edmund Sheffield in the *White Bear* and Edmund Fenton in the *Mary Rose*, mistaking the lights of the Spanish ships for Drake's signal, found themselves off Brixham and almost within the crescent of the Armada itself. Thanks to Drake's dereliction of duty three important ships, with the commander-in-chief in one of them, were in danger of being cut off and destroyed by the Spaniards. Hugo de Moncada in command of the Spanish galleasses prepared to pursue them but, for some reason, Medina Sidonia called him back. It had been close to a disaster for the English – and it was Drake's fault.

Meanwhile, Drake himself was laughing all the way to the bank. He had come across the *Rosario* and had allowed his reputation to work its special magic on the Spanish commander. So awestruck was Don Pedro to be facing the almost legendary Drake that he considered it quite appropriate to surrender without a fight, even though his ship was more powerfully armed than Drake's *Revenge* and he had aboard over three hundred élite Spanish pikemen and musketeers. It may have been a chivalric decision in his own eyes but in those of his commander, Medina Sidonia, it was a craven one. Drake responded in kind, according Don Pedro all the honours of war – after all, it cost him nothing to be polite to so feeble an opponent – and entertained him to dinner in his cabin. Drake was very pleased with himself. At that moment, a king's fortune was being taken ashore and he did not intend to share it with any of his fellow commanders, now floundering about in the Channel. But not every English captain was prepared to be Drake's dupe and several, notably the Yorkshire-born Martin Frobisher, accused the vice-admiral of trying to 'cozen us of our shares of fifteen thousand [sic] ducats'. Frobisher threatened Drake that unless he paid up he would 'spend the best blood in his belly'. It says much for Lord Howard – something of a shadowy figure, surrounded by such famous sea dogs as Drake, Frobisher and Hawkins – that he was able to reconcile Drake and Frobisher and restore order among the English captains. Nevertheless, Drake's greed had threatened the safety of the English fleet and he deserved, no less than Don Pedro de Valdés, to be court-martialled whatever his previous achievements. In the event, neither man suffered for his dereliction of duty. Drake's fame was never higher than in the aftermath of the Armada's defeat, while de Valdés spent some time in London, in luxurious imprisonment as a guest of Drake, before returning to Spain when a suitable ransom had been paid. His men, however, were far less lucky, becoming virtual slaves of the gentry of Dorset and Devon.

# The Escape of the *Goeben*

The two most famous examples of cowardice in British naval history are both far from straightforward if 'cowardice' is taken to imply that the men in question – John Byng and Ernest Troubridge – were physically afraid of what might happen to them if they acted in a certain way. In the case of Byng – who was cleared of any hint of cowardice by court-martial and yet tainted by the court of history with that very crime – there were extenuating circumstances (see p. 35). In the case of Ernest Troubridge we need to examine his 'cowardice' in the context of the problems of high command. Troubridge felt that he had greater responsibilities to his crew and his country than to himself and if these involved not risking action then he was prepared to bear the burden of guilt. It was the classic confrontation

The German battlecruiser *Goeben* became known as 'the ship that changed the world'. Evading British attempts to stop her, the *Goeben* reached Constantinople in 1914, and was a major factor in persuading Turkey to enter the First World War on the side of the Central Powers.

between moral and physical courage, and one is left with the thought that perhaps Sir Christopher Cradock showed less moral courage in seeking hopeless battle at the Coronel (see p. 163) than did Troubridge in avoiding it off Sicily.

In the last days of peace, in late July 1914, Rear-Admiral Sir Ernest Troubridge – a giant of a man with the most famous name in the navy but 'not much up top' – was in command of a squadron of armoured cruisers in the Mediterranean, as second-in-command to Admiral Sir Archibald Milne – the preposterous 'Arky-Barky' (see p. 90). On 30 July, Milne received a telegram at Malta warning him that hostilities with Germany might break out at any time. In the event of war he was to bring to action and destroy the German battlecruiser *Goeben* and the light cruiser *Breslau*, which had been sent into the Mediterranean, presumably to threaten France's communications with her North African colonies. The Admiralty was at pains to say that Milne should not act against 'superior forces' unless he was in company with contingents from the French Navy. But this was extremely misleading. Milne had with him, after all, the two battlecruisers *Indomitable* and *Inflexible*, which presumably would not have been considered an inferior squadron to the German one. In the event of war, Milne would be free to engage the *Goeben*, but in the last few hours of peace he had to confine himself to shadowing the German squadron. The *Goeben*'s commander, Admiral Souchon, was on a secret mission to Turkey but he wanted to keep the British in the dark as long as possible about his destination. He knew that with the British ultimatum due to run out at midnight on 3 August he would have to break away from his shadows or else they would attack him. Working up to full speed Souchon managed to pull away from Milne and headed across the western Mediterranean towards Troubridge's squadron of armoured cruisers, which were patrolling off the island of Cephalonia, between the Adriatic and the Ionian Sea.

So it fell to Troubridge to intercept the Germans now that they had eluded Milne. But the message and the warning to avoid 'superior forces' that the Admiralty had sent to Milne applied equally to Troubridge. It placed him in a difficult situation. After all, if the Admiralty had felt uncertain about Milne's two battlecruisers facing the *Goeben* how would they feel about four armoured cruisers? Was Troubridge entitled to intercept the *Goeben* and bring it to battle without contravening the Admiralty warning of 'superior forces'?

Troubridge's four cruisers were far from being the equal of Milne's battlecruisers, but neither were they negligible opponents. Admittedly two of them – the *Black Prince* and the *Duke of Edinburgh* – were nine years old but the other two – the *Defence* (flagship) and the *Warrior* – were only six years old. Each of the cruisers carried 9.2-inch guns and between them they had a broadside heavier than that of the *Goeben*'s ten 11-inch guns. On the other hand, though they were known as armoured cruisers, their armour protection was just half of the *Goeben*'s and would be easily penetrated by a Dreadnought's main armament. Furthermore, the *Goeben* was faster and could outrun and outmanoeuvre the four cruisers if she got into any difficulties. Lacking the advantage of hindsight, Troubridge did not know what we know now, which is that at the battle of Jutland both the *Defence* and the *Warrior* were destroyed with ease by the big guns of the German fleet – a clear indication of what would have happened if they had been engaged by *Goeben*.

As the *Goeben* fled eastwards only one British ship from Milne's squadron had managed to keep pace with her, the cruiser *Gloucester*, which sent a string of reports to both Milne and Troubridge. On the night of 6/7 August Troubridge set an interception course which would bring him into action with the *Goeben* at approximately 0600 hours on 7 August. It was at this moment that Troubridge fell prey to the doubts of his flag-captain, Fawcett Wray.

During the night before the engagement Wray visited his commander and they talked over the squadron's chances. Wray was clearly pessimistic and did everything he could to weaken Troubridge's confidence. He must have seen the way in which the admiral was torn and put all the pressure he could on his commander's weak intellect. Troubridge feared that if he did not fight the 'name of the whole Mediterranean Squadron' would 'stink'. Wray left Troubridge alone for nearly an hour and then returned to see if the admiral had taken the bait. He opened by telling Troubridge that he did not relish a battle with the *Goeben*, as it was bound to cause the destruction of the squadron. In Wray's own words, it was 'suicide'. Troubridge was agonized by this thought but replied, 'I cannot turn away now, think of my pride.' Wray had manoeuvred the admiral into a situation where if he fought it would only be for personal advantage – to save face – rather than for the good of the men under his command or the country he served. Wray had managed to personalize Troubridge's decision in such a way as to trivialize it. He told Troubridge, 'Has your pride got anything to do with this, sir? It is your country's welfare which is at stake.' Wray was reminding the admiral of his higher duty, compared to which personal pride was as nothing. This appeal to the patriotism and sense of duty of a proud but intellectually limited man like Troubridge was shrewd and decisive.

Troubridge now conferred with his navigation officer, asking if in his opinion the four cruisers would be able to close in on the *Goeben* to enable their main armaments to operate at short range. The officer, hardly any keener to fight than Wray, said categorically that it would be impossible. One has only to think of the way the three smaller cruisers *Exeter*, *Achilles* and *Ajax* fought the *Admiral Graf Spee* off Montevideo in 1939 to see how such an action could have been managed. But Troubridge was looking for excuses not tactical suggestions. The navigation officer had merely said what the admiral had wanted to hear before calling off the interception. Wray was jubilant, telling Troubridge that 'it was the bravest thing' he had ever done. As he did so he saw that the admiral was sobbing uncontrollably.

Few agreed with Wray, either at the Admiralty or among the general public. In most people's minds Troubridge's action was a clear case of dereliction of duty and was 'deplorable and contrary to the tradition of the British Navy'. This was all very well, but Troubridge was entitled to point out that everything hinged on the interpretation of the words 'superior force'. If the *Goeben* constituted a force superior to his squadron then he had acted correctly in not engaging her. The Court of Inquiry set up by the Admiralty did not see it that way. Ignoring their own instruction they suggested that Troubridge 'had a very fair chance of at least delaying *Goeben* by materially damaging her'.

On 5 November 1914 Rear-Admiral Ernest Troubridge faced court-martial on the grounds that he did 'from negligence or through other default, forbear to pursue the chase of His Imperial German Majesty's ship *Goeben*, being an enemy then flying'. Apparently the Admiralty felt it had a strong case against Troubridge but in court it saw much of its evidence torn asunder by the brilliant defence QC, Leslie Scott. Their Lordships stood condemned by their own misleading message to Milne ordering him not to engage a superior enemy. What could they have meant other than the *Goeben*, which was the only substantial German ship in the Mediterranean? If Milne had been warned not to tackle the *Goeben* without French help, why should Troubridge be indicted for not doing what his commander had been ordered not to do with a force far stronger than four armoured cruisers? Troubridge was acquitted on this technicality, yet his reputation was gone. Everyone knew that he had lost his nerve and failed to do what hundreds of naval officers had done throughout Britain's history, 'turned a blind eye' to orders and thrown themselves on their enemies. He had allowed himself to rationalize a military situation which had fed the fears which everyone experiences before a battle. He had failed the test of command and, in allowing the German battlecruiser *Goeben* to pass unhindered, he had opened a Pandora's box whose repercussions are still with us today. The arrival of the *Goeben* at Constantinople persuaded Turkey to enter the war against the Entente. As Winston Churchill later wrote, 'For the peoples of the Middle East the *Goeben* carried more slaughter, more misery and more ruin than has ever before been borne within the compass of one ship.' Churchill was not exaggerating. With some justification the *Goeben* has been called 'The Ship that Changed the World'.

# To Encourage the Others

The execution of Admiral Byng on the quarterdeck of the *Monarch* in 1757 has come to stand as a symbol of the fate that awaits those commanders who fail in their duty to their country. In the words of the great French writer, Voltaire, who took an unusual interest in the admiral's fate and lobbied for his pardon, Byng died *pour encourager les autres*. Yet though this has become the accepted explanation of Byng's punishment there can be little doubt that the truth lies elsewhere. Byng was sacrificed as a scapegoat to cover the disastrous policy failures of the Duke of Newcastle, and the rapacity with which the politicians fell on Byng shows that in the world of military incompetence the failures of individual commanders are as nothing compared to the failures of their political masters.

In February 1756, before war was officially declared between Britain and France, word reached London that the French had assembled a fleet of twelve battleships at Toulon under Admiral de la Galissonière, and were planning to land the Duc de Richelieu with 16,000 troops on the British-held island of Minorca. The British government, fearing that the French were also planning an invasion of England and on the advice of Lord Anson, gave Minorca a lower

Admiral Byng was executed, in the words of Voltaire, 'to encourage the others'. His failure to relieve Minorca from the French led to the loss of the island. But Byng was really a victim of the incompetence of the Duke of Newcastle's government.

priority than it probably deserved and allocated the reinforcement and relief of the island to Admiral the Hon. John Byng. Byng was the highest ranking naval officer below Lord Anson, and had little to gain from such a risky undertaking, particularly as there were signs that the expedition was going to be seriously undermanned and under-resourced. At 52, Byng had shown himself to be a capable if not outstanding officer and his lukewarm attitude towards the command should itself have been a warning to his political masters. He was the wrong man for the job. Nevertheless, he eventually accepted the task though not without telling a friend, 'I shall think myself fortunate if I am so happy to succeed in the undertaking.'

Byng's words were not signs of cowardice or lack of spirit. They were justified by the deplorable problems he found himself confronted with before he could even get his ships to sea. Eight of his men-of-war were quite unfit for action, while four others were so seriously undermanned that they could not sail until their numbers were made up. When he sought to draw men from other ships in harbour he was firmly prevented by order of the Admiralty. The best ships and crews would be kept to protect England. Even those men he was allocated – many pressed in Ireland or taken directly from hospital – were so poor in quality that he considered his ships 'the worst manned of any perhaps in His Majesty's Navy'. Pressured to sail on 7 April, Byng knew that he was 400 men short of full complements at a minimum, with a further 389 in the early stages of sickness. Even before he reached the Mediterranean the truth was clear – Byng's fleet was not fit to meet the French in battle. So depleted were his crews that he was forced the use some of the troops he was transporting – the 7th Fusiliers – as deckhands. The fault was not his, yet once he had left England he would bear the blame for any disaster that occurred.

Byng was not alone in his uncertainty. When he arrived at Gibraltar he found the Governor, Thomas Fowke, unwilling to give more than the minimum help, for fear of being too weak to resist a French attack there. Byng was supposed to transport troops from Gibraltar to Minorca – where the French had already landed and were currently besieging the British fortress of St Philip's Castle – but he allowed himself to be talked out of it by Fowke. In the end, he merely picked up three extra ships and a few officers on leave from Minorca, and set off for the Balearics. Fowke was as much a victim as Byng. His own shortages of manpower were products of governmental neglect. Even though it had been known for a year that the French were planning to attack British possessions in the Mediterranean no attempt had been made to reinforce the garrisons there.

With a fleet of thirteen ships–of–the–line Byng at last reached Minorca on 19 May. To his immense relief he saw that the Union flag was still flying above the castle, where the 82-year-old General Blakeney with just 2,000 men was putting up a remarkable resistance against the Duc de Richelieu and his 16,000 troops. Blakeney's predicament was itself a product of the government's parsimony. He was short of 34 officers: a second-in-command, all four colonels of regiments and 29 subalterns. However, before Byng could relieve the British garrison he would have to settle accounts with the French fleet under de la Galissonière. Although numerically stronger, Byng was in reality outclassed by the heavier guns and superior sailing qualities of the French. Nevertheless, true to the tradition that a British admiral must throw himself upon an enemy, however strong, Byng closed on the French admiral and made the signal for a general chase. But Byng's subsequent actions were dominated by his attempts to conform slavishly with the Admiralty's Fighting Instructions, which had been promulgated in the late 17th century as an attempt to bring order to the naval mêlées of that period. But Byng was no master of the Instructions and found it difficult to reconcile them with his need to come to grips with the French. His inadequate signalling left many of his captains baffled.

In fact, Byng erred in seeking immediate action. The French instruction to their admirals was to avoid action with British squadrons if it was possible to achieve 'ulterior objectives'. De la Galissonière did not need to defeat Byng; he merely needed to prevent him relieving the island. As a result, the French manoeuvred skilfully, preventing the British fleet from achieving decisive contact. Where engagements did take place the British ships were sometimes isolated by concentrations of French ships – a strategy Nelson would later perfect – and suffered heavy damage. At the end of a day's desultory fighting the British had suffered losses of 42 killed and 265 wounded, most on the *Defiance*, while the French had lost 26 killed and 136 wounded.

During the engagement Byng had moved like a man in the dark, proving himself incompetent if hardly cowardly. He even managed to get between the French and the island, yet he made nothing of this slight advantage. He still had several options open to him: to blockade the island and prevent the French ships returning to harbour, which might have forced de la Galissonière to fight; or to sever the French supply line to Toulon. Either of these would have been better than what he did, which was to call a council of war – always a sign that the admiral has lost his authority and is looking for a consensus for doing something he is afraid to do himself. He asked his captains – naval and army – to decide whether there was any real chance of relieving Minorca, to which they replied that there was not. He then questioned whether a further engagement with the French might endanger Gibraltar, to which they replied that it would. It was therefore decided to withdraw to Gibraltar.

So Byng sailed away, without landing any reinforcements, leaving Minorca's British garrison to fend for itself. This was dereliction of duty, as King George II was the first to point out. He said of Byng, unfairly, 'This man will not fight.' When de la Galissonière's report of the engagement reached Paris – tragically for Byng, earlier than his reached London – it became apparent that the French ships had not suffered heavily and that none of the British ships 'had stood the fire of ours for long'. This was enough to set the witch-hunt in progress – Byng had lacked aggression. Blakeney surrendered St. Philip's Castle on 27 June, after a siege of 70 days during which the poor old man had never spent a night in bed in spite of his gout. In England one might have supposed the Tower of London had fallen. The Duke of Newcastle, fearing that the opprobrium for the fiasco would fall upon him, decided that Byng must take the blame. When the admiral's despatch reached London the politicians printed only that part of it that would condemn him, suppressing the rest. They also revealed that Byng's flagship, the *Ramillies*, suffered no casualties at all in the engagement, a clear indication that Byng had held back from the fight.

Newcastle instructed Anson to undertake 'the immediate trial and condemnation of Byng'. When he arrived at Portsmouth, Byng was informed of His Majesty's displeasure and was arrested, clapped in irons and placed in a room without even a bed. A regicide might have expected better treatment. He was indicted and found guilty, not of cowardice, but of failing to do his utmost to take, sink, burn and destroy the ships of the enemy. The only possible verdict was guilty, and even though the admirals who formed the court-martial immediately asked for the death penalty to be set aside, there was no chance of that. Byng, had he been allowed to live, might have been able to demonstrate the incompetence of the Duke of Newcastle and his gang of cronies. In spite of William Pitt's powerful argument for clemency – and petitions from Voltaire and Richelieu in France – Byng was executed on the foredeck of the *Monarch*, a ship he once commanded, on 14 March 1757. Thus died the most famous symbol of failure in naval history. He was buried in the family vault in Southill, Bedfordshire, where his monument bears the inscription, 'To the Perpetual Disgrace of Public Justice, the Hon. John Byng, Esq., Admiral of the Blue, fell a Martyr to Political Persecution, March 14th in the year MDCCLVII; when Bravery and Loyalty were insufficient Securities for the Life and Honour of a Naval Officer.'

# The 'Triumphs' of Admiral Barroso and Admiral Tamandaré

The savage wars between President Francisco Solano López's Paraguay and the Triple Alliance of Brazil, Argentina and Uruguay, involved some fierce fighting between the rival navies on the River Parana. The allied navy was under the command of the Brazilian Admiral Barroso, a man notable more for his instinct for self-preservation than his military ability. The Brazilians, with their fleet of ironclads, had an immense material advantage over the primitive Paraguayan navy. But what the Brazilians lacked in abundance was the courage to use their weapons to achieve a decisive victory. Admiral Barroso inspired his men only with thoughts of avoiding action, concealing themselves from danger and retreating at the first opportunity.

The war broke out in 1864, by which time López had collected a fleet of six old steamers, armed with a few smooth-bore guns, honeycombed with rust. Against this the Brazilian navy consisted of 40 such steamers, mounting 250 guns. In addition, the Brazilians had 20 small ironclads, heavily armoured and carrying a variety of modern British-made rifled guns. In terms of the opposition the Brazilian fleet was immensely strong. However, its two leaders, Admirals Tamandaré and Barroso, were both tentative and cowardly. Barroso led the first expedition against López's fleet, moving so cautiously that it took him 42 days to cover just 100 miles up the Parana River.

In spite of the anxiety the Brazilian commander clearly felt, he still failed to take any sensible precautions against ambush, although the river was edged on each bank by thick jungle. The Paraguayans, in fact, had used this cover to conceal some artillery. López sent his steamers into action with orders to his men to board the Brazilian vessels, but no one had brought any grappling hooks. Barroso was asleep in his cabin as the Paraguayans steamed up to his ironclads and tried to scramble aboard, many of them missing their footing and falling into the piranha-infested waters. Everywhere was confusion. The Paraguayan sailors showed the courage of desperation – López had told them to succeed or he would have them tortured to death – but the Brazilian firepower was overwhelming and the four remaining Paraguayan steamers were forced to beat a not-very-hasty retreat. Barroso pursued them, finding it extremely difficult not to overtake them. For this triumph, which Barroso merely overheard from the comfort of his cabin – for he certainly never emerged while the fighting was still going on – the admiral was made a Baron. The outcome of this engagement – named the battle of Riachuelo – was most unusual. The victorious Brazilians fled down river, while the defeated Paraguayans were able to salvage the guns from their capsized warships and consolidate the positions they had held before the battle.

Admiral Tamandaré now arrived to support Barroso, bringing with him substantial reinforcements. The Brazilians sent four ironclads up the Parana to a point where they encountered López's defeated army retreating across the river in small boats. Eyewitnesses gave the wretched Paraguayans up as lost only to be amazed when the Brazilian ironclads allowed themselves to be driven off by soldiers in canoes.

On 21 March 1866, Tamandaré swung into action, bringing with him three ironclads and a gun-platform armed with a massive 150-pound rifled gun. These four ships, accompanied by numerous wooden craft, were brought to battle by a single Paraguayan raft, bearing a single smooth-bore gun. What followed defies belief. In an engagement lasting some hours the Brazilians rained shells on everything in sight except the Paraguayan vessel, which inflicted enormous damage on the Brazilian squadron before it was finally sunk. After his success Tamandaré pushed on up river but was held up for several weeks by a single Paraguayan fort boasting just one gun. So many Brazilian shells landed around the fort that the Paraguayans collected them, melted them down and cast new ammunition for their own cannon.

The Brazilians moved on and besieged Curupaity. On some days they would fire upwards of 4,000 shells without damaging the fort at all or causing any casualties. It was only the eventual recall of Tamandaré, to be honoured with the naming of a battleship after him, that allowed his replacement Admiral Ignacio to restore some sanity by bursting past the Paraguayan position with nine ironclads. Even so the Paraguayans were not finished. They kept moving the same guns up river so the Brazilians found themselves held up time after time by the same guns. On 1 March 1866 the Paraguayans carried out a sudden raid by 24 canoes on a squadron of Brazilian ironclads. Two ironclads were sunk and their crews – surprised asleep on deck – were wiped out. On other ships the crews fled below decks and battened down the hatches, until reinforcements came to their rescue and swept the decks with grapeshot. It was the same story everywhere: Brazilian indolence and cowardice pitched against the desperate courage of the few Paraguayans. When López was killed and Paraguay finally accepted defeat the country had been almost depopulated of adult males. The reputations of Admirals Barroso and Tamandaré survived intact and each lived to see his name proudly borne by a brand-new Brazilian battleship. One English eyewitness, striking a sour note, commented that in England, rather than being made a baron, Admiral Barroso would have been shot for cowardice.

A caricature of 'Black Charlie' Napier (1786–1860) as a parliamentary candidate. Napier's colourful naval career culminated in his controversial command of Britain's Baltic fleet in the Crimean War.

# 'Black Charlie' Napier in the Baltic

The appointment of Sir Charles Napier to command Britain's Baltic Fleet in the event of war against Russia in 1854 was a particularly bad one. Known as 'Black Charlie', he was an embittered old man subject to fits of paranoia in which he doubted his own legitimacy and questioned why he was the only small and dark one in his family. When his appointment to command the Baltic Fleet was made public it brought forth a wave of criticism from serving officers.

Controversy followed Napier wherever he went. When he had applied to command the Mediterranean Fleet three years before, the then Prime Minister, Lord John Russell, replied that the post needed 'an officer on whose secrecy and discretion the Queen's ministers can fully rely. I am sorry to say that, notwithstanding your many brilliant exploits, I could not place in you that implicit confidence which is required.' Russell was right, as Napier's performance at a Reform Club banquet on the evening of 7 March 1854 was to show. Rising to speak, after wining and dining well, Napier established an unusual 'first' in diplomacy by informing Her Majesty's Government, as well as the assembled notables – both military and civil – that when he got to the Baltic he would take the opportunity of declaring war on Russia. Admittedly the wine had been flowing, but Sir Charles was surely going far beyond his brief as an officer of the crown when he promised all present 'a prosperous war'. Sir James Graham, the First Lord of the Admiralty, rose next to speak and surprisingly endorsed Napier's sentiments, partly no doubt to cover the admiral's gaffe. But it was too much for *The Times*, which next day reported Napier's speech in full and asked by what authority he was usurping the power of the sovereign to declare war. Questions were asked in Parliament about Napier's indiscretion, but those who knew him best expressed no surprise for 'Black Charlie' Napier, though an excellent seaman, was a man renowned for his intemperate boasting.

---

'Lads, war is declared with a numerous and bold enemy. Should they meet us and offer battle, you know how to dispose of them. Should they remain in port, we must try and get at them. Success depends upon the quickness and precision of your firing. Also, lads, sharpen your cutlasses, and the day is your own.'

**Admiral Sir Charles Napier, 1854**

Charles Napier, British commander in the Baltic during the Crimean War, was quite unsuited to fighting a modern naval battle in the age of steam and ironclads. His reference to using cutlasses presupposed that boarding would still take place, even though long-range guns made this quite impossible.

---

# CHAPTER 2: THE TALE OF A TUB

Battleship development in the second half of the 19th century followed some unusual routes, more than one of which was a dead end.

## The Round Ships

One of the most interesting ideas in the 1860s was the circular ironclad devised for the Russian Fleet by Admiral Popov. Following on from the monitors invented by the Swede John Ericsson, Popov created two of the strangest vessels ever built – named the *Admiral Popov* and the *Novgorod*. Both had circular hulls, carried a heavy main armament of 12-inch guns and had thick armour plating. Unfortunately, both were total failures. Popov, it seems, had failed to cater for the need to keep a straight course. On their trials up the River Dnieper the two ships were caught by the current, whirled helplessly round in circles and spun far out to sea. It was as if the two ironclads were caught in a permanent whirlpool. Their wretched crews could do nothing to control them and lay about the deck hanging on and prostrate with sea-sickness. These two prototype frisbees later found a permanent anchorage as floating forts and tourist attractions.

The revolutionary ironclad *Novgorod* was circular in shape and proved impossible to steer. Along with her sister ship, the *Admiral Popov*, she ended her days as a curiosity and tourist attraction.

The *Hoche*, like most French warships of her time, bore all the signs of having been designed by committee. Absurdly top-heavy, and prone to roll to an alarming degree, she was noted less for her fighting qualities than for the excellence of her accommodation.

# Le Grand Hôtel

The shipbuilders of the 1880s were responsible for some of the most extraordinary monstrosities ever to take to the water. Advances in gunnery and armour-piercing shells made it increasingly necessary to protect battleships with heavy armour. But the more protection a ship needed the heavier and larger she became and the area that needed to be protected increased proportionately. It was a vicious circle. One answer was produced in Britain in the shape of the preposterous battleships *Victoria* and *Sans Pareil*, widely known as the 'pair of slippers' for their very low freeboard, and 'one punch monstrosities' for their single massive turret whose 16.25-inch guns had a lifespan of just 75 shots. The French, ignoring the quip that 'the camel is a horse designed by a committee', produced an extraordinary quartet of battleships over a twelve-year period, during which the *Hoche* and her sisters *Marceau*, *Magenta* and *Neptune* were subjected to such an accretion of bits and pieces by one department or another that they eventually ceased to resemble battleships at all. The *Hoche* was so extraordinary that she was described by one foreign critic as 'a half-submerged whale with a number of labourer's cottages built on its back'. A French critic, more charitably, dubbed her '*Le Grand Hôtel*'.

During the 1880s the French followed the highly inefficient policy of simultaneously working on a number of different classes of ships and constantly tinkering with the designs of each. Although begun in 1880, the *Hoche* and her sisters took over twelve years to complete, during which time every new naval development was added, irrespective of its compatibility with the original blueprint. The *Magenta* was a notable victim. Her original design called for a ship of 9,800 tons, three 13.4-inch guns on a central line and a top speed of 14.5 knots. After the keel had been laid down, it was decided to change the armament to two 13.4-inch and two 10.8-inch guns in a lozenge formation. Two years later a new *Conseil de Travaux* changed the format again, to four 13.4-inch guns and no 10.8-inch. This naturally added substantially to the ship's tonnage. The decision was made to lengthen and broaden the ship and increase its top speed to 16 knots, thus demanding more boiler-room space. Next it was decided that the *Magenta* should have massive military masts added, along with an armoured conning tower. And so Topsy kept growing! Next it was decided to add torpedo nets and searchlights. Then it was a battery of quick-firing guns. By the time the *Magenta* was completed in 1893 she was some 300 tons overweight and had lost 30 per cent of her planned stability. Like her sisters the *Magenta* was dangerously unstable with a superstructure so massive that successive *Conseils de Travaux* were accused of behaving like medieval bishops constructing a Gothic cathedral. To others she was 'a three-storeyed chateau' rising 40 feet above her defensive armoured belt, with 60 guns of five different calibres. If the *Magenta* had trained her guns to one side at speed she would have heeled over and probably capsized. Even with just a five-degree heel her armoured belt was completely under water, making the ship a helpless target; a fifteen-degree heel would have simply flooded the boilers and sunk her. Her captain raised the only word in her defence when he said, 'A ship may go into battle only once in its life, and for 30 years it will be inactive. The superstructures, annoying in battle, notably improve habitability for ordinary life.' One may now better understand the description of the *Hoche* as *Le Grand Hôtel*. The French designers never seemed to understand that the vast superstructures of these ships, high above the defensive armour, would have made them easy targets for enemy fire, if the basic instability of the ships did not sink them first. Even when, in later years, the *Hoche* had her superstructure lightened she still found it impossible to steam at high speed without much of her freeboard under water. Fortunately, these ships never saw action so that it is possible to agree with the captain of the *Magenta* that, useless as they might have been as warships, they provided comfortable accommodation for their crews.

# Battlecruisers

There are times when even the greatest reformers can become a menace. When they mount their hobby-horses it is time to stop indulging them and to lock them away with their toys. And rarely can this have been more urgent than in the case of Lord Fisher and the love of his old age – the battlecruiser, the fast, sleek, beautiful 'killer' ship. Unfortunately for Britain, Fisher was not locked away and continued to bewitch his listeners, luring them to destruction on the rocks of his irrationality. For the harsh truth was that the battlecruiser, as envisaged by Jacky Fisher, was a disaster with a capital D.

Since the 16th century the battleship had dominated naval warfare but as the tasks of the navy proliferated in the 19th century, involving commerce-protection, blockading, reconnaissance and, in the case of Britain, anti-slavery duties, the need arose for a new kind of ship to replace the frigate. It had to be fast, strong enough to deter most aggressors and suitable for long-range cruising – hence 'the cruiser' was born. By the late 19th century the role of the cruiser had been more accurately defined in terms of defending communications and attacking enemy commerce, and for this there was the need for vessels stronger than existing cruisers and fast enough to escape from a battleship should they meet one. All naval powers built armoured cruisers to fill this need but one man – the brilliant Admiral Sir John Fisher – envisaged a new kind of cruiser which would combine the firepower of a battleship with the speed of a cruiser. He called his 'dream ship' the *Uncatchable*.

In the creation of any major warship three elements need to be kept in balance – protection, speed and firepower. Should any one of the three become dominant then the design is likely to fail. Speed could only be increased at the cost of protection and vice versa. This was a fundamental of warship design but unfortunately Fisher refused to maintain a sense of balance. Once the *Dreadnought* had been launched and had revolutionized the world of battleship design, Fisher turned his attention to his idea for the *Uncatchable*. It was intended to be not so much an armoured cruiser as a 'battlecruiser', in that in hitting power it would be the equal of a battleship and in speed – which would be its protection instead of heavy armour – it would be as fast as a cruiser. When these 'battlecruisers' first saw the light of day they were as revolutionary as the *Dreadnought* had been. Fisher's *Invincible*, *Indomitable* and *Inflexible* carried 12-inch guns and could travel at over 27 knots. They seemed to be the answer to Britain's naval problems with Germany – until one looked at their armour protection, just 6 inches amidships and 4 inches in the bows. Big they might be, and fast, but they were dangerously vulnerable. They would be 'easy meat' for any battleship. This serious distortion of the vital equation involved in building warships worried many informed commentators. Brassey wrote with remarkable prescience in 1908:

> Vessels of this enormous size and cost are unsuitable for many of the duties of cruisers, but an even stronger objection to the repetition of the type is that an admiral, having 'Invincibles' in his fleet will be certain to put them in the line of battle, where their comparatively light protection will be a disadvantage and their high speed of no value.

Tragically, Brassey was quite right. He did not live to see his prediction come true in the Denmark Strait, on 24 May 1941, when the greatest of all battlecruisers, *Hood*, succumbed to the power of the battleship *Bismarck* (see p. 172).

Fisher's obsession with speed and hitting power at the expense of protection was not shared by everyone. German designers saw value in the concept of battlecruisers, but their sense of moderation enabled them to achieve a better balance in their first ship, the *Von der Tann*, which was superior to the *Invincible* in every way but gun size. As the Germans matched each class of battlecruiser built by Britain it was noticeable how much less emphasis they placed on extravagant looks, speed and gunnery. They built their ships to survive punishment, if necessary, and were already regarding the new type as offering a fast wing for the main battlefleet, rather than a roving commission as Fisher had originally contemplated. The British battlecruisers increasingly became a component of the main battle fleet. As Brassey had warned, they would be expected to participate in a main fleet action. Whereas the *Von der Tann*, *Moltke*, *Seydlitz* and *Derfflinger* were able to exchange fire with the British super-dreadnoughts of the Queen Elizabeth class at Jutland, their British rivals were not even able to resist the fire of the German battlecruisers, let alone the German battleships. Clearly the Germans had achieved a far better balance between speed, protection and hitting power. And the reason for that was that they were not subjected to the increasingly unrealistic demands of Admiral Fisher. With the laying down of the *Lion* and her sisters, and later the *Tiger*, British battlecruisers were now substantially bigger than the latest battleships and carried the same armament. As they grew ever larger, protection was sacrificed to maintain or increase their speed towards the target of 30 knots. By comparison, the latest German battlecruisers were smaller, slower, less well armed but infinitely stronger fighting vessels. With war against Germany imminent the First Lord of the Admiralty, Winston Churchill, chortled that the British had an 'undoubted superiority in our ships, unit for unit'. But he was wrong – as events were soon to show.

By late 1911 Fisher had become completely obsessed by his battlecruiser dream. On 10

The battleship *Tiger* typified First Sea Lord 'Jacky' Fisher's unrealistic approach to warship design in the years leading up to World War I. With her elegant lines, she was more of a work of art than an effective fighting ship. Her gunnery proved deplorable both at the Dogger Bank and at Jutland.

November he told Churchill that he must 'reduce armour and increase subdivision . . . You only want enough thickness of armour to make the shell burst outside and in most places where the armour is put you don't want it all.' He carried on by emphasizing, 'Hit first, hit hard, and keep on hitting – when you like, how you like and where you like.' He never mentioned the enemy hitting back. When the Director of Naval Ordnance and the Admiralty Controller reminded Churchill that there was still a need to build battleships, Fisher was outraged, calling them 'Slugs' who wanted to perpetuate battleships as heavily armoured as tortoises. His sense of balance seems to have left him completely in this minute to Churchill:

A nightmare! The British Fleet were Spithead Forts, splendid armour but they couldn't move. The first desideratum is Speed. Your fools don't see it – They are always running about to see where they can put on a little more armour! to make it safer! You don't go into battle to be safe! No, you go into Battle to hit the other fellow in the eyes first so that he can't see you. Yes! you hit him first, you hit him hard and you keep on hitting. That's your safety! You don't get hit back.

Soon Fisher was on the track of the 15-inch gun for his battlecruisers and speed – much more speed. As he said to Churchill, 'There must be sacrifice of armour . . . There must be further VERY GREAT INCREASE OF SPEED.' Fisher named his new wonder ship the *Incomparable*. She would carry ten 16-inch guns, bigger than anything ever built. When he was told that such heavy armament would reduce the speed his response was predictable: reduce the thickness of the armour. When he heard that the Germans were working on a diesel engine for their capital ships, Fisher snapped, 'They have killed fifteen men in experiments and we have not killed one.'

When war came Fisher found himself increasingly isolated at the Admiralty. Yet he continued to force his plans through. 'Battlecruisers and more battlecruisers, is the watchword. Cumbersome battleships are rotten.' By putting pressure on his protégé, Admiral Jellicoe, commander-in-chief of the Grand Fleet, as well as on the battlecruiser commander, Admiral David Beatty, Fisher kept the battlecruisers coming. Two new and improved 'Tigers' were laid down – *Repulse* and *Renown* – armed with 15-inch guns and with just 6 inches of armour protection. Fisher's fantasies were completely out of step with the realities of the war at sea. He gloated that the battlecruisers *Invincible* and *Inflexible* had sunk the German armoured cruisers *Scharnhorst* and *Gneisenau* at the Falklands, without suffering any casualties. Yet that outcome had been inevitable: it was battlecruisers against armoured cruisers, with every advantage in the British favour. But how would a battlecruiser like the *Indefatigable* fare against even the oldest and weakest German battlecruiser, the *Von der Tann*? Fisher would get his answer at the battle of Jutland.

In May 1915 Fisher was pushing back the barriers even further. He asked Cammell Laird what was the biggest and the longest ship that they could build. He was planning the *Incomparable*, which would be 1,000 feet long – twice the length of the best German battleships – with an armament of six 20-inch guns and a top speed of 35 knots. As this monster was to weigh just 40,000 tons, its protection would have been flimsy in the extreme. Anyone who opposed these ideas was referred to as belonging to the 'bow and arrow party'. After *Repulse* and *Renown*, came the most magnificent – and tragic – of British battlecruisers, the *Hood*, which represented everything that was good – and bad – in the genus. But the destruction of three battlecruisers – *Invincible, Indefatigable* and *Queen Mary* at Jutland in 1916 – jolted Fisher temporarily. On 15 June Jellicoe told him the obvious truth, which was that the British battlecruisers had inadequate armoured protection compared with the German ships. Undeterred, Fisher wrote back, 'Never meant to get in enemy's range.' The old man was incorrigible.

Even out of office Fisher continued to ride his hobby-horse, and before he resigned as First Sea Lord he planted enough seeds to maintain a healthy stock of grotesque new warships. There was a submarine armed with a 12-inch gun which would have sunk had it been fired, and by 1918 Fisher was working on a submarine battlecruiser of 30,000 tons, with eight 18- or 20-inch guns. At best it was a byway, at worst a dead end. Aircraft were coming to influence warship design and the future lay not with the battlecruiser or indeed with the battleship, for that matter, but with the aircraft carrier. By a supreme irony the last British battlecruisers – the craziest warships built for the Royal Navy – the *Furious, Courageous* and *Glorious* (known alternatively as the *Spurious, Outrageous* and *Uproarious*), the former with a single 18-inch gun and virtually no armour at all, were converted into aircraft carriers and saw useful service in the Second World War.

# Ships That Torpedo Themselves

Weapons systems are generally designed to operate within a range of climatic conditions. However, when they are exposed to conditions far beyond the norm there is always the danger that they will malfunction. This can be unfortunate if the weapon is of prime defensive importance – as with the 'Sea Wolf' anti-aircraft missile system during the Falklands War of 1982. But if the weapon is offensive in character then the worst that can usually happen is a failure to strike the enemy. However, there have been two recorded occasions of weapons turning upon their masters and, in one case, inflicting decisive damage. The weapon was the torpedo and the victim the British cruiser *Trinidad*.

On 29 March 1942, *Trinidad* was escorting convoy PQ13 in Arctic waters when it was attacked by three German destroyers. It was so cold that day that spray froze instantly as it landed on the decks. After an exchange of gunfire *Trinidad* fired three torpedoes at the Z26, but two of them were so iced up that they failed to leave their tubes. The third torpedo malfunctioned when the oil in its motor and gyroscope froze, causing it to change direction, swing round and return the way it had come. The torpedo hit the cruiser amidships, damaging her severely. It was only with extreme difficulty that *Trinidad* limped into Murmansk for repairs.

Luckier than *Trinidad* was the Chilean ironclad *Huascar*, when it tried to torpedo the corvette *Abtao* in 1879. The *Huascar*'s commander, Admiral Grau, closed to within 200 yards of the unsuspecting *Abtao* and fired the torpedo. It travelled straight for about 100 yards before suddenly turning to port, making a wide semi-circle and returning straight back towards the *Huascar*. Lieutenant Diaz Canseco, alive to the danger, leapt overboard, swam towards the torpedo and forced it to change direction with his hands. Admiral Grau was so disgusted with the new weapon – for it was the first time he had ever fired a torpedo – that he took his remaining supply and buried them in a cemetery.

# The Art of Self-Defence

The British Task Force sent to the Falklands in April 1982 operated on shoestring resources, and was clearly the minimum that could have carried out the operation successfully. It was a risk that would never have been taken in the context of a wider war. Too much of Britain's limited naval capacity was involved, and the need for aircraft carriers, destroyers and frigates to defend themselves against potentially overwhelming air power placed an unreasonable burden on their defensive missile systems. The two aircraft carriers – *Invincible* and *Hermes* – were able to carry just twenty Sea Harriers to provide both air defence and strike capacity. Apart from the Sea Harriers the task force could rely on only the 'Sea Dart' missiles of the Type 42 destroyers – *Coventry*, *Glasgow* and *Sheffield* – and the close air-defence system 'Sea Wolf' carried by the frigates *Broadsword* and *Brilliant*. The fact that by 1982 the Royal Navy was essentially an anti-submarine force meant that the Falklands operation would test the adaptability of the defence systems to their utmost – and beyond.

Of the two main forms of missile defence – 'Sea Dart' and 'Sea Wolf' – the former was known to be not totally reliable. In addition, the Argentinians had bought 'Sea Dart' from Britain and their pilots could be expected to know how best to evade it. Furthermore, it had been designed to operate against high-flying Warsaw Pact aircraft and was least effective against low-level attack. In view of the nature of the fighting, in the mist and heavy cloud of the South Atlantic, it could be assumed that the Argentinian planes would come in low to deliver their attacks. This would mean that ships equipped with 'Sea Dart' would be almost helpless and totally dependent on the two frigates that had the close-range defence of 'Sea Wolf'. This was poor planning by the Admiralty, which had failed to equip its ships with appropriate defences. Without 'Sea Wolf' the Type 42 destroyers were forced back on their 'historical leftovers': 40-mm Bofors and 20-mm Oerlikons of World War Two vintage. The American Vulcan Phalanx system was available for anti-aircraft defence and the Task Force should have been equipped with this before it left Britain. It was asking too much of men to go into battle defensively naked.

The much vaunted 'Sea Wolf' system turned out to be something of a 'Jekyll and Hyde'. On 12 May, four Argentinian Skyhawks came in to attack the destroyer *Glasgow* and the frigate *Brilliant*. The latter fired her 'Sea Wolf' and two of the attacking planes exploded, while another flew into the sea. However, an hour later, a further attack was made under the level at which 'Sea Dart' could operate. When 'Sea Wolf' was switched on it became confused by the multiple targets and closed down. There was nothing for it but to fire the Bofors guns and hope for the best. The Skyhawks released three bombs. One bounced over *Brilliant* and another smashed through the hull of *Glasgow* without exploding. The problem was that 'Sea Wolf' had been designed to engage a single incoming plane and its computerized operating system was confused by the appearance of four planes simultaneously. The missile systems were clearly inadequate to defend the Task Force and the loss of a carrier to an Exocet missile or a bombing attack could have signalled the end of the entire campaign. Unless the Harriers could break up the incoming flights of Argentinian planes the navy was bound to suffer heavy losses in ships. But as the Task Force was not equipped with AEW – Airborne Early Warning – would the Harriers have time to intervene?

The navy's confidence in its ability to win and maintain aerial superiority had been based on their misplaced belief in their anti-aircraft missile systems. Had they fully appreciated the drawbacks, notably of 'Sea Wolf', it is doubtful if the operation would have been undertaken in the first place. In the event it was the Sea Harriers that stood between the Task Force and total disaster. The heavy losses among the destroyers and frigates can be attributed both to the inadequacy of their missile defences and to the advanced role they were asked to play in the absence of AEW. No weapons system is infallible, but that which the British took south to the Falklands was dangerously flawed.

# Sir Percy Scott Sticks to his Guns

For a nation whose survival for so long depended on the strength of her navy, Britain has suffered more than any other from failures in naval gunnery. For much of the 19th century the navy was required to do little more than show the flag in distant parts and display itself as the world's greatest fighting force. With its fighting qualities taken for granted by friend and foe, the navy began to fall back on less warlike manifestations of its inner strength: smart uniforms and bright paintwork. Gunnery practice became 'the Cinderella of all drills', with practice shells being more often than not thrown overboard as the smoke caused by firing them spoiled the paintwork. One British battleship had flannel nightcaps placed on the gun barrels to keep them clean, while its watertight doors had been so thoroughly polished over a twelve-year period that they were worn away and no longer watertight. The height of incompetence was reached at the bombardment of the Alexandrian Forts in 1882, when eight British battleships fired 3,000 heavy shells and achieved just ten hits on the target – completely random fire might have achieved better results.

Improvements in British gunnery owed much to the work of a young naval officer, Percy Scott, for whom such incompetent gunnery was nothing less than a national scandal. When Scott first joined the navy Sir Edward Seymour told him, 'The chief things required in a man-of-war are smart men aloft, cleanliness of the ship, the men's bedding and the boats. Her gunnery is quite a secondary thing.' And in Scott's view this attitude continued to prevail in the second half of the century as much as it had in the first. Each year every man-of-war was inspected by an admiral, but in his report there was never any mention of efficiency at gunnery, a feature not added until 1903. Scott recorded one admiral's report on the *Astraea* in 1901:

> Ship's company of good physique, remarkably clean and well dressed; state of bedding, specially satisfactory.
>
> The stoker division formed a fine body of clean and well-dressed men.
>
> At exercise the men moved very smartly.
>
> The ship looks well inside and out, and is very clean throughout.
>
> The tone of the ship generally seems to me to be distinctly good.

Scott reports that the *Astraea* was, in fact, a fine gunnery ship, but nobody aboard gained any credit for that.

Scott served with the Mediterranean Fleet during its attack on Alexandria in 1882 and was astonished to find that the Admiralty was satisfied with the fleet's gunnery on that occasion, in that it was better than that of the Egyptians. Scott was not amused, commenting that many of the British shells had been duds anyway, only half filled with powder or with faulty fuses, and would not have exploded even had they hit the targets.

In 1886 Scott was appointed to the battleship *Duke of Edinburgh*, the most modern turret ship of her time. Even so he found he was wasting his time trying to preach the gospel of gunnery. There was a far more powerful god in the fleet than the one he worshipped. Appearance was everything as he soon found:

> So we gave up instruction in gunnery, spent money on enamel paint, burnished up every bit of steel on board, and soon got the reputation of being a very smart ship. She was certainly very nice in appearance. The nuts of all the bolts on the aft deck were gilded, the magazine keys were electro-plated, and statues of Mercury surmounted the revolver racks. In short, nothing was left undone to insure a good inspection.
>
> In those days it was customary for a Commander to spend half his pay, or more, in buying paint to adorn H.M. ships, and it was the only road to promotion. A ship had to look pretty; prettiness was necessary to promotion and as the Admiralty did not supply sufficient paint or cleaning material for keeping the ship up to the required standard, the officers had to find the money for buying the required housemaiding material. The prettiest ship I have ever seen was the *Alexandria*. I was informed that £2,000 had been spent by the officers on her decoration.
>
> In these circumstances it was no wonder that the guns were not fired if it could be avoided, for the powder then used had a most deleterious effect on the paintwork, and one Commander who had his whole ship enamelled told me that it cost him £100 to repaint her after target practice.

Scott found that his ideas for improving gun-sights were not welcomed by the Admiralty, and he was even warned that his efforts to instigate improvements were harming his chances of promotion. But Scott refused to be silenced. When the *Terrible* left England for service at the Cape in 1900, Scott found that all her gunsights were inaccurate, and her main armament so bad that scoring a hit on a moving target would just be a matter of luck. Furthermore, Scott found that this was true for every ship tested. When Scott tested the new gun-sights of the *Centurion* in 1904 he found them inaccurate and refused to pass them. This irritated the Admiralty which tried to cajole him into doing so. When Scott refused to be bullied the Admiralty sent an inspector of their own choice who immediately declared the sights acceptable and the ship then sailed to China where, in Scott's words, 'it was quite unfit to go into action'. The problem was that if what Scott said was true – as it undoubtedly was – then the gun-sights of all the ships in the navy were inefficient and the guns of the whole fleet needed to be resighted. To Scott's chagrin the highly incompetent First Lord, Lord Selborne, claimed to be making gunnery his prime concern. This was pure nonsense; until Selborne was replaced in 1904, there was not the slightest chance of a general improvement in the gunnery of the Royal Navy.

In 1905 Percy Scott was appointed 'Inspector of Target Practice' and at last he had the chance to get things done. With Sir John Jellicoe, as Director of Naval Ordnance, real improvements were possible – and not before time. At fleet target practice – even at point-blank range – less than 50 per cent hits were achieved and some ships still achieved a nil score. Scott was now on the trail of director firing which he eventually managed to force on a reluctant Admiralty in time for the First World War. But it was no easy task.

---

*'The holding of a number of patents would, in their Lordships' opinion, constitute a grave objection to his being selected for any scientific or administrative post in Her Majesty's service.'*

**The Admiralty on Sir Percy Scott's attempt to patent his inventions in 1896**

The Admiralty positively discouraged serving naval officers from improving their technical capabilities. Engineer officers were not regarded as 'gentlemen' and, as Sir Percy Scott found, 'clever' officers were unpopular throughout the service.

---

Even though director firing had proved itself by 1905 the Admiralty boycotted it until 1911 when, on the insistence of Sir John Jellicoe, director firing was installed in the *Neptune*. In the six 'wasted years' – as Scott saw it – the Admiralty reached an amazing decision. In order to cope with the smoke from forward turrets obscuring the sighting of the rear turrets, British battleships practised for battle in such a way that no forward firing took place. Nor could any enemy – real or imaginary – be allowed to operate except in good weather and with the wind blowing towards them, thus dispersing the smoke from the British turrets and not impairing the sighting of the British guns. It was not until Winston Churchill became First Lord of the Admiralty that director firing was generally introduced into the Grand Fleet but by then a blunder of astonishing proportions had been perpetrated. The *Dreadnought*, launched in 1906, had a design fault by which the mast which carried the observation platform for controlling the guns was erected abaft the funnel, with the result that the gun control officer was both roasted and – half the time – smoked into the bargain. On one occasion, apparently, the mast got so hot that the wretched observer had to stay aloft for days and have his food hoisted to him for fear that he would be scalded as he descended. Acting on this experience, the next two classes of battleships were built with the mast in front of the funnel. But the Admiralty did not thank Percy Scott for his advice and reverted to the old style of placing the mast abaft the funnel in all the super-dreadnought battleships and battlecruisers launched up to 1912. Scott constructed a model to demonstrate this fault and showed it to Winston Churchill who immediately saw the problem. But how could it be remedied? To change the funnel and the mast around in more than a dozen ships would cost half a million pounds. Nevertheless, Churchill stood by Scott and forced the matter through.

But in solving one problem the Admiralty designers introduced another even worse one. They removed the strong tripod masts, capable of carrying the weight of a director-tower, and replaced them with lighter structures incapable of carrying the extra weight. Again Scott sought out Churchill, but this time the Admiralty was adamant that it would not give in and it was not until much later, during the war, that they were forced to carry out the repairs that Scott had recommended.

Sir Percy Scott has been called the father of modern naval gunnery, but he would have been the first to demolish the idea that he had achieved a thorough reform of the bad practices which had developed after the Napoleonic Wars and had continued throughout the 19th century. So entrenched was the conservatism of the Admiralty that British gunnery remained poor during most of the major engagements of the First World War – Coronel, Dogger Bank, the Dardanelles and particularly Jutland. And the problem was not even solved by the outbreak of the Second World War. In the final battle with the *Bismarck*, the battleships *Rodney* and *King George V* – even at point-blank range – fired a total of 719 shells at the German ship without managing to sink her. One can imagine how Scott would have felt if he had heard Admiral Tovey telling his fleet gunnery officer that he would have more chance of hitting the *Bismarck* if he threw his binoculars at her.

# The *Thunderer*

Even though breech-loading naval guns had been demonstrated as early as 1860 the British Admiralty was slow in making the transition from the tried and tested muzzle-loaders that had served Britain so well since the time of Sir Francis Drake and the Armada. Yet there seemed

The *Thunderer* was regarded as something of a hoodoo ship. Equipped with muzzle-loading guns rather than breech-loaders, she marked a retrograde step by the Royal Navy. The disastrous explosion aboard the *Thunderer* in 1879 finally convinced the Admiralty of the need to adopt breech-loading guns.

little point in building bigger and better ships when their main armaments suffered the extraordinary drawback of having to be loaded externally. The shells were now far too large to be loaded manually and so ever more weird methods had to be adopted to lift the massive weights into the barrels. A huge 16-inch gun, weighing in at 80 tons, was built for HMS *Inflexible*. A shell from this monster could penetrate 24 inches of armour plating. But instead of reacting with appropriate fearfulness the world's naval architects could only gasp with astonishment at the lunatic obstinacy of Britain's naval designers. Rather than equipping the *Inflexible* with breech-loaders for her huge revolving turret, they had designed a deck housing to which, after each firing, the turret had to return so that it could have its barrels reloaded by a hydraulic system within the housing. What would have happened had the battleship been under fire and the deck housing smashed is not difficult to imagine. The great ship would have been totally disarmed and helpless. Enemy ships of far less strength than the *Inflexible* could have closed to point-blank range and pounded her with their smaller guns.

Eventually it took a disaster aboard the battleship *Thunderer* to make the Admiralty see the error of their ways. On 2 January 1879, the *Thunderer* was taking part in gunnery practice in the Gulf of Ismid. One of her 12-inch, 38-ton Woolwich muzzle-loading guns – a mere baby compared with *Inflexible*'s over-fed youngster – was being charged with 85 pounds of powder and a common shell when the shell exploded in a barrel of the ship's forward turret. The muzzle of the gun was blown off, causing terrible damage in which two officers and nine men were killed, and 35 others seriously wounded by flying metal splinters. The accident was probably caused by double-loading the muzzle, but the Committee of Inquiry at first tried to claim that the shell had shifted after being hydraulically rammed home. Whatever the true cause, the accident was a clear pointer to the dangers inherent in clinging to the outworn habit of muzzle-loading. The breech-loading turret had been adopted in other navies and Britain risked losing her naval supremacy by building ever larger models of an outdated system. The *Thunderer* disaster eventually convinced the Admiralty that the time had at last come to accept that change was necessary.

---

*'Even if the propeller had the power of propelling a vessel it would be found altogether useless in practice, because of the power being applied in the stern it would be absolutely impossible to make the vessel steer.'*

### Sir William Symonds, Surveyor of the Navy, 1837

This statement by an Admiralty expert was all part of the attempt to hinder progress in naval technology so that the advantage Britain had gained with her wooden-walled fleet over the French could be maintained without undue expenditure and the need to replace ageing vessels. The result, of course, was to leave Britain far behind her competitors, notably France.

---

# Powder B

On 10 September 1905 the Japanese battleship *Mikasa*, flagship of Admiral Togo at the battle of Tsushima (see p. 3), was rent by a series of explosions while at anchor. Six months later the

Brazilian battleship *Aquidaban* was also torn asunder by an internal explosion. Both of these disasters were apparently due to the unsound storage practices employed in both navies for explosive powder. Yet it was not until 1907 when the French battleship *Iéna* suffered a similar fate that governments began to investigate the growing problem of unstable powder, in the case of the French the notorious 'B Powder', a smokeless nitro-cellulose mixture which was extremely volatile. Unless the temperature of the powder was rigidly controlled, a difficult task for ships on Mediterranean and Caribbean duty, it was liable to explode without warning.

The loss of the *Iéna* provoked an enquiry at which it was revealed that not long before, the battleship *Admiral Duperré* had nearly suffered the same fate and had only been saved by immediate flooding of the magazines. The matter had been hushed up and no effort had been made to instigate reform. In fact, nothing was done until on 29 September 1911 the battleship *Liberté* blew up at anchor in Toulon. The crew of the stricken battleship behaved with astounding bravery. As one of their officers related:

> Something happened which I cannot praise too highly. When the fire broke out many jumped overboard. When they heard the bugle calling them to 'Fire Stations', they began to swim back to the ship, while others who had already been picked up by ships nearby had jumped overboard again and swum back to the *Liberté*. Most of these men are dead now.

The explosion was so enormous that a piece of wreckage 40 tons in weight flew 150 metres across the harbour and landed on the top of the aft turret of the battleship *République*. The body of the *Liberté*'s bugler was also found on the *République*.

Another court of inquiry was held which discovered that it was 'poudre B' which had accounted for the *Liberté* as it had accounted for the *Iéna*. Even after the *Iéna* disaster had shown that powder B needed to be kept away from heat, the magazine of the *Liberté* had been situated in an area where pipes from the boilers were routed. The potency of the deadly powder was demonstrated yet again in 1921. Shells from the *Liberté*, which had been at the bottom of the harbour for ten years, were brought to the surface and taken by lighter out to sea. Before the lighter could dump her cargo the powder B exploded and blew her and her crew to pieces.

# Smoke Signals

During the 17th century the giving of salutes by warships became so excessive and wasted so much gunpowder that it placed a real financial burden on the England of Charles II. Ridiculous as it may seem the gunners resorted to their weapons every time anyone went ashore, and if it should be a lady the seamen would fire seven guns and play a tune on the trumpets. In 1675 a merchant ship in the Thames failed to give an adequate salute to a man-of-war, whereupon the warship fired a shot at her to make her stop and apologize. On this occasion, the gunner went aboard and fined the merchant skipper six shillings and six pence for the cost of the powder.

The matter of wasting powder was raised in the House of Commons. Apparently East Indiamen meeting English warships in the Channel had to salute with seven guns, while the man-of-war replied with five. At Plymouth Castle each man-of-war saluted with nine guns, the castle replied with the same and then the warship fired three more to express its thanks. And so it went on. An English captain named Holden, invited to dinner on one of the ships he was escorting to Tangier, was given a five-gun salute when he left her, to which he replied

*Plus ça change, plus c'est la même chose.* The *Blücher* capsizes in the North Sea, 23 January 1915 (top), while its namesake shares a similar fate in Oslofjord, 9 April 1940 (bottom).

The first and last ships of their kind. The British battlecruiser *Invincible* in 1907, its date with destiny at Jutland still nine years in the future (top). The battlecruiser *Hood* in 1938 – an appointment with the *Bismarck* in the offing (bottom).

with three, apparently on the basis that between Englishmen the vote of thanks required two guns less. But with foreigners the English insisted on having a reply to a salute with the same number of guns. When one Venetian ship saluted an English vessel with eleven guns, she was snubbed with a reply of just five. On the King's birthday every ship in the fleet – and there were hundreds, large and small – fired thirteen guns. When one British admiral entered Malta the Knights of St John gave him a 45-gun salute, lasting two hours. Every English ship then replied with 21 guns. On St. George's Day, after the King's health had been drunk, every ship in the fleet fired 25 rounds. And if a ship's captain should die his gunners might fire anything between 40 and 100 rounds.

It was an expensive folly which imposed an unnecessary burden on the fragile economy of the Stuart state – but it must have been fun.

# What's in a Name?

On 23 January 1915, the German armoured cruiser *Blücher* rolled over and capsized with the loss of over 900 men, after being battered by the British battlecruisers at the battle of the Dogger Bank (see p. 169). The *Blücher* was far too weak and too slow to stand in the line of battle with the faster German battlecruisers under Admiral Hipper, which managed to escape when a signalling error by Lieutenant Ralph Seymour, aboard the British flagship *Lion,* caused the other British ships to call off their pursuit.

On 9 April 1940 the German heavy cruiser *Blücher* rolled over on her side after suffering the ignominious fate of being torpedoed by a Norwegian fort in Oslofjord, during the German invasion of Norway. Her commander, Rear-Admiral Kummetz, had completely under-estimated the strength of Norwegian resistance and had slowly sailed up to the Oscarsborg fort until, at point-blank range, his ship had been virtually lifted out of the water by two 11-inch shells from the fort's antiquated guns, as well as by two torpedoes. Over 1,000 lives were lost.

'Hood' has been a famous name in the Royal Navy since the late 18th century when the brothers Samuel and Alexander gave sterling service to their country in the wars against the French. Several British warships had carried the name, including a pre-Dreadnought battleship, launched in 1891, and the most famous of all British battlecruisers. But was it a lucky name? At the battle of Jutland in 1916 the commander of the 3rd Battlecruiser Squadron was a descendent of the two great Hoods, Rear-Admiral the Hon. Horace Hood, flying his flag in the *Invincible*. At 1829 hours on 31 May, the *Invincible* was struck by a shell from the German battlecruiser *Derfflinger* on her 'Q' turret and promptly exploded in an astonishing mushroom cloud of smoke, the third British battlecruiser to perish in that fashion in a matter of hours. So shallow was the North Sea at this point that as the ship broke in half her stern and bows projected from the water, making a huge 'V' hundreds of feet high. Rear-Admiral Hood perished with over 1,000 of the *Invincible*'s crew. Just six men survived.

Twenty-five years later another British battlecruiser – this time carrying the great name of *Hood* – was again facing German warships in action (see p. 172). On 24 May 1941 the *Hood* was struck by a salvo of shells from the German battleship *Bismarck,* which penetrated her thin deck armour and caused an enormous explosion in her magazine. Like the *Invincible* at Jutland, the *Hood* perished in a vast cloud of smoke, thousands of feet high. Of her crew of over 1,400 men only three survived.

# CHAPTER 3: THE PRICE OF ADMIRALTY

Blunders in wartime are rarely simply the result of human failure or mechanical malfunction in the battle zone. On too many occasions they are caused by factors over which the man on the spot has no control, such as faulty intelligence, inept strategic judgment and even simple administrative errors. Such blunders are the 'price of admiralty' that every serving mariner – from whatever nation – has to pay over and over again in each successive war.

## Friendly Fire

On 22 February 1940 the German First Destroyer Flotilla – six destroyers led by Commander Fritz Berger in *Friedrich Eckoldt* – set out to intercept British trawlers operating on the Dogger Bank. It seemed a simple mission – codenamed 'Caviar' – and Navy Group West (which controlled the operation) was alerted by the Luftwaffe that 'air reconnaissance' would be available to 'cover the destroyers' departure and return'. In addition, apparently, 'Bomber forces will also be at readiness.' Nobody quite understood this last reference but assumed that it meant that bomber support would be available if the destroyers were to run into formidable opposition – an altogether unlikely event.

At 1913 hours the *Friedrich Eckoldt* detected the sound of an aircraft overhead, apparently a bomber. But was it friendly or not? As the plane made no attempt to identify itself two of the destroyers fired a few random shots, whereupon the plane returned fire with its machine gun. Then, as the moonlight struck the side of the plane, a lookout on the *Max Schultz* called out 'It's one of ours', claiming to have seen the German insignia. But was he mistaken? On the *Friedrich Eckoldt* Berger was certain that if German bombers had been in the vicinity he would have been told. Suddenly, at 1944 hours, the *Leberecht Maas* radioed that she had spotted the plane again, coming out of the clouds. On his radio receiver Berger heard a dull explosion, followed by another. The plane had dropped two bombs, hitting the *Leberecht Maas* amidships. Berger immediately turned back to help his struggling colleague.

As it happened, X Air Corps had decided to carry out an attack on enemy shipping in the North Sea on the same day as the destroyers began 'Operation Caviare'. Navy Group West was accordingly informed that two squadrons of Heinkel He-111 bombers would be hunting British shipping that night, but someone forgot to warn the destroyers. One of the Heinkels, flown by Warrant Officer Jäger, became detached from the others. Jäger's observer, Sergeant Schräpler, spotted a ship below which he later described as 'rectangular' and clearly a merchantman – in fact it was one of Berger's destroyers. When asked at the court of inquiry how much experience he had had in identifying ships from the air at night, Schräpler replied, 'None at all. That was the first time.' Both plane and destroyers were unaware of each other's identity owing to a simple breakdown in communications between the Luftwaffe and the navy – and the consequences were severe. Convinced that the ships were hostile Jäger decided to attack and struck the *Leberecht Maas* with two bombs.

Commander Berger raced back to help, only to find that the *Leberecht Maas* had broken in half and was sinking. He immediately ordered the other destroyers with him to lower their boats and try to rescue the survivors. A few minutes later there was another explosion and a bright flash of light in the darkness. Captain Böhmig of the *Theodor Riedel*, engaged in trying to rescue the men swimming in the sea, suddenly heard the message, 'Sounds of submarine, strength five decibels, to starboard.' So there was a British submarine, after all, Böhmig thought. It must have been that which sank the *Leberecht Maas*. At once he ordered depth charges to be launched but his own ship was almost shattered by their explosions, damaging its steering mechanism and making it go round in circles – at the mercy of the submerged British submarine. The sound of depth charges being fired convinced the other German captains that Böhmig must have located a submarine. Meanwhile, lookouts on the *Erich Koellner* called out that they had also spotted a submarine. This put Commander Berger in an unenviable situation not unlike the British cruiser captains on the Broad Fourteens in 1914 (see p. 60). As Berger later explained: 'I was by now convinced that a submarine was present . . . to date British bombers had failed to score a single hit even by day, was it likely that they had suddenly scored a series of hits by night?' So, while Berger and his captains scurried about in the dark looking for a submarine, for Jäger and his crew it was a 'red-letter day', having sunk two enemy vessels in one night.

Berger, fearing that his ships might be 'sitting ducks' during a rescue operation, made the heartbreaking decision to abandon the men in the water and to leave the area at full speed. So quickly did the destroyers leave that one ran over its own rescue launch, killing its own men and drowning the recently rescued survivors from the *Leberecht Maas*. Signals now reached Berger thick and fast. In the darkness his crew panicked, sighting submarines all around and torpedo tracks making towards them as if drawn by a magnet. What they could see, in fact, was their own bow wash illuminated by the moon. Hysterical lookouts next claimed to see a conning tower which one of the destroyers tried to ram only to find at the last moment that it was the bow section of the doomed *Leberecht Maas*, slipping beneath the waves.

Berger was by now thoroughly confused. He had just come across what he believed was the stricken *Leberecht Maas*, even though he had been heading in the opposite direction, away from her. And then the truth struck him: a second destroyer had been hit and was sinking – the *Max Schultz*. There must be a submarine – perhaps more than one. It was his task to save the remaining four members of his squadron. The survivors from his two wrecked ships would have to be abandoned. With a heavy heart he called off the rescue operation and ordered the destroyers to head for home. Nobody from the *Max Schultz* survived and just 60 from the *Leberecht Maas* were pulled from the sea.

The disaster that struck Berger's flotilla was a combination of friendly fire and sheer hysteria. There had been just one bomber – Jäger's He-111 – which had achieved the remarkable tally of sinking two destroyers with just five bombs – and at night as well. There had been no British submarines at all. All sightings were the products of minds confused by their own bow waves and the effects of moonlight through mist.

Jäger, meanwhile, had every reason to be satisfied with his haul. He reported his first success as a '3,000 ton steamship'. Unfortunately, the position he gave for his 'kill' was exactly the same as that currently occupied by Berger's flotilla. Rear-Admiral Otto Ciliax was immediately concerned, yet how could the pilot confuse a single merchant ship with six destroyers? We will never know why Jäger's observer made such an elementary error. In his excitement he showed as little control as his naval colleagues below, who saw periscopes, conning towers and torpedo tracks where none existed. At last the truth began to materialize. However unpalatable the news was, Hitler had to be informed and he demanded an immediate enquiry. Enemy action was conclusively ruled out. It had been an administrative error, a tragic and unnecessary example of friendly fire, which cost Germany two new destroyers and the lives of 578 seamen.

# The 'Livebait Squadron'

On 22 September 1914 there occurred in the North Sea what the eminent American naval historian, Arthur Marder, has called a 'deplorable incident', and one which raised major questions about the efficiency of the British Admiralty to run a modern naval war. Three obsolete armoured cruisers of the Bacchante class – *Aboukir*, *Hogue* and *Cressy* – crewed mainly by over-age reservists and fifteen-year-old cadets, and cruelly nicknamed 'the livebait squadron', were sunk 'before breakfast' by a single U-boat. In all, 62 officers and 1,397 men were lost through sheer carelessness. It was such a blow to British prestige at the time that details of the disaster were hidden from the general public. The fact that these three old ships had been cruising, unescorted and at just ten knots (to conserve coal) on the 'Broad Fourteens' – an area known to be the haunt of enemy submarines – and had been there on and off for much of the previous six weeks, made the losses unforgivable. The Court of Inquiry which followed the disaster revealed so much ineptitude at all levels that the repercussions were felt throughout the entire navy.

The Bacchante class cruisers – over fourteen years old and quite unfitted for modern naval threats like submarines, mines and torpedoes – have unkindly been compared to 'sea elephants'. Over 12,000 tons in weight – 'twelve thousand tons of old iron going to rust' was one opinion – they were long, slow, thinly armoured and packed a feeble punch compared to the latest German cruisers. They were armed with two 9.2-inch and twelve 6-inch guns, but half of the latter were under water much of the time in heavy seas and unusable. Shortages in manpower had meant that the cruisers were crewed partly by 400 fifteen and sixteen-year-old cadets taken from the Britannia Royal Naval College, Dartmouth.

The Bacchantes formed part of 'Southern Force', which supported the Harwich destroyer flotillas and was commanded by Rear-Admiral Arthur Christian, who flew his flag in the cruiser *Euryalus*. The Bacchantes themselves comprised the 7th Cruiser Squadron and were commanded by Rear-Admiral Henry Campbell, with the *Bacchante* herself as his flagship. Campbell's areas of operations were supposed to be the Dogger Bank and the Broad Fourteens, off the Dutch Coast, though nobody – least of all Campbell – seemed to have a very clear idea as to their function there. On 17 September, bad weather had caused the usual destroyer escorts to put into harbour, and Admiral Christian in the *Euryalus* had been forced to return to Sheerness to recoal and to repair an aerial antenna. Christian claimed the weather was too bad for him to transfer his flag to another one of the cruisers. Christian's excuse that he needed coal – though later accepted by the inquiry – was an odd one as he still had 200 tons more than the *Aboukir*, which continued the cruise. He apparently passed over control to Captain Drummond and left the other Bacchantes bravely but dourly to continue their cruise. In the eyes of many observers this was tantamount to cowardice on the admiral's part and certainly at least dereliction of duty. Admiral Campbell, meanwhile, was safely in harbour at Chatham with the *Bacchante* undergoing repairs to her engines, and claiming that he did not know where his squadron was and that it was nothing to do with him anyway, as Christian was in command. While Christian and Campbell were vying with each other to shirk the unpleasant responsibility of leading 'the livebait squadron', great decisions were being taken elsewhere.

The cruiser *Aboukir* goes to the bottom, with her sister ships *Hogue* and *Cressy*, soon to share the same fate, in the background. The German U-boat U-9 sunk all three in less than half an hour on the Broad Fourteens in September 1914.

On 17 September a meeting took place at Loch Ewe between First Lord of the Admiralty Winston Churchill, Admiralty Chief of War Staff Doveton Sturdee, Commodore Reginald Tyrwhitt and Commodore Roger Keyes. They agreed that the old armoured cruisers had no business to be exposed to such danger and should be withdrawn from their patrol. The following day Churchill recommended to the First Sea Lord, Prince Louis of Battenburg, that the Bacchantes should be brought back. Battenburg agreed at first but then allowed Sturdee to persuade him instead to send the following telegram to Admiral Christian on 19 September: 'The Dogger Bank patrol need not be continued. Weather too bad for destroyers to go to sea. Arrange for cruisers to watch Broad Fourteens.' Churchill later insisted that he never saw this fateful message which condemned the old cruisers to patrol the intensely dangerous area between the Dutch coast and the German minefields which had been laid nearby. To make matters worse, neither Christian nor Campbell was with the cruisers at the time that this order was relayed to them. Thus it fell to Captain John Drummond of the *Aboukir* to lead the three members of the 'suicide club' to their rendezvous with the German submarine U-9.

At 6.20 am on 22 September U-9, commanded by Kapitän Leutnant Otto Weddigen, fired its first torpedo at the leading ship of three British cruisers which had come into sight some 30 minutes before. It was the *Aboukir*, and in spite of having four look-outs on the bridge, nobody aboard the old ship saw the torpedo which destroyed them. It struck between the first and second boiler rooms and disembowelled the cruiser, causing her to list 20 degrees to port.

Captain Drummond was asleep when the torpedo struck and he was later criticized for not being alive to the danger his ship was in. He had been warned just six days before of the likelihood of U-boats in the vicinity but had given the report scant attention and had not even recalled his destroyer escort from Harwich now that the weather had moderated. Even more surprising was the fact that none of his gun crews were at action stations, the guns were unloaded and the only precaution taken was to open the ammunition boxes 'in case of emergency'. It was a thoroughly sloppy display of leadership. Drummond's first assumption was that the *Aboukir* had struck a mine and he therefore looked to the *Hogue* and *Cressy* to effect a rescue and perhaps tow the *Aboukir* back into harbour. Oblivious to the possibility that there was a U-boat in the vicinity, he ordered the *Hogue* to close on the *Aboukir*. This was an astounding decision and contributed a great deal to the tragedy that was to follow.

Drummond now ordered all boats on the *Aboukir* to be swung out prior to launching, only to discover that a sailing pinnace, two cutters and two whalers had been left in Chatham to increase deck space. To save 700 men all that were left were a steam pinnace, a picket boat and a launch. Even then, with the ship listing so far to port it was impossible to launch some of the boats, while the steam-driven derrick needed to launch the pinnace was inoperable. There were now hardly enough boats for a quarter of the crew.

Meanwhile, Captain Nicholson on the *Hogue* was fully aware of the risk he was taking in closing up on the stricken *Aboukir*. He therefore signalled Captain Johnson in the *Cressy* to keep his distance and maintain a sharp look-out for submarines. Nicholson then closed in on the *Aboukir* and came to a full stop. In U-9 Weddigen simply could not believe his eyes – a stationary target! At 6.55 am U-9 fired two torpedoes at the *Hogue* which ripped her armoured sides away before exploding her magazine. Within minutes the old cruiser began to slip beneath the waves, following closely on the *Aboukir*, which had just turned turtle and submerged.

Captain Johnson on the *Cressy* was faced with a dilemma. The sea was by now covered with over a thousand men from the *Aboukir* and *Hogue*, and there were no destroyers to help in the rescue. If he raised full speed to save his ship from the unseen assailant all these men would die. In a moment he reached a decision and told his second-in-command, 'I won't leave those men. I will take my chance.' He slowed down and lowered all his boats, as well as dropping lines and climbing nets over the side to help the struggling survivors. He also took the important step of ordering all watertight doors to be closed. Yet, curiously, he did not order his men to action stations and his guns remained unmanned. Suddenly, a cry was heard that a U-boat had been sighted – wrongly as it proved – and a 12-pounder gun crew rushed to action stations and opened fire on where it believed a periscope had been spotted, claiming an immediate 'kill'. In fact, all the *Cressy* had hit were pieces of floating timber from her ruined sisters. The gunners next opened fire on a Dutch trawler nearby – luckily without scoring any hits – claiming that she had directed the U-boat's attacks and was a German spy-ship.

As the rescue operation continued the *Cressy* found that she was in danger of running into an area where hundreds of heads were bobbing in the water. Captain Johnson therefore ordered his engines stopped. In U-9, stationed diametrically opposite to where the *Cressy* was firing, Weddigen could hardly contain his excitement – another stationary target. At 7.17 am he fired both stern tubes at the *Cressy*, blowing a gaping hole in the cruiser's side and flooding her boiler rooms.

The agony of the old ships was over as the *Cressy* joined her sisters at the bottom of the North Sea, but the human tragedy had only just begun. By an oversight life-jackets had not been issued when the ships' companies had joined their vessels at Chatham and hundreds of lives were to be lost among the many non-swimmers and injured men. Only eight lifeboats had survived the sinkings and these were now packed with up to 600 men, while nearly 1,800 more were swimming and drowning among the flotsam of the Broad Fourteens. Yet just 50 miles away eight destroyers led by Commodore Tyrwhitt were heading towards them though they had heard nothing from the three stricken ships, and were not steaming at full speed. Those who survived that day owed their lives to a number of British and Dutch trawlers that came upon the scene and succeeded in rescuing perhaps 400 of the swimmers.

When the Admiralty received full details of the disaster their Lordships were struck by a storm of criticism. Reasonable questions were asked such as why the cruisers were operating to no apparent purpose, unescorted and exposed in such a dangerous area, and why so many Dartmouth boys were serving in three old hulks? Criticism swung towards Admirals Christian and Campbell. Why had neither been present when the U-boat attacked? The First Lord, Winston Churchill, instead criticized the cruiser captains and wanted to court-martial them all.

The board of inquiry findings were neither fair nor very illuminating. Certainly the Admiralty telegram of 19 September to Admiral Christian – a telegram sent by Doveton Sturdee – was the major cause of the disaster, but Captain Drummond, the captain of the *Aboukir* and senior officer present after Christian had retired from the scene, was blamed for not instructing his squadron to zig-zag and for ordering the other two ships to close in to help his stricken vessel. Both Nicholson of the *Hogue* and Johnson of the *Cressy* were criticized for stopping their ships and presenting the U-boat with such an easy target. Yet while these three brave men were pilloried in public Prince Louis of Battenburg exonerated both Christian and Campbell – hardly surprising in light of the fact that Campbell was a personal friend of the King and was said, by some, to have been dining with His Majesty the night before the disaster occurred, when he should have been flying his flag in the *Aboukir*. But the men who escaped criticism were those who deserved it most: the 'meddling civilian' Winston Churchill and the incompetent Admiralty Chief of Staff Doveton Sturdee, whose telegram to Christian had sent all those men and boys to their quite unnecessary deaths. And as if to prove that the Admiralty learns nothing from its fiascos, U-9 and Weddigen were able to 'ambush' the cruiser *Hawke* some two weeks later and sink it with the loss of a further 400 lives. One of the *Hawke*'s survivors – Boatswain Sidney Austin – had only joined the ship six days earlier after having served on the *Hogue* and having survived the earlier disaster.

# The Scattering of Convoy PQ17

The appointment of Sir Dudley Pound as First Sea Lord in June 1939 has been called a stop-gap appointment, made as a result of the death or sudden ill-health of far more able and desirable candidates. The result was that Pound, a man once told by Sir Ernle Chatfield that he was specifically *not* going to be First Sea Lord, and who was regarded as lacking both the character and the ability for the job, found himself at the head of the nation's naval affairs until his death in 1943. During much of that time his own health was suspect. Even at his best his work for the navy reflected a plodding mentality rather than a first-class intellect. In his career he had never cultivated popularity; neither had he attracted it. Contemporaries spoke of his 'pig-headedness' and his unwillingness to see the other point of view. To Pound, apparently, initiative was a dirty word.

The ill-fated Convoy PQ 17 at Hvalfiord, Iceland, July 1942. The scattering of PQ 17 at the behest of First Sea Lord Sir Dudley Pound – who feared the German battleship *Tirpitz* was closing on the convoy – led to the greatest convoy disaster of the Second World War.

One of the greatest maritime disasters of the Second World War – or indeed of any war – was the 'Massacre of Convoy PQ17' in July 1942. To describe its losses of 26 merchant ships containing 210 crated aircraft, 430 tanks, 3,350 vehicles and 100,000 tons of stores, no word other than 'catastrophic' will suffice. In one day the Germans destroyed the work of months. The responsibility for this resounding Allied defeat can only be laid at the door of one man: First Sea Lord Sir Dudley Pound.

Hitler's invasion of the Soviet Union in June 1941 imposed a new responsibility on the Royal Navy. The British felt obliged to supply their Soviet allies with as much military material as they could. Once the United States of America entered the war the burden of supplying tanks and planes was increasingly borne by the United States, yet the responsibility for shipping them to the Soviet Union still lay with the over-stretched Royal Navy. Initially the Soviets had offered to supply the necessary merchant ships to carry the supplies themselves but heavy losses to U-boats and the Luftwaffe, operating from bases in Norway, made it inevitable that Britain would have to shoulder the burden. And so the Arctic convoys began runs to Murmansk and Archangel, vulnerable to the whole gamut of enemy threats: mines, surface ships, submarines and aircraft. To escort these vital convoys the British stretched the resources of their Home Fleet to breaking point. Faced by the ever-potent threat of German battleships like the *Tirpitz*, *Scharnhorst* and *Gneisenau*, the commander-in-chief, Admiral Tovey, had to be prepared to use his own capital ships and aircraft carriers to protect the convoys. Yet he knew that he could not take such valuable assets within range of German bombers from Norway.

To do this job he had to turn to the escort vessels, destroyers, corvettes and even submarines. Losses were to be expected among both merchant ships and escort vessels. The only thing that mattered was to keep the losses within manageable proportions.

The risks that each successive convoy ran strained the nerves of everyone from merchant skippers to Admiralty Sea Lords. By the time the large convoy to be known as PQ17 was due to sail, Pound was clearly depressed by losses and anguished at the thought of what might happen if the battleship *Tirpitz* should ever get loose among a convoy. He began to fall victim to his own fears and always postulated the most disastrous scenarios. The pressure of work was weakening a man who was in the process of a long mental disintegration. He ought to have been retired before he could do any serious damage. But it was left too late.

Convoy PQ17 sailed for the Soviet Union on 27 June 1942. Special Admiralty instructions had been issued for this convoy to the effect that British surface forces would defend it only as far as the west of Bear Island, but not beyond. The job of protection for the final part of the journey would be left to submarines alone. But one aspect of the Admiralty instructions was particularly contentious and caused an immediate rift between the First Sea Lord and the commander-in-chief, Vice-Admiral Tovey. Pound, fearing the intervention of powerful German surface units, notably the *Tirpitz*, had overridden existing convoy instructions forbidding the convoy to scatter 'unless the escort has been overwhelmed'. He now contemplated ordering PQ17 to scatter if the *Tirpitz* should be in the vicinity. Tovey was furious at this intrusion in the affairs of the men on the spot and reminded Pound that the convoy was far better concentrated in the face of aerial attack and that scattering was absolutely a final resort, only to be taken in the most extreme circumstances.

PQ17 was to have the close support of six destroyers, two anti-aircraft ships, four corvettes and two submarines under the overall command of Commander J.E. Broome, a most experienced and able naval officer. In addition, the convoy would be escorted as far as Bear Island by a further force of four cruisers and three destroyers under Rear-Admiral Hamilton. Tovey himself and much of the Home Fleet would give distant cover in case heavy German surface ships should be committed.

By the time PQ17 sailed, British Intelligence at Bletchley Park had a clear idea of what U-boats and bombers the Germans were going to commit against the convoy. They had no information to suggest that the *Tirpitz* was going to leave Trondheim. The Admiralty therefore informed Hamilton that there had been no movement by major German surface units. On 3 July, however, evidence came in that the pocket battleship *Admiral Scheer* was moving north from Narvik to Altenfiord, while the *Tirpitz* and the heavy cruiser *Hipper* had left Trondheim possibly for the same destination. Tovey, with the main units of the Home Fleet, thus faced the likelihood that the Germans were planning a major sortie, possibly against PQ17.

It was now that the First Sea Lord began to exercise his influence on the fate of the convoy. On 3 July he entered the Admiralty Operations Room and began to study the plotting table on which the movements of the main units, British and German, were shown. He was tired and seemed irritated, perhaps by the pain of his osteo-arthritis. His mind was clearly on just one track: he wanted to know about the *Tirpitz*. Could she be advancing on the convoy at that moment? He was told that Bletchley Park were at that moment decoding the latest Enigma receipts and that soon they would have a much clearer view of what the *Tirpitz* was doing. But Pound was disinclined to wait and left the Operations Room. When the Enigma decrypts arrived they clearly indicated that the *Tirpitz* was expected at Altenfiord: she was not bearing down on the convoy as Pound had feared. The Operations Officer, Commodore Denning, then prepared a message for Tovey and Hamilton, but before he could send it Pound came in and asked to see it first. Denning had intended to send the relatively comforting news that *Tirpitz* was heading for Altenfiord and not towards the convoy. But Pound took a different view. The Enigma decrypts proved that the *Tirpitz* was at sea, and therefore could be heading for PQ17. Denning contested this point, arguing that there had been no sightings from the British submarines patrolling the North Cape and that the Germans had always been very cautious in their use of the battleship. But Pound rounded on him and asked, 'Can you assure me that *Tirpitz* is still in Altenfiord?' This was more than anyone on the British side could know at that time. Pound was dissatisfied and left to continue his own private musings. Late the same evening Denning received the news he was waiting for: a new decrypt from Bletchley Park saying, 'No own forces in operational area. Position of heavy enemy group not known at present but is main target for U-boats when encountered.' The Germans had given Denning conclusive proof that *Tirpitz* had not left Altenfiord.

Denning took the decrypt and set off to find Pound. Instead he met Rear-Admiral Clayton, who was on his way to a special meeting called by the First Sea Lord, and who agreed to take the message himself. Denning, meanwhile, drafted signals to be sent to Tovey and Hamilton. Normally he would have sent these on his own initiative, but in the event he decided to wait. When Clayton returned it was with the gravest possible news. Pound had decided that in view of the U-boat threat Admiral Hamilton would be ordered to withdraw from the escort and head westwards at high speed. Even worse, because of the possible threat from the *Tirpitz*, the convoy would be told to disperse. Denning was distraught. There was no need for this desperate reaction but Clayton warned him that 'Father [Pound] says he's made his decision and is not going to change it now'. It was one of the worst decisions of the war.

Three starkly worded signals were now made by the Admiralty. There was no attempt to explain why they were made and the only assumption possible by the commanders at sea was that Pound had received devastating information of a massed attack by German surface craft. The signals were:

**2111: Most immediate. Cruiser force withdraw westward at high speed.**
**2123: Immediate: Owing to threat from surface ships, convoy is to disperse and proceed to Russian ports.**
**2126: Most immediate. My 2123/4. Convoy is to scatter.**

Why had Pound not allowed Denning to send the information from the Enigma decrypts to Hamilton and Tovey and let them judge what the situation demanded? Why, when there was no evidence to suggest the *Tirpitz* was heading towards the convoy, did the First Sea Lord give way to his fears and panic? He was deliberately flouting Atlantic Convoy Instructions which forbade convoys to scatter unless the enemy had already engaged and overcome the escorts. Yet there were no sightings whatsoever of German surface ships. And why was the *Tirpitz* a greater threat to the convoy than the packs of U-boats would be to individual ships once they were forced to scatter without any naval support? Pound was an authoritarian figure of the old school who had made up his mind and thought it weakness to go back on his first thoughts. He lacked any appreciation of how the Germans might see the situation. Had he known that Hitler had absolutely refused to risk his valuable surface vessels – particularly the *Tirpitz* – in attacks on the convoy and that the German crews were sitting in frustration in Altenfiord questioning the Führer's decision, he might have thought differently. What made Pound's signals worse was the barely suppressed tone of panic that these few clipped phrases contained. Anyone receiving them must have expected to see the *Tirpitz* and all the legions of Hell bearing down on them.

Sir Dudley Pound (rear of the dinghy, left) returns to shore after a flight in an RAF flying boat, from which he had watched HMS *Hood* fire her 15-inch guns. The photograph was taken in 1938, shortly after Pound – then Second Sea Lord – took up the post of commander-in-chief of the Mediterranean Fleet.

Pound had blundered, terribly and irrevocably. He was interfering – disastrously as it turned out – with the operational control of his commanders. He had no experience of command at sea in the present war and was dominated by the rigid controls possible within peacetime operations. He lacked the flexibility essential when dealing with an opponent and laid his dead hand on the operational skills of far more able men. He was old, ill and incompetent. He had offered his resignation to the Prime Minister earlier in the year on the grounds of ill health, but Churchill had urged him to continue. Now that error of judgment on Churchill's part was going to cost his country dear.

Until the receipt of Pound's signals PQ17 had enjoyed a relatively peaceful voyage. But the 'Most immediate' signals changed all that. Everyone went to action stations and waited for the sound of gunfire. Once the 'Scatter' order had gone out Commander Broom, together with his escort vessels, joined Admiral Hamilton in the flight westwards. It was a sickening moment. The wretched merchant ships, after being led into the lion's den, were now being abandoned. It was *sauve qui peut*, and yet there were no enemies in sight – an amazing situation. The Royal Navy was running away from shadows in an old man's mind.

Commander Dowding – who was responsible for the convoy – now saw his escorts disappear to the west leaving his merchant ships alone, at the mercy of U-boats, surface vessels and the Luftwaffe. PQ17 was still 600 sea miles from the Soviet Union and it was every ship for itself from now on. Admiral Tovey found Pound's signals unacceptable. As he wrote later:

> The order to scatter the convoy had, in my opinion, been premature . . . its results were disastrous. The convoy had so far covered more than half its route with the loss of only three ships. Now its ships, spread over a wide area, were exposed without defence to the powerful U-boat and air forces. The enemy took prompt advantage of this situation, operating both weapons to their full capacity.

In the event, the Germans had no need of the *Tirpitz*. The job of destroying the convoy was far easier for bombers and submarines. In the next few days the Germans sank 23 of the merchant ships with enormous losses in tanks, planes and equipment. Eleven of the convoy reached Russia through the skill and courage of their crews.

Sir Dudley Pound had some explaining to do. To say that he lied to the cabinet is too harsh: perhaps he was confused. His allegation that he had information 'on the night before the order to disperse was given that the *Tirpitz*, having eluded our submarines, would, if she continued on her present course, be in a position to attack the convoy early next morning . . .' is quite untrue. The Enigma decrypts that were received by Commander Denning bore no such interpretation. Nor, in view of the massacre that ensued, was he justified in his statement that it would be safer for the convoy to scatter than to encounter the *Tirpitz*. Even a battleship as powerful as the *Tirpitz* would have taken a long time to sink 23 ships, not to mention the fact that its attention might have been distracted by attacks from swarms of escort vessels, including Hamilton's cruisers. It was a poor attempt to justify a terrible mistake.

Sir Dudley Pound did not long survive this disaster. His ill-health was apparent to everyone. General Allanbrooke commented unkindly that business at Chiefs of Staff meetings got through very much quicker when he was asleep, which he apparently was much of the time. The general wrote, 'Am getting more and more worried by old Dudley Pound as First Sea Lord . . . He is asleep 75 per cent of the time he should be working.' Another officer wrote, 'After a not very long time I noticed that Pound was drooling down the stem of his pipe – not just a drop, for I was at least five yards away. He may not have been asleep but he was quite 'out for the count'. Some officers felt that Churchill was sticking with Pound because he was afraid to appoint a First Sea Lord such as Andrew Cunningham whom he could not control so easily. The result was that there was talk of raising the matter in the House of Commons. Eventually Pound suffered a stroke and became partly paralysed, forcing the Prime Minister to accept his resignation on 10 September 1943. He died just six weeks later, on 21 October.

# Force Z and the Art of Gunboat Diplomacy

Britain's neglect of her Far Eastern defences, particularly the main naval base at Singapore, was one of the greatest miscalculations of the inter-war period. Her promises to Australia and New Zealand that in the event of war with Japan a major British naval force would be available to send east at short notice, was soon exposed as mere wishful thinking. In order to minimize the weaknesses of Britain's position east of Suez, the myth of 'Fortress Singapore' was created, notably after 1940 by Winston Churchill, who spoke of the base as if alone it would deter the Japanese from acts of aggression. But for a state prepared to challenge the Americans in the Pacific and attack Pearl Harbor, Singapore posed no great threat. Thus when Churchill made the following statement he was being thoroughly dishonest:

As Singapore is as far away from Japan as Southampton is from New York, the operation of moving a Japanese Army with all its troopships and maintaining it during a siege would be forlorn. Moreover, such a siege . . . would be liable to be interrupted, if at any time Britain chose to send a superior fleet to the scene.

Having begun the war as First Lord of the Admiralty, Churchill knew better than anyone that Britain did not have a superior fleet to Japan's, nor could such a fleet possibly be spared even if it existed. Britain's priorities in 1941 were with the preservation of the homeland. If naval strength was needed in the east it would have to be symbolic. But what Churchill intended as symbols of British strength were regarded by the Japanese as exactly the opposite – symbols of weakness and of self-sacrifice. The Japanese could well understand the *kamikaze* nature of Force Z that Churchill sent east on 25 October 1941.

The big question was: what could Britain spare? The first plan was to send four of the old Revenge class battleships to Ceylon, but there was no way of disguising the fact that these would simply be blood sacrifices. They were no match for the modern Japanese ships and would succumb easily to air attack. Churchill soon rejected this feeble response and instead decided to make a gesture that the Japanese would understand. Britain would send her latest battleship – the *Prince of Wales* – which was the best she had. British power in the Far East had depended on prestige for so long that sending the *Prince of Wales* would clearly demonstrate Britain's firm commitment to the colonies. In fact, Churchill's gesture was redolent of 19th-century gunboat diplomacy. Malay or Chinese pirates might once have quailed at the sight of British naval strength, but the Japanese – disciples of the British and, in eastern eyes, their successors – would assess the British commitment on its merits. And these were not very great.

The choice of the *Prince of Wales* was predictable as she was, in spite of her lamentable display against the *Bismarck* (see p. 172), the newest and strongest of British battleships. But to choose as her partner the old First World War battlecruiser *Repulse* was less comprehensible. Although *Repulse* had been modernized in the 1930s and carried 15-inch guns, her thin protection would make her easy meat for Japanese battleships or even, perhaps, a group of heavy cruisers, who could also match her top speed. And against the powerful Japanese fleet air arm the two capital ships would be mere sacrifices unless accompanied by a British aircraft carrier to provide air cover. Initially Force Z was to include the carrier *Indomitable*, but when she ran aground in the West Indies, the decision was taken to go ahead without her. Anyone with even the slightest conception of the vulnerability of capital ships to air attack should have recognized the folly of this decision. If the order to send two capital ships to Singapore was a gesture – as has been widely suggested – it was a gesture of despair.

The choice of Sir Tom Phillips to command Force Z was an unusual one. Phillips had up to that point been Deputy Chief of Naval Staff and had no experience at sea in the present war. He was Pound's protégé and a firm believer that ships and guns could triumph over air power. As such he was an inappropriate choice to command a squadron against as powerful an air power as Japan. With just four destroyers to escort them, the two British capital ships were sailing to certain destruction under Phillips – and Churchill and Pound appeared content to let it happen.

With the Japanese attack on Pearl Harbor and their simultaneous invasion of Malaya, all the strategic assumptions behind Force Z's despatch were destroyed. Phillips could not cooperate with the American Pacific Fleet because it had ceased to exist, nor could the British ships act as a deterrent to the Japanese in approaching Malaya. The Japanese had simply swept away the comfortable and static strategy of a previous age and presented the British with a stark choice – fight or flight. Unwisely, Phillips decided to fight. He seemed to think he could get by without even the feeble fighter cover that could be provided by the RAF in Singapore. He was determined to strike at the Japanese transports at Singora and Khota in Northern Malaya, hoping thereby to smash the invasion forces. Phillips was relying on having the advantage of surprise. His thinking was profoundly flawed. Japanese air strength in Indo-China amounted to 144 bombers and fighters, all highly trained in anti-ship action. To achieve surprise was almost inconceivable in view of this air strength, not to mention Japan's numerous surface ships and powerful submarine fleet.

Phillips' confidence was misplaced and redolent of an earlier age:

> We may have the luck to try our mettle against the old Japanese battleship *Kongo* or against some Japanese cruisers and destroyers . . . Whatever we meet I want to finish quickly and so get well to the eastward before the Japanese can mass too formidable a scale of attack against us, so shoot to sink.

Yet Phillips knew that he could rely on no fighter cover from the RAF, which had told him before he sailed that they could not cover the Singora area. They had also warned him that the Japanese had strong bomber forces in Southern Indo-China and Thailand. In spite of this Phillips insisted on carrying out his sortie. It has been suggested that Phillips was a victim of his own inexperience. Had he personally experienced the effects of aerial attack, as had anyone who had served in the Mediterranean, for example, then he could not have taken Japanese air power so lightly. The problem was that Phillips came from the tradition of Admiralty men who had resisted every naval innovation from steam power to the submarine. Even as late as August 1940 he favoured battleship building over aircraft carriers and had called the capital ship 'the foundation of our naval strength'. In his words, those who favoured naval air power over naval gunnery were 'misguided persons'. He was about to learn the hard way, but he would not live to benefit from his lesson.

It was one of six Japanese submarines, placed on picket duty to cover the landings, which first sighted Force Z, and called up Admiral Kondo with two battleships, six cruisers and a swarm of destroyers to meet the British squadron. There was just a chance that Phillips would have the opportunity to try his 'mettle' against Japanese battleships. But three reconnaissance aircraft put a stop to that by radioing the position of Force Z to the 22nd Air Flotilla at Saigon. Phillips, meanwhile, with the element of surprise now lost, decided to call off the sortie and return to Singapore. At that moment 85 Japanese bombers, some with torpedoes, others with armour-piercing bombs, were flying south to intercept Force Z.

Early on 10 December Phillips received a report of fresh Japanese landings at Kuantan, and decided to investigate. The *Repulse* signalled that she had spotted a Japanese reconnaissance aircraft but Phillips stuck to his decision and kept heading for Kuantan, not even bothering to call up available air support from airfields in southern Johore and Singapore. Even First Sea Lord Dudley Pound was later to express his concern at this omission. One explanation advanced is that Phillips assumed that fighter cover would be sent when he announced that he was heading for Kuantan. Apparently it was necessary to read the admiral's mind rather than have him break radio silence. In the event, the report of landings at Kuantan was a false one. Phillips and Force Z were to perish as the result of 'a wild goose chase', in a sense a microcosm of the strategic thinking that had sent them to Singapore in the first place.

Phillips now found something else to occupy his mind: the investigation of a small steamer towing a string of barges rather than making a high-speed return to Singapore. Never has there been a more inappropriate moment for two British capital ships to carry out the function of a sloop or corvette. Force Z's last chance to escape had gone. At 10.30 am *Repulse*'s radar picked up the first wave of Japanese aircraft and everyone went to anti-aircraft positions. Phillips' confidence in his high-angled anti-aircraft guns was about to be tested – not in an exercise at Scapa Flow – but against a skilled enemy in the Gulf of Siam. Omitting to order the normal precaution of a smokescreen, Phillips decided to fight it out in the open. At first the Japanese bombers achieved a straddle on the *Repulse* but next came the torpedo-planes which, ignoring the storm of flak being fired at them, achieved the first hit on the *Prince of Wales*. Using 24-inch torpedoes which carried 1,200-pound warheads – far more powerful than the British 18-inch models with 300-pound heads – the Japanese blew a hole 12 feet in circumference in the hull of the *Prince of Wales*, which allowed over 2,000 tons of water to gush inside. The explosion also knocked out the electric power supply and this stopped half the ship's pumps. The great battleship was stricken. The pride of the Royal Navy had been found wanting by the first attack of Japanese torpedo planes and later investigations suggest that design and construction faults had made her far less powerful in combat than had been believed at the time. Worst of all, the crew was not working at peak efficiency, particularly the damage control parties who made a number of mistakes which contributed to the ship's loss.

Meanwhile, *Repulse* was putting up a better show than the flagship. Though doomed by her admiral's mistakes, she was not going to succumb easily. She signalled to Singapore that Force Z was under attack and asked for air cover, and then successfully combed nine torpedoes fired at her. But her luck could not hold and she was next attacked from both sides by torpedo bombers and received one hit. Even so, she kept steaming at 25 knots and her guns kept firing.

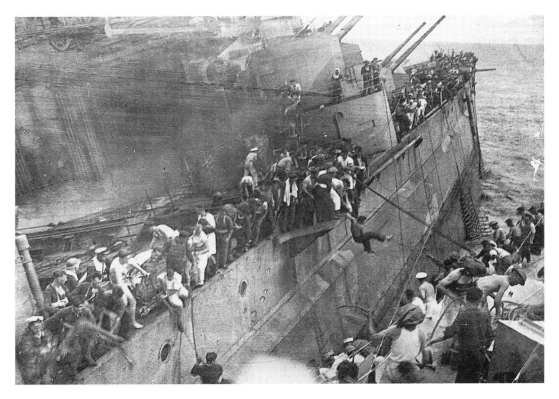

The doomed British battleship *Prince of Wales* sinking after an attack by Japanese bombers off Malaya, December 1941. Her commander, Sir Tom Phillips, had fatally underestimated Japanese air power in the Far East.

Two more torpedoes now hit the virtually stationary *Prince of Wales*, which was clearly doomed. The Japanese switched to the *Repulse* and overwhelmed her, hitting her with four torpedoes. As the battlecruiser rolled over, the destroyers *Electra* and *Vampire* managed to save 796 out of the crew of 1,300. While *Repulse* was going through her death agony, the *Prince of Wales* had managed to limp away at eight knots. But she was sinking and a further bomb hit ended all hope. Fortunately the destroyer *Express* was able to take off many of the crew before she finally went under, taking with her both her captain and Admiral Phillips.

The destruction of Force Z had cost the Japanese just eight aircraft – a powerful refutation of Tom Phillips' belief in the efficacy of naval anti-aircraft gunnery. Ironically, as the two great ships were still settling on the floor of the ocean, a flight of RAF Buffalo fighters arrived over the scene, prompting the remaining Japanese bombers to break off and flee for home. The fighters were able to patrol the skies while the destroyers carried out the mournful task of picking up survivors. It is pointless to speculate on the effect their arrival would have had an hour before. It is just as pointless to look for villains to explain this humiliating defeat. Fools there were in plenty – starting from the top with Churchill and Pound, and including Sir Tom Phillips, who was too brave for his own good. The 'band of brothers' mentality had no part to play in a war against technically superior opponents; it merely stretched the casualty lists.

# The Indianapolis 800

On 16 July 1945 the American cruiser *Indianapolis* left San Francisco Harbor carrying a most important cargo – a 200-pound metal cylinder containing uranium and the detonating mechanism for an atomic bomb. Her orders were to deliver the cargo with utmost speed to the Pacific island of Tinian, where a Boeing B-29 bomber known as *Enola Gay* was waiting to deliver the world's first atomic strike against the city of Hiroshima. Captain Charles McVay of the *Indianapolis* was left in no doubt as to the importance of this cargo. His instructions were to guard it with not only his life but that of his ship as well. If the *Indianapolis* were sunk the 'cargo' was to have absolute priority in any lifeboats. Aware of the urgency of the mission McVay broke the world speed record between San Francisco and Pearl Harbor. Just six hours later, having refuelled, he was on his way again to Tinian, still 3,300 miles away. On 26 July the *Indianapolis* anchored off the small island and delivered its cargo. It had been a quiet trip, and with the war in its final stages McVay and his crew must have thought that they had already experienced their 'date with destiny'. But they were wrong.

Captain McVay's next orders were to cross the Philippine Sea to Leyte, where he was to report for training to Task Force 95.7 under Rear-Admiral Lynde D. McCormick, then flying his flag in the battleship *Idaho*. This order had been sent to McCormick so that he could make the necessary arrangements for *Indianapolis*'s arrival. But when the message was received on the *Idaho* it was wrongly decoded as being addressed to 75.8, not Task Force 95.7, so McCormick ignored it. It had carried the classification 'Restricted' instead of 'Secret' and was not thought important enough to query. This initial blunder was to have tragic consequences for the *Indianapolis*. Nobody at Leyte knew that she was coming, or why.

The *Indianapolis* was to sail from Guam without escort, a clear indication that no enemy submarine activity was expected on her chosen route. But this was just not true. The American destroyer *Underhill* had been torpedoed to the west of Guam on 24 July and the navy later admitted that McVay had not been told that there were four Japanese submarines operating in the Western Pacific at that time, including one on 'Convoy Route Peddie' (Guam to Leyte), which the *Indianapolis* was due to take. In the face of this it is difficult to understand how McVay could have been told by Captain Oliver Naquin, surface operations officer at Guam, that the chance of him meeting a Japanese submarine was 'practically negligible'. As the *Indianapolis* set sail Guam made a routine transmission to 'interested parties' of the cruiser's anticipated movements. This message was received at Leyte, but Rear-Admiral McCormick for one found it confusing. He had not received the first coded message explaining why the *Indianapolis* was joining him and so he assumed that there was every chance that the cruiser would be redirected – perhaps towards Okinawa – before she ever reached Leyte. Nor was his superior, Vice-Admiral Jesse Oldendorf, any wiser than McCormick. He gathered that *Indianapolis* was coming but when he did not know. Both admirals simply put the matter down to administrative muddle – it happened all the time – with no serious consequences.

At just after midnight on 30 July the *Indianapolis* was crossing the Philippine Sea, travelling at 17 knots in calm conditions. She was not zig-zagging, as would have been the case had anyone on board remotely suspected that she might encounter an enemy submarine. Suddenly five torpedoes from Captain Hashimoto's *I-58* ripped into her. The impact was tremendous and the ship began to sink with alarming speed. Captain McVay ordered Lieutenant Orr to make sure that the radio room was sending a distress signal before he rushed off to check the inclinometer which showed that the *Indianapolis* had a list of eighteen degrees. There was little time to order the crew to 'abandon ship' and the bugler, when ordered to sound the 'abandon' signal, first could not locate his bugle and when he did find it was overtaken by events and never made a sound. McVay was still worried about this distress call. Had the radio room sent off a distress signal or not? He sent Commander Janney to check and then followed up himself. A signal had been sent – but who had heard it and what would they do about it? The *Indianapolis* was now going under, carrying some 400 of her crew with her. But McVay and between 800 and 900 crewmen went over the side and were soon bobbing around amongst the debris of the cruiser and in the thick, oily seas which clogged their lungs and choked them. All the survivors could do now was to keep afloat somehow, a few on rafts and others with lifebelts, and wait to be rescued.

But blunder after blunder now conspired to delay the rescue of the crew of the *Indianapolis*, exposing them to a martyrdom almost without parallel in the history of sea warfare. Shortly after *I-58*'s successful attack Hashimoto reported the sinking of the *Indianapolis* to Tokyo. American Naval Intelligence had broken Japanese codes some time before and knew that *I-58* was operating in the area that the *Indianapolis* had been routed to travel. Yet, in spite of the fact that Hashimoto was reporting that he had sunk a large American vessel – battleship or cruiser – nobody put 'two and two together' and concluded that it had been the *Indianapolis*. Washington took no further action on the intercepted message in the knowledge that Pearl Harbor would have the same information. But at Pearl Harbor Commander-in-Chief, Pacific Fleet, Fleet Admiral Chester Nimitz, did nothing either, claiming after that they thought *I-58*'s message was simply a deception. If either Washington or Pearl Harbor had followed up this lead the crew of the *Indianapolis* would have been rescued in the first 24 hours and hundreds of lives saved.

Meanwhile, for the hundreds of swimmers in the Philippine Sea the first sharks were beginning to arrive . . .

One thought stayed in Captain McVay's mind throughout and this helped to sustain him in his ordeal. Surely once the *Indianapolis* failed to arrive at Leyte, a full search would be set in motion. But the *Indianapolis* was about to be lost in a kind of cartographical limbo. Removed from the plotter's charts for the Marianas after she left Guam, she was never placed on the charts for the Philippines Sea. She simply disappeared on the demarcation line between the two different commands and neither did anything about it. She became an administrative error.

But what of the distress message sent from the *Indianapolis?* Had nobody picked it up? The simple answer is that we will never know for certain. After the disaster stories circulated that some ships had received a message and done nothing about it but nothing was ever proved and the official naval records are adamant that no distress message was received by any ship in the area. After the war a crew member from an ocean going tug alleged that the tail end of a distress message had been received by his radio operator. It gave no identification or position but did say that 'We are torpedoed and sinking fast. We need immediate assistance'. In the confusion no action was taken by the tug. Yet rumours of this kind are rife in wartime and individual memories can often play one false in the tense atmosphere of active operations. In so vast an area of military operations as the Pacific ocean, with the radio waves filled with messages from hundreds of vessels, mistakes of this kind were always possible. In the case of such a disaster as the *Indianapolis* suffered there will always be an understandable tendency of those who are grieving to look for scapegoats. Sometimes, however, the fault lies less in the hands of individuals than in that generality, the 'fog of war'.

Meanwhile, the survivors of the *Indianapolis*, some on rafts but most swimming without life-preservers, bobbed up and down on 'a painted ocean', while the sharks, growing more confident all the time, began picking off stragglers. Marine Captain Parke strung out a hundred feet of line attached to a cork life ring and this helped the men to cling together in the ocean, while they sheltered the weak and the wounded in the circle of swimmers, hoping to keep the sharks at bay. As one survivor wrote, the sharks tended to single out their victim 'and no amount of shouts or pounding of the water would turn him away. There would be a piercing scream and the water would be churned red as the shark cut his victim to ribbons.'

Lieutenant Stuart Gibson was operations officer at Leyte on 31 July. He was one of the few men at Leyte who knew that the *Indianapolis* had been expected that day and was now overdue. But he told nobody as he saw his job as reporting arrivals, not non-arrivals. It was a small point, to be sure, but he was sincere in his belief that he could not be blamed for doing his job 'to the letter'. Gibson later successfully used this interpretation of his duty as a defence but such lack of initiative was rightly condemned by Admiral King as 'stupid'. The following day, Lieutenant Edward Henslee, plot supervisor at Leyte, also became aware that the *Indianapolis* had not arrived. Suspecting a delay or reassignment he simply chalked in the cruiser for the next day and said no more. Meanwhile, the plotters at Guam had removed the *Indianapolis* from their board, assuming that she had arrived at Leyte. If any of the officers had taken the trouble to check they could have set in motion a rescue operation for the hundreds of desperate survivors now spending their second day in the sea.

At Leyte, on 1 August, the *Indianapolis* was still not officially listed as missing. Her ETA had merely been put back day by day – but she was in fact 36 hours overdue already. Meanwhile, Admiral McCormick in the *Idaho* had sailed out of Leyte on a routine exercise. He knew that the *Indianapolis* was supposed to join him but he had no idea when and thought he might pass her on the way out. If not, she was sure to be in harbour when he returned.

In the water the *Indianapolis*'s medical officer, Dr Haynes, struggled hard to stop the men, who were suffering agonies of thirst in the burning heat, from drinking sea water. Many of the survivors were becoming delirious. The cry went up that there were 'Japs' in their group and fights broke out everywhere. Knives were drawn and blood flowed – and the sharks came.

One swimmer tried to help another floating in a life-jacket only to find that he was dead and from his waist down there was nothing left. One by one the survivors died and slipped beneath the surface or were pulled down by the sharks.

On their fourth day in the water the first sighting of the survivors took place – entirely by chance. Lieutenant Wilbur Gwinn, flying a twin-engined Ventura bomber, spotted a huge oil slick which he followed until he noticed heads in the water. At 11.25 am the first news of the *Indianapolis* reached a world which seemed to have forgotten that the cruiser had ever existed. Shortly afterwards the first help began to arrive. Lieutenant Adrian Marks reached one group of survivors in his Catalina flying boat, making it a base on the sea to which some 30 of the survivors could cling. Soon the airwaves were singing just one word – *Indianapolis* – and recriminations were starting, as well as alibis.

Rescue craft were still unbelievably slow in reaching the survivors and they were forced to endure a fifth day in the water, which cost many more lives to exhaustion and shark attack. It was only when the destroyer *Helm* reached the scene that the true horror of the tragedy was revealed. There were many more heads bobbing in the water than there were bodies. The sharks had ripped away lower limbs and torsos, leaving arms and upper bodies intact. In most cases identification was impossible. Commander Hollingsworth wrote,

> All bodies were in extremely bad condition and had been dead for an estimated 4 or 5 days. Some had life jackets and life belts, most had nothing . . . Bodies were horribly bloated and decomposed – recognition of the faces would have been impossible. About half of the bodies were shark-bitten, some to such a degree that they more nearly resembled skeletons.

There was no possibility of giving the bodies formal burial; most were simply weighted and sunk on the spot. Of the 1,196 crew of the *Indianapolis*, just 316 men survived. It was the greatest disaster at sea in the history of the US Navy.

Fleet Admiral King had already sent a stinging despatch to Nimitz at Pearl Harbor, criticizing him for allowing an unescorted ship to be routed in an area where Japanese submarines were known to be operational. The scramble for scapegoats had started.

A court of inquiry was quickly convened, but its impartiality was suspect as one of its judges was to be Vice-Admiral George Murray, who had been responsible for re-routing the *Indianapolis* after her voyage to Tinian. Murray and his operations officer – Captain Naquin – were deeply implicated in the loss of the cruiser and the failure to rescue the survivors. Naquin, when asked by the court to give his opinion on the likely danger of the *Indianapolis* encountering a submarine on the route that he had prepared for her, replied as he had earlier to McVay, that the risk was 'practically negligible'. Incredibly this was accepted by the court and he was released from questioning by Admiral Murray. Nobody raised the obvious question: if the risk was 'negligible' how had the cruiser met her end. It was little more than a charade. The court rightly concluded that the delay in mounting a rescue mission was caused by the failure of officers at Leyte to report the non-arrival of the *Indianapolis*. This was obvious and yet officer after officer was able to pass the blame onto someone else. But the American people needed a scapegoat: somebody had to be held responsible. At last the court found its man – Captain Charles McVay, commander of the *Indianapolis*. He would be court-martialled on the grounds of 'culpable inefficiency' and 'negligently endangering the lives of others'.

At first Nimitz rejected the court's decision to put McVay on trial, agreeing that his failure to zig-zag was an error of judgment, but suggesting that a letter of reprimand was surely punishment enough. But he was overruled by Chief of Naval Operations, Admiral Ernest King. King needed a 'show trial'. Too many families in America wanted to know whose negligence had allowed their sons and husbands to die so horrifically. It was even suggested that King had a score to settle with McVay, whose father had reprimanded him when he served under Admiral McVay in the Asiatic Fleet in the 1930s. Whatever King's reasoning, the captain of the *Indianapolis* was to endure a personal martyrdom to cover the disgraceful negligence which ran throughout the entire Pacific operation. McVay was to be accused of failing to zig-zag and of not giving the order to abandon ship quickly enough. As if the American Navy had not injured its reputation enough already, King chose to summon Captain Hashimoto of the submarine *I-58* to give evidence against one of his own officers! After Japan surrendered Hashimoto was flown to America and even given $100 to buy presents for his wife and children.

King eventually nailed his man – McVay was found guilty of failing to zig-zag and lost seniority. But nobody asked the burning question: if the threat of enemy submarines was 'negligible' why would the *Indianapolis* be expected to zig-zag, a manoeuvre only adopted where the threat of a torpedo attack was serious. The American Navy was only interested in finding a scapegoat and now they had their public victim – Captain Charles McVay was the man responsible for the loss of the *Indianapolis*. It was a burden he carried alone until 1968, when he shot himself in the front garden of his house in Litchfield, Connecticut.

# Operation Catherine

First Lords of the Admiralty should confine their most imaginative thoughts to the 'port-and-cigars' stage of dinner. Well-fed and well-wined, their guests will probably share with them the fantasies of minds liberated from the humdrum world of politics and 'the possible'. But danger lies in failing to differentiate between those flashes of inspiration and the objective data which should form the basis for planning naval operations. One of the most notable exponents of the school of inspirational planning was Winston Churchill, First Lord of the Admiralty at the outbreak of both world wars. In September 1939 – just as in August 1914 – Churchill had a new idea: not Antwerp and Borkum this time; instead nothing less than the whole Baltic Sea. This Napoleonic conception was named 'Catherine' after Catherine the Great, Empress of Russia. In the end, Britain – and Churchill himself – was saved from the First Lord's excesses by the personality of the First Sea Lord, Sir Dudley Pound (see p. 63), a man as dull and professional as his political counterpart was inspired and amateurish.

After just three days in office as First Lord of the Admiralty, Winston Churchill had produced a lengthy war-winning memorandum suggesting a naval operation against Germany in the Baltic. This was the first sight anyone had of 'Operation Catherine', a plan to send a powerful squadron of ships – three 'Revenge' class battleships, an aircraft carrier, five cruisers, two destroyer flotillas, submarines and, presumably, numerous auxiliary ships as well as some 'turtle-backed blistered tankers' carrying three months' supply of oil – into the Baltic. Churchill's plan was both original and substantial. To combat the inevitable threat from German aircraft and submarines he proposed to equip each of the battleships with 2,000 tons of extra armour, while removing two of their 15-inch turrets. The battleships, thus armoured, would have their maximum speed reduced to just 15 knots but this would be more than offset by their new invulnerability. In any case, 15 'mine-bumpers' would precede the fleet through the narrow, heavily mined waters between Denmark and Sweden. The aim of this force would ultimately be to sever Germany's iron supplies from Sweden. For some curious reason Churchill believed that this would encourage the Scandinavian countries to join the war against Germany, perhaps drawing Soviet Russia in as well – even though Stalin had just signed the Non-Aggression Pact with Hitler. The climax of his memorandum to the Sea Lords was the statement that the plan was 'the supreme naval offensive open to the Royal Navy'.

Once this idea was rooted in the First Lord's mind it was Sir Dudley Pound's job to remove it with as little damage as possible to the patient. In the first place Churchill had given far too little thought to where he was going to find the massive amount of armour plating necessary. At a time when Britain could not even send a fully equipped armoured tank division to France it was incumbent on the government to devote available resources to producing new tanks. And what was the Home Fleet Commander-in-Chief, Sir Charles Forbes, going to say when he found that three of his very limited supply of battleships were going to be castrated by losing their turrets and turned instead into the metal juggernauts of some maritime fantasy? Most important of all, however, Churchill was underestimating the potency of air power, just as he would two years later when he sent the *Prince of Wales* and the *Repulse* unprotected to their doom in the waters off Singapore (see p. 68). As events were to show, even the Japanese super-battleships *Musashi* and *Yamato* were vulnerable to air power, so what chance had three ancient, pre-Jutland battleships? As Forbes would have said, far better to let them earn their keep escorting convoys or using their 15-inch guns to bombard coastal positions than to squander them like 'sitting ducks' to the Luftwaffe.

Pound was wise enough not to meet Churchill head on. He simply hung on to his coat tails and tried to wear away the edges of this most ridiculous plan. In public Pound would acquiesce with Churchill's thinking but behind the scenes he would keep pecking away until the First Lord realized that what he wanted was impossible. On 20 January 1940, 'Operation Catherine' was shelved, mostly through Pound's skilful rearguard action. In the end the plan was scrapped by Churchill himself. Pound had managed to demonstrate to the First Lord that Britain and France might need to be able to fight Germany, Italy and even Japan, and could not spare the naval forces needed to keep the Swedish iron ore cut off from Germany in the Baltic. If Churchill could guarantee that the *Rodney*, *Nelson*, *Queen Elizabeth*, *Warspite*, *Barham*, *Malaya*, *Valiant* and the remaining two 'R' class ships could successfully face the might of Japan and Italy, then Pound was all in favour of spoiling three of Britain's limited supply of battleships and locking them into an open-ended operation in the Baltic. While a substantial part of Britain's naval strength was in Baltic waters, would Britain be strong enough to face Germany's U-boats in the Atlantic and the North Sea, not to mention the battlecruisers *Scharnhorst* and *Gneisenau*, the new German 'pocket-battleships', the powerful heavy cruisers like *Prinz Eugen* and *Blücher*, and most frightening of all – the *Bismarck* and *Tirpitz*, which were nearing completion?

Yet 'Catherine' was not defeated without casualties. The able Naval Staff Director of Plans, Captain V.H. Danckwaerts, was sacked because of his total opposition to the plan. Pound survived – only just – but it had been one of his hardest battles. On the day the plan was finally shelved Pound's memorandum painted a domesday scenario – of a fleet mauled by air attack, mines and torpedoes, without a secure base in the Baltic, suffering such losses that its effect on naval strength might encourage Italy and Japan to join the war against a failing Britain.

Pound's victory may have put an end to 'Operation Catherine' but it had taken six months, used up valuable Admiralty time and cost the services of at least one able man in Danckwaerts. And it was not a complete victory for Churchill was incorrigible. Thwarted over the Baltic, his active mind was already moving towards new areas of amphibious operations and, in choosing Norway, he was curiously replicating the thinking of that other military dilettante – Adolf Hitler.

# Scapa Flow and the Submarine Peril

As First Lord of the Admiralty at the outbreak of war in 1914, Winston Churchill has won warm acclaim from historians for the way in which the Royal Navy was 'on station' on 4 August when war was declared on Germany. From Scapa Flow in the Orkneys, where Jellicoe's mighty Grand Fleet was stationed, right down to the Channel, where three squadrons of pre-Dreadnought battleships were situated, the North Sea had become a 'no-go area' for Germany. British battleships, it was claimed, would block exits to north and south, while cruisers and destroyers of the Harwich patrol protected the east coast of England against possible German attack. Quite literally, the German fleet was 'locked out of the world'.

But if Churchill and his naval planners were feeling pleased with themselves they were in for a shock. Mistakes had been made – at least one so staggering that it seems impossible that it could have escaped anyone's notice: there was no suitably situated, fully prepared and fortified base on the east coast for the Grand Fleet. Scapa Flow had no anti-submarine defences – mines, nets or booms – whatsoever, nor were there any fixed guns, searchlights or other fortifications. At the outbreak of war Scapa Flow simply offered open house to visiting German U-boats. The British planners had underestimated the threat of the submarine and believed Scapa Flow was out of their range – but they were wrong. The oversight was incredible. Given the fact that the nation's security rested on the Grand Fleet, why had no consideration been given by naval planners to its security?

The problem was that the revolution in Britain's foreign policy between 1904 and 1914 – with the consequent change in Britain's strategic imperatives – meant that the threat to Britain no longer came from the south, as in the past. Naval bases at Plymouth, Portland and Portsmouth were of no use in facing a German threat in the North Sea. As early as 1903 the matter of east coast bases had been raised by the Admiralty and the decision had been taken then to develop Rosyth, in the Firth of Forth. But building work was plagued by friction between the Admiralty and the War Office, for defence of the base would be the Army's responsibility. In any case, it soon became apparent that Rosyth would be too far south for the Grand Fleet to operate an effective blockade on Germany and, with the massive increase in the size of Britain's main battle fleet, Rosyth was just too small.

It was not until 1913 that consideration was given to building a new base, either at Cromarty or Scapa Flow. When the Lords of the Admiralty wanted to build permanent defences at Scapa Flow they found the estimate of £400,000 prohibitive. After all, for that sum one could build a fifth of a new Dreadnought. By the outbreak of the war things were chaotic: Scapa Flow was undefended, Cromarty incomplete and Rosyth far too small. All three were victims of the offensive doctrine which dominated British naval thinking in 1914. Money spent on shore defences was seen as money wasted; it could be used to build and arm more and more Dreadnoughts. There was no safety except in attacking the enemy and sinking his ships.

But the success of the German submarine U-9 in sinking three armoured cruisers in the space of minutes soon made their Lordships reconsider. Now periscopes were seen everywhere. During the first battle of Scapa the fleet was thrown into disarray by the sighting of a periscope – which turned out to be a seal. In the battle of Jemimaville off Cromarty the bow wave of a destroyer was taken for a submarine; guns fired on the phantom sub damaged roofs in the nearby village of Jemimaville and wounded a baby in a cot. While a ship's doctor calmed the child, a young flag-lieutenant delighted the parents with the news that the battle had resulted in the sinking of two U-boats. Admiral Sir Reginald Drax drolly commented that as yet no decision had been taken about striking a medal for the engagement. In his undefended base

Jellicoe was soon calling for protection. While shore defences were hastily erected he decided to take the entire Grand Fleet of 21 Dreadnoughts and eight pre-Dreadnoughts to Lough Swilly on the north coast of Ireland. Round one to the Germans, had they but known it. By sinking three old cruisers, U-9 had literally driven the British out of the North Sea.

Worse was to follow. The Germans laid mines off the coast of Ireland and succeeded in sinking one of the newest of the British battleships, HMS *Audacious*. Beatty complained to Churchill of the lack of a base 'where we can with any degree of safety lie for coaling, replenishing, and refitting and repairing, after two and a half months of war'. According to Beatty the navy had been 'knocked off its perch' by the incompetence of the planners. At the time he wrote these angry words, Beatty and his battlecruisers were in a loch on the Isle of Mull, protected from submarines by picket boats and nets. The hunter had become the hunted. As the dashing Beatty said, 'We have been running hard now since 28th July' and he did not know how long he could go on like that.

The Germans were never able to capitalize on the errors of the British naval planners. That Britain's naval supremacy, won at Trafalgar in 1805, had been temporarily thrown away by the absence of a secure base, by the fear of the U-boat and by the occasional sightings of seals, would not have occurred to German admirals who were still in thrall to a reputation that the British navy of 1914 did not deserve.

The more things change the more they remain the same. The situation in 1939 was a remake of the 1914 film – with the same set, Scapa Flow; the same cast; and the same leading man – Winston Churchill as First Lord of the Admiralty. In September 1939 Churchill visited Scapa to confer with the commander of the Home Fleet and discovered that all the anti-submarine defences established during the First World War, along with the shore batteries, had been demolished as an economy measure and never replaced. Scapa Flow was just as welcoming to U-boats as it had been in 1914 – and this time they came. The loss of the *Royal Oak* to U-47 was the product of the grossest incompetence by the British Admiralty in not ensuring the fleet a well-defended base.

If the fleet at Scapa Flow was open to U-boat attack, it was even more vulnerable to assault from the air. The base's total gunnery strength, to protect the fleet on which the future of the nation depended, was just eight antiquated 4.5-inch anti-aircraft and no close-range batteries at all. Apparently even as late as the early months of 1939 Prime Minister Neville Chamberlain was refusing to increase the defences at Scapa Flow in case it sent the wrong message to Hitler by suggesting that Britain was preparing for war. In the event, the British were very lucky. German bombers attacked Scapa Flow – in its defenceless state – the day after the *Royal Oak* was torpedoed (see p. 113) but found that the fleet was out. Only the *Iron Duke* – flagship of the Grand Fleet at Jutland and now employed as a floating coastal battery – was at home and the Germans took out their frustration on her, hitting her with one bomb so that she had to be beached. The obsolete fighter aircraft sent up to intercept the German bombers were too slow to even catch them. It was a humiliating episode which, in Churchill's words, was a product of 'pre-war neglect'.

# Operation Menace

Admiral Sir Herbert Richmond said of Operation Menace that 'it would be difficult to find, in the whole history of war, a more deplorable fiasco than this'. As a naval historian Richmond always wielded a sharp pen, yet in this case it is difficult to disagree with him. One of the 'actors' in the fiasco – novelist Evelyn Waugh – later described his own experiences through the character of Guy Crouchback, hero of the novel *Men at Arms*.

After the surrender of France in June 1940 Britain was faced with the danger that the French fleet might be taken over by the Germans and used against the Royal Navy. Prime Minister Winston Churchill met the problem head on and ordered British ships to sink the French ships at Oran in North Africa. At Alexandria the French were persuaded to scuttle their vessels, but in other ports – notably at Dakar in West Africa, where the powerful but unfinished battleship *Richelieu* was stationed – the British government faced the awkward problem of having to fire on its erstwhile allies.

The essentials of Operation Menace were that Free French leader Charles de Gaulle would leave Britain in late August 1940 with two battalions of troops, some tanks and aircraft, and would aim to 'hoist the Free French flag in French territory in West Africa'. His aim would be to secure Dakar as a base. The British were prepared to supply the shipping for de Gaulle's expedition but stressed that above all it must appear to be a French operation.

At a meeting on 15 August the Chiefs of Staff in London instructed the joint British commanders of the operation – Vice-Admiral John Cunningham and Major-General Noel Irwin – that the operation should aim to achieve the installation of de Gaulle in Dakar if possible without the use of force, after which the British force could withdraw. 'Surprise rather than force' was to be the order of the day. This hoped-for scenario would see the British task force arrive off Dakar at dawn – having encountered no French naval resistance – whereupon aircraft would drop millions of propaganda leaflets appealing to the inhabitants – notably the servicemen – to put down their arms and welcome General de Gaulle with open arms. The British warships would stay just over the horizon to allow the small French contingent with them to enter the port first. It was imperative that de Gaulle should not appear as a pawn of the British. If the Vichy governor accepted de Gaulle's envoys the British fleet would not enter the port of Dakar at all. If, however, there was resistance – from coastal batteries and from the *Richelieu* – the British fleet would close in to suppress the French fire. British troops would only land in the event of serious resistance, which de Gaulle was at pains to stress was most unlikely.

Some historians have generously described the 'bad luck' associated with this operation. Others, like Richmond, have rubbished both planning and execution. In fact, Operation Menace should have been renamed 'Operation Muddle'. From the start everything that could go wrong did go wrong. So much depended on intelligence information from de Gaulle of his likely reception at Dakar. His agents in the area exaggerated his popularity and the British made the mistake of believing them. When it came to intelligence on Dakar's defences and the suitability of the beaches for landing troops the performance of British intelligence was lamentable. The task force sailed with plans of Dakar dated no later than 1919. One man – Captain Poulter (who had been a liaison officer at Dakar before the war) – knew the truth but he was largely ignored. Once the task force was at sea Poulter produced a 1940 copy of a map – sent to the British War Office in June but completely overlooked – which showed that the Dakar defences were far more formidable than the task force commanders had been led to believe. Instead of the meagre 1,400 Vichy troops expected there would be more than 7,000. In addition, Poulter ominously told Cunningham and Irwin that 'not one man, woman or child is pro-de Gaulle'. This information was simply brushed aside with the words, 'We all regarded him [Poulter] as a Jeremiah.' In fact, he proved to be the only officer on the task force who guessed the truth.

Troops transferring from the French sloop *Commandant Duboc* to a British vessel in Freetown harbour in the humiliating aftermath of Operation Menace. The Anglo-French combined operation aimed at installing General de Gaulle's Free French forces in Senegal was characterized by muddle from the outset.

If there were intelligence failures in planning Operation Menace, attempts to maintain secrecy assumed the level of farce. Young British officers visited London shops demanding maps of Dakar, while Polish and Free French soldiers spoke openly of their destination. Even General de Gaulle was capable of 'gaffes', buying large quantities of tropical gear from Simpsons of Piccadilly and telling sales assistants he needed it for West Africa. French officers at a dinner in a Liverpool hotel openly toasted 'Dakar', while at the Écu de France in London's Jermyn Street, patriotic and drunken Frenchmen toasted 'Dakar' and 'de Gaulle'. As de Gaulle and his staff left Euston Station on 30 August for their 'ultra-secret' destination there were crowds of VIPs, as well as wives and girlfriends, cheering and waving them off. Just as the train was due to pull out a porter rushed up with a case which tipped off his trolley and opened. The wind whipped into the air hundreds of blue, white and red leaflets headed 'Aux Habitants de Dakar'.

Just before the fleet sailed from the Clyde one further incident publicized the operation so well it might as well have been announced in the daily papers. As Evelyn Waugh relates in *Men at Arms*, a lighter came alongside the cruiser *Devonshire*, which was carrying de Gaulle and his party, to deliver some large packages. As the boxes were being taken aboard several broke open and revealed more of the leaflets designed to convince the inhabitants of Dakar to accept de Gaulle. They bore the words *'Français de Dakar! Joignez-vous à nous pour délivrer la France! General de Gaulle.'* Hardly anyone on the cruiser failed to get a copy and soon they were circulating the pubs of Glasgow.

Once the cat was out of the bag, Churchill reasoned, there was nothing to be done but to get on with the operation with all speed. But even here he faced frustration. All the deadlines were immediately thrown out by the late discovery that the top-speed of the French MT convoy was 8 knots instead of the 12 knots promised. Meanwhile, the loading of stores aboard the transports *Ettrick*, *Kenya*, *Karanja* and *Sobieski* had been made without reference to the operational plans. As a result, the weapons and materials needed for the landing were scattered throughout the four ships in no particular order. According to General Irwin, 'No one had the least idea of what was actually down below decks.' It took three precious days to bring order to the chaos.

The next problem had a distinctly French flavour about it. The crews of the French MTs refused to sail until they were paid three months' back pay and had *pâté de foie gras* and champagne added to their rations. No sooner was this settled than one of the French captains refused to sail unless he could bring his mistress with him. Even when the ships did sail two collided in the Mersey and had to return to Liverpool for repairs. Winston Churchill was furious:

> There seems to be an air of negativism, and of undue yielding to difficulties, and a woeful lack of appreciation of the time factor in some of the naval proceedings, which is not in accordance with the best traditions of the Admiralty.

The late summer of 1940 was one of the darkest periods in Britain's history. By day and night the RAF and the Luftwaffe fought it out over the south of England and London reeled under its first bombing raids. Across the Channel the Germans had assembled troop transports and barges for a possible invasion of England, while on the borders of Egypt the Italians were threatening an invasion in overwhelming numbers. And at this pregnant moment Churchill decided to undertake an operation both ridiculous and unnecessary. Naval opinion at the Admiralty was united in its opposition. As one officer wrote, Operation Menace was 'an irritating and irrelevant sideshow'. Another – even more bitterly – saw it as an

> . . . ill-omened operation, sponsored on us by the P.M. in spite of bitter opposition from the Service Chiefs. It is part of the price we pay for having Winston as P.M. . . . I hate this operation. We don't want to dissipate our strength fighting the French, when every blow we can strike should be delivered against the Germans or Italians.

The naval component of 'Force M' comprised the old battleships *Barham* and *Resolution*, the aircraft carrier *Ark Royal,* three cruisers and ten destroyers, with the cruiser *Devonshire* acting as flagship. The Free French sent just three tiny sloops. The decision not to send any British submarines was an undoubted error, as events were to prove. As the fleet made its way south the planners aboard the *Devonshire* did their best to ensure the operation's failure by adding English facetiousness to a general air of incompetence. On arrival at Dakar three 'situations' were apparently possible: *happy* if de Gaulle was met with flowers and dancing girls in grass skirts; *sticky* if there was more resistance than an old gendarme with a stick; *nasty* if the French, remembering past insults and shouting '*A bas les Anglais*', decided to fight with everything they had got. The British had plans for every contingency and codenames for each of them: 'William', 'Conqueror', 'Rufus', 'George', 'Alfred' and so on. On one occasion de Gaulle enigmatically signalled the flagship with the message 'Charles is very pleased with "Charles"'. The operations orders changed every day and General Spears, liaison officer with de Gaulle, wrote in despair that he was being inundated with paper by the planners. 'Their industry was in fact amazing . . . they had plans to meet every emergency, excepting, as it turned out, the one with which we were presently faced.'

Admiral Cunningham and General Irwin – with all their combined staffs – were crowded like sardines into the *Devonshire*, which was quite unsuited to the task of flagship. Irwin's staff of eight had to make do with an office seven foot square, with three typewriters (of which two were broken) and a faulty duplicator, courtesy of War Office Supplies. Ironically, while the commanders suffered, the troops enjoyed the 'holiday of a lifetime'. The British troop transports were liners in peacetime and had not been converted to wartime service. As a result, morning tea was served in cabins by white-coated stewards and there were five-course meals. On one liner the band was still *in situ*. It was certainly a change from war-torn Britain.

Unfortunately nemesis was approaching. When the Vichy government in France got wind of the British operation they ordered Admiral Bourragué at Toulon to sail for Dakar with the cruisers *Georges Leygues*, *Montcalm* and *Gloire*, accompanied by three large destroyers. From Toulon the French squadron – codenamed 'Force Y' – would need to pass through the Straits of Gibraltar but through a series of errors and misunderstandings the British commander there, Admiral Sir Dudley North, chose not to challenge them. This was later – controversially – to cost North his job. The problem was that North had received a signal from the British consul-general at Tangier warning him that the French squadron was approaching Gibraltar. How should he react? The same signal had apparently been sent to the Foreign Office but had been placed at the bottom of a pile of reports and was not decoded and sent to the Admiralty until too late. Thus while North waited for Admiralty instructions, their Lordships remained in ignorance of the movements of Force Y. In fact, Admiral North – for security reasons – had been told nothing about Operation Menace and therefore could not judge how dangerous the French cruisers might be to the British task force. As the French ships passed Gibraltar North even signalled *bon voyage* to them – a ghastly if forgivable error. When the Admiralty learned that the French had been allowed to pass Gibraltar unchallenged they were furious and ordered North to send the battlecruiser *Repulse* in pursuit. But by then it was far too late; the French cruisers were five hours ahead – and faster than the aged battlecruiser. Admiral Somerville, given the unenviable task of pursuing the cruisers, wrote to his wife, 'How the hell I was expected to stop all six I don't quite know.' In the event, Somerville had no chance and the French cruisers reached Dakar to add significantly to its defences. Now was the time to call off the operation but Churchill obstinately pushed on. General Irwin was disappointed:

> Our advice to continue the operation in the face of this access of strength to the defences of Dakar was based too much on the information that the people were ripe for General de Gaulle, and not enough on the obvious military reinforcement to the defence, and it was, in consequence, and in my opinion, not sound.

Force M sailed on to Freetown in Sierra Leone to refuel. Clearly North at Gibraltar must have been one of the few people in the world who did not know its destination. Africans paddling out in canoes to the troopships even called out to the British soldiers, 'Massa, you going Dakar!'

As Force M approached Dakar the betting was that the French would either accept de Gaulle with open arms, or else capitulate after token resistance. Nobody – with the exception of Captain Poulter – expected much resistance. But the British were ready if the French wanted to fight. Apparently the plan was that if the task force was fired on the battleships would bombard the vast stacks of groundnuts piled by the harbour wall of Dakar. Subsequently, it turned out, the battleships deluged this vital target with heavy shells but failed to gain ignition. The Fleet Air Arm then also tried their luck but with even less success. The day before the operation was due to commence de Gaulle organized a party for senior officers at which he was presented with an iced cake inscribed '*A la Victoire*' in pink icing. It seemed appropriate.

On 23 September the Free French sloops entered Dakar harbour, while the British warships stayed well out to sea, over the horizon. At once a thick fog – which in a metaphorical sense had been ever present since the expedition left Britain – enshrouded the coast, reducing visibility to just two miles. Alarmingly, just prior to their arrival, the British learned that the 'friendly colonial gunners' who they had expected to man the port's defences had been replaced by pro-Vichy naval personnel. What was worse, the senior army and naval personnel were known to be rabidly anti-British. The situation report was certainly 'sticky' and it began to look as if de Gaulle had misled the British with reports of his popularity when anti-aircraft fire was directed against the six Swordfish from *Ark Royal*, scattering the tricoloured leaflets over the city. The final rejection came when a Free French sloop flying a large Cross of Lorraine flag and carrying de Gaulle's emissary, Commander d'Argenlieu, sailed into the harbour. D'Argenlieu and his men first tried to negotiate with the Vichy authorities. But the defenders knew a British fleet was just over the horizon and would not receive d'Argenlieu's mission. The local police tried to arrest the Gaullist emissaries who only escaped in a fast motor-boat pursued gallantly but lamely by an old Vichy tug. As one Free French sloop made its escape past the *Richelieu* the French battleship's 15-inch guns swung round to point at her. At any second the sloop would be blown out of the water. The sloop's commander kept his head and ordered his bugler to sound 'attention'. Immediately the gun crew on the battleship abandoned their guns and stood to attention and the tiny sloop raced away into the fog. But all was despondency in the Allied task force: 'Situation sticky' was rapidly becoming 'Situation nasty'.

Admiral Cunningham had no alternative now but to commence a bombardment of the French warships in Dakar harbour, as well as the port defences. In thick fog the battle began. Even at a range of 4,000 metres it was like 'blind man's buff'. The *Richelieu* could fire just one turret against the eight of the two British battleships, yet the discrepancy in strength never seemed very great. The *Barham* and the *Resolution* fired over a hundred 15-inch shells without achieving a single hit. On the other hand, a shell from a coastal battery hit the cruiser *Cumberland*, forcing her to withdraw to Gambia for repairs. It was not a propitious start.

The following day the British renewed the bombardment. First aircraft from the *Ark Royal* attacked the ships in the harbour with 250-pound bombs – poor weapons for penetrating the armoured decks of a battleship. Again no hits were scored. 'We might as well have dropped bricks,' commented one pilot. Later attacks by torpedo planes launched eight torpedoes, but again without any success. Meanwhile, the heavy British ships continued their assault on the *Richelieu*, again without scoring a single hit on a stationary target. Without spotter planes the gunnery of the battleships was quite ineffectual. The most serious damage to the British navy – at least in the eyes of General Spears – was from the constant stream of cigarette ends that de Gaulle insisted on dropping upon the *Devonshire*'s pristine deck.

Back in Britain, Winston Churchill was disturbed by the news he was receiving. After a bombardment of several hours duration the French ships had suffered no damage at all. What on earth was happening? He signalled Cunningham that the 'Matter must be pushed to [a] conclusion without delay'. This was easier said than done.

By the morning of 25 September the fog had lifted. Surely now the British battleships would be able to destroy the *Richelieu* and the Dakar forts? But the single submarine left in Dakar harbour – the *Bévéziers*, named after a rare French naval victory over the English – was about to administer the *coup de grace*. Her commander, Lieutenant-Commander Pierre Lancelot, had trained with the Royal Navy and was able to recognize British signals. Watching the *Barham* raise 'Blue 7' – a turning signal – Lancelot fired four torpedoes at the turning points of the two British battleships, just missing *Barham* but hitting *Resolution* amidships. This was the final straw for Admiral Cunningham. The *Resolution*, listing heavily, retired under a smokescreen.

Ironically, Lancelot later served under Cunningham during the North African landings in 1943. Lancelot introduced himself as the man who had torpedoed the *Resolution*. With true British aplomb Cunningham shook his hand and said, 'Good shot!' before pinning a British decoration on the intrepid Frenchman.

The *Barham* and the *Richelieu* briefly exchanged hits with 15-inch shells, again to little effect, before Cunningham called off the bombardment. It was the same old story – ships were 'helpless' against forts. Would the Admiralty never learn?

Force M left Dakar on 27 September and sailed to Freetown, Sierra Leone, with the *Barham* towing the *Resolution*. It was a thoroughly humiliating retreat and recriminations were severe. Churchill was looking for a scapegoat and found one in Admiral Dudley North, who was dismissed for allowing the French cruisers to reach Dakar via Gibraltar. In the words of Commander Crease, Churchill was determined to have someone at Gibraltar's 'balls for a necktie'. But Churchill was unfair. The whole operation had been a disaster from start to finish. He had forced it on an unwilling Admiralty and he had placed too much reliance on the word of the messianic but opportunist Charles de Gaulle. Furthermore, the forces that Britain could spare were not up to the job. Though the *Richelieu* was incomplete and could only operate one turret, she was a modern ship and more than a match for the tired old warhorses that Churchill sent south. The whole affair aroused unpleasant memories of the pre-Dreadnoughts that Churchill had sent to the Dardanelles, which were apparently good enough to fight the Turks but not the Germans in the North Sea. In the words of Alfred Marder, 'Operation Menace was a classic example of wishful thinking, which is thinking directed more by personal wishes than by objective or rational factors.'

After the war General Irwin revisited Dakar. One senior officer there told him that – as usual – the British had failed to understand the French mentality. How could they have asked so many senior generals and admirals ashore to subordinate themselves to a man as junior as de Gaulle – a mere 'Général de Brigade'. On a lighter note he was gently teased at dinner by the wife of a French battalion commander, 'Why did you keep on shelling my vegetable garden, couldn't you hit anything else?' In a sense this said it all.

# The Floating Whorehouse

The American Civil War contains few stranger episodes than the campaign conducted by Captain John M. Newcomb of the paddle-steamer *Idahoe*, on the Cumberland and Ohio rivers above Nashville, in July 1863. Single-handedly Newcomb saved hundreds of Union soldiers from 'a fate worse than death'.

The Confederate stronghold of Nashville in Tennessee had fallen to the Union in February 1862. At once the Federal commanders found that the South still had a secret weapon which undermined both the health and the morale of their soldiers: the legions of prostitutes who inhabited Nashville's red-light district of opium dens and brothels, known as Smokey Row. For every Union soldier who fell in battle dozens were laid low by venereal disease. By July 1863 Nashville's military commander, Brigadier-General Robert S. Granger, had had enough. Daily complaints by his regimental surgeons convinced him that the only way to restore his men to health was to clear Nashville of its prostitutes. Granger therefore ordered the Provost Marshal, Lieutenant-Colonel George Spalding, to seize all the city's prostitutes and transport them by river to Louisville, Kentucky. Spalding needed a boat and by luck – or mischance –

his choice fell on Captain John Newcomb and the *Idahoe*. Newcomb had no chance to complain – he was going on active service and that was that.

Meanwhile, Spalding had begun rounding up Nashville's 'fallen daughters'. It was not a simple matter and Spalding's troopers suffered casualties. Although many of the women were taken by surprise, others fought back and had to be brought down by flying tackles. Half-naked girls were to be seen leaping from second-storey windows or climbing barefoot up drainpipes in their attempts to escape capture. Others were driven at bayonet point into waiting wagons, where they punched and kicked their captors. In the chaos mistakes were made. Ladies of reputation and breeding who happened to be passing by while the round-up took place found themselves swept up into the wagons with their less fortunate sisters. General Granger was at pains to deny press reports that several straitlaced Nashville dowagers had been arrested by mistake, but there can be no doubt that a number of ladies of blameless reputation experienced a broadening of their education on board the *Idahoe* – soon to be nicknamed 'the floating whorehouse'. Eventually some 150 women were placed aboard the *Idahoe*, much to the consternation of Captain Newcomb, who was now told that it was his responsibility to feed them on the voyage to Louisville. But what Spalding had not told him was that nobody at Louisville was prepared to accept his cargo. Newcomb was forced to set sail without provisions for his passengers, without medical resources and without guards to keep the girls in check.

The *Idahoe* paddled up the Cumberland River and crossed the Kentucky border at Linton, joining the Ohio near Smithland, after a journey of over one hundred miles. In five days Newcomb reached Louisville, where he had every reason to believe that his problems would end. The journey had tried his patience to the limit; the unwilling passengers, when not indulging their fury at the expense of the captain, did what they could to smash the interior of the *Idahoe* to smithereens. At least half of them were confined to bed through sickness and Newcomb had to dig deep into his own pocket to buy them food and medicine from the towns they passed on the Cumberland. At each stopping place Newcomb was refused any help by the military authorities, who even stationed guards to drive back on board any of the prostitutes who tried to escape. The girls made things worse by waving to the men on the river banks and adjusting their dresses to show more shoulder.

Newcomb now found that, like the Flying Dutchman, he was doomed to sail the seas of the world – or the rivers of America – without ever finding a haven. The authorities at Louisville would not accept his cargo, and told him to take the women on to Cincinnati. They did, however, agree to supply him with guards, who spent most of the trip sampling Newcomb's wares – apparently free of charge.

News of his coming passed up the river like wildfire and Cincinnati was ready for the invasion from the south. As Newcomb hove into view local Union commanders ordered their troops into battle stations to drive the *Idahoe* away. Meanwhile, Newcomb's own crew had to stand ready to repel boarders as men rowed out from the shore to try to take advantage of his predicament and pay his cargo a visit. The incredible battle continued, with Newcomb repelling the civilian boarders but quite unable to break through the line of grim-faced Union troops protecting the harbour at Cincinnati from the corruption aboard the *Idahoe*. Newcomb at last managed to get a telegram through to Secretary of War Stanton in Washington asking what he should do next. Stanton, his mind preoccupied by reports of the fighting at Gettysburg in Pennsylvania, was furious. Someone had blundered. Who was responsible for organizing this fiasco? Stanton decided that Granger had exceeded his brief by sending the prostitutes north and ordered Newcomb to take the women back to Nashville, incidentally warning Granger that if he did not accept them he would be looking for a new job.

Thirteen days after he had left the Nashville waterfront Captain Newcomb was back, with the *Idahoe* still laden with its cargo of 'frail sisterhood'. Within hours the 'sisters' were at work again in their old haunts in Smokey Row. But Newcomb's journey had not been in vain. Although driven away by the righteous folk along the Ohio River, he had brought to the attention of the national government in Washington the danger the prostitutes posed for federal soldiers of occupation in Tennessee and Kentucky. In Nashville a chastened General Granger at last found the answer: legalize prostitution but insist that the 'sisters' submit to medical inspection. Everyone was delighted: prostitutes, clients, the people of Nashville and especially the army commanders, who saw cases of venereal disease reduce to a trickle. Only Captain Newcomb had cause for complaint. In spite of his heroism in conducting over a hundred enemy combatants through a war zone, he found it difficult to gain reimbursement for the money he had spent on feeding them, or the damage they had inflicted on his vessel. Moreover, he became a figure of fun everywhere he went, known ever afterwards as the 'captain of the floating whorehouse'. Even after the war, as the *Idahoe* worked the rivers of the south, children would line the banks of the rivers chanting, 'Here comes the whorehouse!' Newcomb had paid a high price for his war service.

# The Nile – by way of Bantry Bay

It was not Nelson's fault if the French fleet he defeated at Aboukir Bay in 1798 was crewed by gangs of naked ragamuffins. Nor did it detract one iota from his victory that many of the French ships were at half complement because so many of their sailors were ashore when the British descended on them. A report written just days before the battle told General Bonaparte, 'On the whole our ships are very poorly manned, and . . . it needs much courage to command such an ill-prepared fleet.' The French were never short of courage, but they were ill-equipped because for five years naval affairs had been in the hands of doctrinaire revolutionaries who made political correctness a *sine qua non* for officers seeking promotion. The results were farcical. At a time when men such as Jervis, Barham and Nelson were moulding the finest naval force in Britain's history, the French were responding with its very antithesis – a navy to set men like Duquesne, Jean Bart, Tourville and Suffren turning in their graves.

The outbreak of revolution in France in 1789 hit the French navy hard. Many officers were drawn from the lesser aristocracy and they fled the country in fear of their lives. Nor were their fears exaggerated. Discipline in the navy collapsed, with officers insulted and beaten up on their own ships and threatened with the gallows or the guillotine. Some officers, who tried to restore order, were hanged from lamp-posts by mutineers in Toulon in 1792. Everywhere senior officers were deposed by committees of sailors and replaced by more popular men, regardless of rank or ability. In 1791 the Assembly abolished the officer corps and introduced a new system of ranks which were to be filled by loyal revolutionaries, while political commissars were given the task of running French ports – with what result can best be left to the imagination.

A career open to talent was one thing, but where was the talent? Lists of officers were displayed in every port so that any suspected of disloyalty to the Revolution could be denounced. Many able men succumbed to enemies eager to settle old scores. Violent revolutionary rabble-rousers soon dominated every ship, with officers afraid to contradict them. Standards of seamanship and gunnery soon fell away. In 1794 the two admirals commanding the French fleet had been mere lieutenants just three years before, while of the 26 captains one had been a common sailor and another a boatswain; the rest came from the merchant service and had no experience of commanding a warship in action. In the French Atlantic Fleet, stationed at Brest, one captain died when he fell from the rigging having taken *egalité* a little bit too far: unable to order his men aloft, he had been forced to lead them there.

Vice-Admiral Morard de Galles lost his headsails when he could not persuade even 30 men to come on deck to trim them. De Galles asked to be relieved of command, but the ferocious revolutionaries of the Committee of Public Safety told him that if he knew what was good for him he would continue to serve his country by attacking a passing Dutch convoy. When he ordered the fleet to go into action the men refused to fight and demanded to return to Brest. The admiral was helpless to impose discipline and was promptly arrested on the grounds of his noble background and imprisoned by Deputy St André. The deputy then rounded up all the men who had obeyed the admiral's orders and sent them to Paris where they were guillotined. He then dismissed all officers of the fleet who had served prior to 1789. At the great Mediterranean base of Toulon they matched their brothers at Brest in the madness of their actions. The naval base was dominated by the local Jacobin committee and when the crew of a frigate mutinied the Jacobins put the captain on trial and condemned him to death for the crime of being an aristocrat. The year 1794 marked a low point in the history of the French Navy, and December of that year saw the extraordinary 'voyage to nowhere'.

After the French defeat by Admiral Howe on the 'Glorious First of June' the politicians of the Convention began to demand more action from their fleet. So critical did they become that as a gesture of defiance to the British the whole fleet was ordered to sea in December, in appalling weather conditions. There was not the slightest chance of them encountering any British ships – all of which were snugly in harbour during the impossible sailing conditions of a North Atlantic winter – nor were the French commanders aware of any master plan or purpose to justify them risking their ships and crews in the howling winter gales. None of the French ships was provisioned for more than a fortnight at sea and many were still carrying severe battle damage from their struggle against Howe six months earlier. The result was a tragedy. Three ships-of-the-line simply capsized and were lost with all hands, another was leaking so badly that 50 of her crew drowned while still aboard. Two others, wrecked by the wind, struggled into neutral harbours. The rest of the fleet was blown out to sea and only managed to return to Brest after twelve weeks. Short of provisions, and with many of their crewmen dead from starvation or exposure, the remnants of the fleet reached port in a more dreadful condition than if they had suffered a major defeat in battle.

But even now the French navy had not reached rock bottom; they were about to be ordered to invade Ireland. It comes as no surprise to learn that the idea came from a cavalry officer – the brilliant General Hoche – and not from one of France's fast-diminishing stock of capable sailors. In December 1796, the Brest fleet of seventeen ships-of-the-line and thirteen frigates, with a force of 20,000 soldiers, set out for Ireland. Hoche, with Admirals Bruix and Morard de Galles and their staff, crowded into one frigate – suitably named the *Fraternité* – thus ensuring that if this one ship were lost or captured the whole command structure of the expedition would be gone in an instant. The first problem they faced was how to avoid a blockading British squadron. There were two ways of leaving Brest harbour – by the westward or the eastward channel. At dusk on 16 December, Admiral Morard de Galles signalled by gunfire and lights that the fleet were to take the westward channel. Unfortunately, his signals were so confusing that chaos broke out. First a French ship ran aground and began firing distress guns, confusing everyone. Then a British frigate, Sir Edward Pellew's *Indefatigable,* sailed into the harbour and began a pyrotechnic display of guns, lights and rockets which baffled all the French captains. In the confusion half the French ships followed the wrong channel and failed to make the rendezvous, including the *Fraternité* with the commander-in-chief, Hoche, aboard. It was a bad start, from which the expedition never recovered. Only one flag officer – Admiral Bouvet – reached the rendezvous, and it fell to him to lead the fleet to Bantry Bay, while Hoche and Morard de Galles searched way out into the Atlantic, looking for their commands.

Planning a large amphibious operation was quite beyond the French at this time. They had sailed at the wrong time of year and landing so many troops in the stormy Bantry Bay was an impossibility. Each time they tried to come close to shore they were driven further out into the Atlantic storms by contrary winds and blizzard conditions. The poorly clad sailors were quite unable to sail their unhandy ships in such weather and it eventually fell to General Grouchy, commanding the expedition in the absence of Hoche, to order a return to France. Before he could do so a great storm swept the bay, causing ships to run aground and drag their anchors. Ironically, Hoche and Morard de Galles in the *Fraternité* did eventually reach Bantry Bay, only to find that Bouvet and Grouchy had gone. The only sign that the French had ever been there was the presence of the badly damaged ship-of-the-line *Révolution*, floundering about in heavy seas. As ironical in its way was the fact that the *Droits de l'Homme* was destroyed on the return journey by the British *Indefatigable*.

With the *Révolution* and the *Droits de l'Homme* gone, it was time for Napoleon to take over and restore French fortunes. He would use the fleet to take him across the Mediterranean to Egypt. On 1 July 1797 a meeting of truly epic proportions was avoided by only a matter of a few hours. The French invasion force reached Alexandria shortly after Nelson's ships had left. Had the two fleets met the whole future of the world would probably have been different. It is difficult to see how the French, undermanned, poorly equipped and weighed down with stores and soldiers, could have survived an encounter with the British. And the capture or death of Napoleon in 1798 raises more 'ifs' than any comparable event in history. But fate decreed otherwise. The two men did not meet and the destruction of the French fleet – 1,700 sailors short of its full complement – was postponed just long enough to save Napoleon from getting his feet wet. A month later Nelson returned to annihilate Admiral Brueys-d'Aigalliers' fleet in Aboukir Bay, a great victory and yet in a sense merely the logical outcome of five years of political interference in naval affairs which had reduced the French navy from its apogee after Chesapeake in 1781 to its nadir at Bantry Bay in 1797.

# CHAPTER 4: A LIFE ON THE OCEAN WAVE

## The Rulers of the Queen's Navee

It was revealed in 1815 that although the national rate for lunacy was one per 7,000 of the population, the rate in the navy was considerably higher, at one lunatic per 1,000. In fact, lunacy was a growing problem and the navy was forced to establish an asylum at Hoxton in London to cater for its more serious cases. Although excessive consumption of strong liquor – most commonly the pint of rum the men were served daily – must have been a factor, along with the consequences of venereal infection, the biggest cause was apparently the fact that men hit their heads so often on the low beams below decks. The madness of so many members of the Royal Navy may in some way have accounted for the often almost insane courage shown by British seamen in innumerable battles throughout the ages. But the lunacy of their commanders has not always had such positive effects. Often merely a product of a 'mild distemper', the eccentricities of serving naval officers have been more often the subject for amusement than serious concern. However, they have also been at the root of mistreatment of sailors and have sometimes fuelled sadistic tendencies to flog and torture (see p. 92).

Some eccentric naval officers were far removed from the world of the Marquis de Sade or Herr Krafft-Ebing. Under the benign influence of Rear-Admiral the Hon. Henry John Rous, the captain of the *Harlequin* had his boat crew turned out in harlequin suits, while the men of the *Caledonia* were resplendent in tartan. Not to be outdone, the men of the *Blazer* set a fashion for striped blue and white jackets, and the crew of the *Vernon* turned out in red serge frock coats and red comforters. One captain – 'Nobby' Ewart – seeing one of his boat crew with a black eye, ordered all the others to paint the same eye black. It was all good harmless fun.

The most famous of the eccentric admirals was Sir Algernon Charles Fiesché Heneage, better known as 'Pompo'. Pompo was harmless enough though resistant to anything resembling progress; technology, engineering, science and so forth would have earned his most scathing criticism. For Pompo appearances were everything. His affectation was such that he could not bear to think of a common sailor washing his clothes and so he took 20 dozen shirts to sea and sent the dirty ones home on every available ship bound for England. Even while rounding Cape Horn, with seas raging and men's thoughts on the Almighty and His wondrous works, Heneage was thinking of his shirts, and how he could transfer them to a passing ship. On one occasion a ship's carpenter was arrested for entering the admiral's cabin without being announced by an appropriate officer, and on another the same man was clapped in irons for going to Pompo's cabin to shut his portholes when the sea was splashing in. In the event the cabin was flooded but no one lower than a petty officer was allowed to swab it out. Pompo's hair was set in curls and he once told a gunnery officer, adopting the affected style of speech which was his hallmark, 'Vot larvely hair you haf. Vot do you put on it? Myself I break two eggs ofer my head efery morning.' On one notorious occasion a seaman took a step forward and steadied Pompo as he was climbing up a gangplank, which had the effect of turning him puce with rage. 'Dat man!' shrieked Pompo. 'He touched me!'

Admiral Sir Archibald Berkeley Milne – of Troubridge and *Goeben* fame (see p. 32) – was as ridiculous as Pompo but had the misfortune to carry his eccentricities into a world war. On

Augustus Earle's (1806–38) 'Life on the Ocean', a somewhat romanticized view of a midshipman's berth on a British wooden-walled battleship of the early 19th century. Life on board ship was not always so relaxing, as those serving under Rear-Admiral Charles Prothero discovered to their cost.

one occasion a common seaman brushed against his coat, whereupon he shuddered, took out a handkerchief to brush the point of contact and then threw the soiled linen overboard. His main claim to fame was his command of the Royal Yachts, though how this qualified him to be commander of the British Mediterranean Fleet at the outbreak of war in 1914 is beyond anyone's comprehension. He was known – not very affectionately – as the 'Great Arch Bark' or 'Arky-Barky'.

Rear-Admiral Charles Prothero – Prothero 'the Bad' to the men who served under him in the British navy in the mid-19th century – was a man of bearlike size and strength, with a big black beard and a hooked nose that would have earned him Shylock's or Fagin's part in amateur dramatics. Commanding a ship where his predecessor had had a rich supply of the milk of human kindness, Prothero thought everyone had got soft. Bumping into a midshipman on the bridge, he lifted the offender by one huge hand on his collar and dropped him over the side of the bridge onto the deck. Inspecting the midshipmen's quarters he found that several of them had got chests of drawers alongside their hammocks. Inquiring what the articles were, Prothero was told that his predecessor had allowed extra furniture to make their lives more comfortable. Prothero exploded, 'When I was a midshipman I lived in my chest and sometimes bathed in it too. Throw them over the side.'

At the battle of Jutland in 1916, Rear-Admiral Robert Keith Arbuthnot was commanding the 1st Cruiser Squadron, flying his flag in the *Defence*, which was blown to kingdom come by the German High Seas Fleet. Arbuthnot would have resented his aerial departure, preferring instead to go ten rounds with the Kaiser or any of his ravening Huns. Arbuthnot ran Pompo close in his eccentricity, offering his dinner guests a pair of boxing gloves and a chance to spar with him or watch his beloved daughter do her physical jerks. Few admirals boxed their physical training instructors for fun but Arbuthnot was a huge man and made of stern stuff. Unlike Pompo, however, Arbuthnot was anything but harmless. After his crew had been sent on a cross-country run in newly issued boots, one man suffered so badly from blisters that he missed the boat back. Arbuthnot sentenced him to death for desertion and had the decision upheld by the Admiralty. Sanity was restored only when a personal appeal by the First Sea Lord had the sentence moderated. His men hated him and one night three of them set on him in Chatham and beat him black and blue – unfortunately for them, two of his assailants ended up in hospital. But it was Arbuthnot's obsession with uniform that made his men wish they had never been born. Strict regulations were included in the admiral's published work, *A Battleship Commander's Order Book*, which included everything any captain needed to know to make his men's lives a misery: it read more like the Index of the Spanish Inquisition. So strict was Arbuthnot's sense of discipline that after he had left one ship, the chief bosun's mate watched a seagull pass over the ship and drop its guano on the deck with a splat. 'That could never 'ave 'appened in Sir Robert's day,' said the mate – and he meant it.

The problem with Victorian admirals was their age. So many of them were little more than exhibits in a maritime museum. In 1840 the ages of admirals were released by the Royal Commission into Navy and Military Promotion. The figures for vice-admirals and above are very revealing:

Over 90 years of age ............................................................................................1
Between 90 and 80 ...............................................................................................7
Between 80 and 70 .............................................................................................25
Between 70 and 65 ...............................................................................................7
Under 65 ..............................................................................................................1

In 1867 Britain's senior admiral was Sir William Bowles, who had fought at Copenhagen in 1807 and had known Nelson. Sir Provo Parry Wallis was next, who had fought in Spain in 1810 and known Wellington. Admiral John Bullen, hero of the battle of Mud Island in 1777, had only just died and been replaced at the top of the list. No test of competence or health could change the list; only the Grim Reaper could do that and he seemed to do it very slowly. Perhaps a lifetime's exposure to sea salt preserved old admirals. During the Napoleonic Wars the navy had expanded enormously and hundreds of men had reached the rank of captain. But after 1815 the navy contracted and these men could find no employment except as dead-wood on half-pay, blocking all the lines of promotion to able, younger men. The result was that by the time the navy was needed again, against Russia in 1854, the most senior admirals – who would at last get a posting, like Price (see p. 18) – were decrepit. The results were all too apparent. Even junior officers were old – one man had been a commander for 47 years, another a lieutenant for 60 years, still another a master for 61 years and one poor man a purser for 64 years. Obviously the navy was a job for life.

# The 'Cat'

Flogging was an important feature of both army and navy life in Britain for more than 250 years, reaching its apogee in the 18th century, when British soldiers were known as the 'Bloodybacks' and sailors kept at their guns less from love of such fighting admirals as Nelson, Rodney, Hood and Jervis, than from fear of the lash. In a sense Britain's military and naval success during this

'The Point of Honor' by George Cruikshank. By the 18th century flogging was considered to be essential for maintaining discipline in the Royal Navy. But it was subject to gross misuse, and often virtually amounted to a death sentence for minor offences.

period was due to the fact that soldiers and sailors feared their own commanders more than they did the enemy. That this was not necessary was displayed time after time in the war of 1812 by American ships, many of which fought as well as or even better than their British opponents, without the threat of the whip. And as a supreme irony, some of these American ships were crewed by British deserters from the Royal Navy who were looking for a more humane regime and better conditions.

During the 19th century, with the humanitarian moves towards abolishing slavery in the Empire, improving conditions in factories and mines, extending education to all and emancipating women, the preservation of flogging – particularly in the navy – ran counter to all these progressive tendencies. The 'cat o' nine tails' ruled the ships of Her Majesty's Navy in a way that nothing else could. It was a power given to a captain over his crew – a virtual power of life and death, for some punishments for relatively trivial offences amounted to a death sentence. Six dozen lashes – a frequent sentence for a minor misdemeanour – represented up to 500 or more stripes on the back from a cat o' nine tails. Yet sentences of 500 lashes were often given – which some men survived – and 1,000 lashes, which hardly anyone lived through. For striking an officer, often under severe provocation, a man would be literally flogged to death, the last 100 or so lashes being administered to a corpse. Flogging round the fleet – during which the victim was rowed from ship to ship and beaten alongside each – was, in fact, a desperately drawn-out death sentence, far more horrible than hanging. During this torture the man was frequently brought round with rum and wine so that he could feel the agony of his punishment. It was frequently the case that the flogging ripped all the flesh from the back and revealed the bones. Men who survived a lengthy flogging often succumbed at a later stage from the massive infections that often set in.

Flogging – in some quarters known as the 'English vice' – encouraged sadism among officers who had often picked up the habit in their public schools. It is remarkable how this kind of physical punishment has been considered a vital element in the achievement of discipline in both schools and in the services. Its psycho-sexual origins might have surprised its greatest supporters, of whom there were many who would have seconded the admiral who suggested that the British race had been brought up on flogging and had not done so badly for all that.

One ridiculous case of flogging involved Admiral Sir William Cornwallis who, in a drunken state, one day ordered an officer to strip and receive a flogging. Punishment was duly carried out with 'all hands up to witness punishment'. However, the following day, when he was more sober, Cornwallis remembered what he had done and offered the aggrieved officer a cane and asked him to avenge himself by beating the admiral. The officer wisely broke the cane in half and threw it overboard. However, the episode illustrates how this severe punishment could be administered at whim.

Some captains punished their men from sheer sadism. Aboard the *Hermione* its commander was notorious for his cruel punishments, apparently liking to hear the crack of the whip and see the white flesh lacerated. He flogged the last man down from the rigging each day, or the last man up. The result was that men fell – and died. When two men fell in their hurry to get down and fractured bones he simply commented, 'Throw those lubbers overboard.' One man was flogged for smiling after being struck by the boatswain. Once the captain demanded to 'see the man's back' and kept flogging him until he could see the bones. Stories of such brutality are endless.

Even in the middle of the 19th century the future Lord Fisher served on a vessel where the captain flogged every seaman aboard out of sheer cruelty. Instead of being shot – Fisher's solution – the captain was promoted. Yet Fisher was not averse to flogging when it suited him – he had a man given 36 lashes for being late back to his ship.

---

*'As if British youths have not been birched and caned from time immemorial, not only at our public schools but elsewhere; and yet the race has not turned out badly on the whole.'*

**Vice-Admiral Penrose Fitzgerald**

Almost all naval officers had enjoyed a public school education where 'beating' was an everyday event. They in turn carried on the notion that men would not work or fight properly unless more frightened of punishment than they were of the enemy. The British sailors who deserted to the Americans in the War of 1812 proved how mistaken an idea this was.

---

# Hard Tack

Nobody ran away to sea to eat well. Salt beef was part of the standard diet in the days of sail and was often served up in a very poor condition. On visiting a naval stores on Ascension Island in 1839, Captain Dalrymple Hay found that the beef stored there had been salted 30 years earlier in 1809. It was apparently still edible, though best boiled and grated with a nutmeg grater. Pork did not last so well but the biscuit had provided home for generations of weevils and maggots, so it was obviously sustaining. In fact, the local sailors had an interesting tactic for getting the best out of their biscuits. They filled a sack with the biscuit and then left a fish on the top, so that the maggots came out of the biscuit and infested the fish which could then be thrown away. Each sack needed several fish. It is a pity nobody thought of eating the fish and throwing the biscuit away.

The sailors had their own distinctive names for their food – not quite *haute cuisine* but very much to the point. Thus salt beef was 'salt 'oss', and was served twice a week at dinner. In the 1870s the navy was still using meat from casks packed in the year that Nelson fell – at Trafalgar, in 1805. One piece of beef was so tough that a sailor carved it into the shape of a frigate, sandpapered it, varnished it and then glued it to a low beam. It was as hard as mahogany as many a cracked skull bore witness in after years. Not everyone was enamoured of 'salt 'oss', one man claiming that the beef, 'must have been in the cask since the creation of the world. It was the kind of flavour you would expect an Egyptian mummy to give off if it were boiled.'

Yet for all the complaints it was a better diet than was enjoyed by soldiers in the army. Admittedly no ships carried cooks – and there was no real attempt to design a balanced diet – but the sailors got the 4,000 calories or so that were needed by men involved in heavy manual labour. The main problem was that long periods at sea denied men access to fresh fruit and vegetables. This was sometimes overcome by ingenuity in the culinary arts – Sir Sidney Smith, among his many eccentricities, establishing a fad for cooked rats, claiming rat was better than duck. To furnish his table baited hooks were let down into the provisions hold and a number of rodents thus acquired.

If the sailor's food was rarely injurious to his health, his drinking water was usually bad and sometimes lethal. In 1845 the warship *America* was becalmed off the coast of South America. Water became short and the men's ration was reduced to half a pint a day, yet the captain always found enough to water his personal livestock and chickens which supplied his table. His men were flogged for drinking his bath water and when a petty officer used a sponge to gather moisture he was broken down to able seaman. Men drank sea water and went mad, others laced their water with vinegar and one died. Natives from a nearby island offered to sell them water but the captain refused and the men saw no fresh water for a further 97 days. On his return to England the captain was court-martialled and severely reprimanded for returning home without orders. At no stage was the subject of the crew's water supply mentioned.

If the water was bad the rum was worse – it just seemed better. The issue of this powerful spirit was quite deliberate. A sailor's life was so hard and so brutal that it was better if the men were at least partially drunk most of the time. Before going into action it was usually the case that the crew of even the best ordered English men-of-war were roaring drunk. Battle usually had a sobering effect and the mechanics of gunnery had been so beaten into the men that they hardly needed to think about it all. This was for the best, thinking was bad for a sailor. Naturally, many men suffered from liver disorders as a result of excessive rum consumption while others went mad through alcohol poisoning. A ration of half a pint of rum was enough to keep even the most ardent spirits subdued.

# Admiral Hosier's Ghost

In 1726 Rear-Admiral Francis Hosier led an expedition to the Caribbean to prevent the Spanish treasure ships sailing from Porto Bello. Although at this time medical science had developed no reliable diagnosis of the tropical disease prevalent in the West Indies, their effects were so well known that the instructions given to Hosier – to remain on station and prevent the treasure ships leaving harbour, without using force against the Spanish defenders – were tantamount to a death sentence. Some thirteen years later, to commemorate Admiral Vernon's attack on Cartagena, the poet Richard Glover wrote the gruesome ballad known as *Admiral Hosier's Ghost*, from which this extract is taken:

> I, by twenty sail attended,
> Did this Spanish town affright;
> Nothing then its wealth defended
> But my orders not to fight,
> Oh! That in this rolling ocean
> I had cast them with disdain,
> And obeyed my heart's warm motion
> To reduce the pride of Spain . . .
>
> Unrepining at thy glory,
> Thy successful arms we hail;
> But remember our sad story,
> And let Hosier's wrongs prevail.
> Sent in this foul clime to languish
> Think what thousands fell in vain,
> Wasted with disease and anguish,
> Not in glorious battle slain . . .

Hosier's disaster was such a terrible one that when Campbell published his famous *Lives of the Admirals* in 1744 he was too upset to relate the details, saying, 'I cannot prevail upon myself to enter into the particulars of a disaster which I heartily wish could be blotted out of the annals of this nation.'

The problem was that in 1726 Britain and Spain were not at war and so when Hosier's fleet arrived off Porto Bello, the Spaniards simply refused to send their treasure ships out to sea. Instead they unloaded the treasure and left the empty ships riding provocatively at anchor, leaving Hosier with nothing to do but wait. From an unhealthy anchorage Hosier chose to blockade the Spanish port – waiting for further orders or for domesday, as far as he was concerned. From June to December 1726 the only activity aboard the British ships was dying. Most died from yellow fever – 'yellow jack' or 'black vomit' as it was known to the 18th-century sailor. When his crews had been diminished so far that they could scarcely operate the ships, the dogged Hosier sailed to Jamaica, picked up more men and then returned to his deadly anchorage to carry out his orders. Although the total number in the fleet at the outset equalled some 3,300 men, Hosier managed to lose over 4,000 from disease. Nor were the officers immune. Hosier himself died in August 1727, to be followed by the next in line, Commodore St. Lô, and then after him Rear-Admiral Hopson. When this gruesome martyrdom was at last ended, late in 1727, Hosier's body was returned to England in the ballast of the insanely named sloop *Happy*.

Who was to blame? The Admiralty for sending men to die in an area known for its unhealthiness? Or Hosier for obstinately maintaining his blockade long after it had ceased to have any purpose? It was all the same to the victims who died of yellow fever like hundreds of thousands of British and French sailors in the 17th and 18th centuries. Hosier was not ignorant of the dangers of disease and informed the Admiralty that his men had 'contracted scorbutic and other distempers, as renders them weak and useless, and the number of men in each ship being so many, it makes it dangerous to those that are well to be near them in the ship'. Yet he persevered with an action which common sense showed was certain to destroy his entire force. He died obeying orders. It was a good epitaph for an 18th-century admiral.

# Commodore Anson's Voyage

The circumnavigation of the world by Commodore Anson in the years 1740-44 is one of the most famous voyages in the history of the Royal Navy. And yet possibly we remember it for the wrong reasons. Certainly Anson's taking of the great Manila galleon after a stern fight and his rich haul of over half a million pounds made the voyage truly remarkable, yet those with an interest in the welfare of common seamen are entitled to point to the devastating effects of scurvy on Anson's crews. Of 1,955 men who left England aboard his six ships, some 60 per cent died of scurvy, not one of them being of commissioned rank. There is clearly a story here

Commodore Anson's (1697–1762) circumnavigation of the globe culminated in the capture of the galleon *Nostra Signora de Cabadonga* – shown here alongside Anson's flagship, the *Centurion*. This dramatic event overshadowed other, less successful, aspects of the voyage.

of inadequate medical treatment which should have shamed Anson and coloured the reputation of this memorable voyage.

The conquest of scurvy – a painful, loathsome and frequently fatal disease – was one of the prime achievements of naval doctors in the 18th century. Yet scurvy had been known since the trans-oceanic voyages of the 16th century and the beneficial effects of citrus fruits – limes, lemons and oranges – had been known for almost as long. As a result there was little need for the disease to be a particular threat at the time that Anson sailed, unless inadequate measures were taken at the outset to cope with it. In fact, Anson had great difficulty finding enough men to crew his six ships. As a final desperate measure, 32 men were taken directly from Haslar Hospital in Gosport and some 500 invalids from the out-pensioners of Chelsea Hospital in London. Anson was shocked at the decrepit state of these elderly men, most over 60 years of age and some much older than that. The 500 who had to set off to walk to Portsmouth numbered just 259 on arrival – the fitter and younger men having taken the opportunity to desert. It was so outrageous an example of Admiralty incompetence that what happened next came as no surprise.

The six ships of Anson's fleet set off at the wrong time of the year and were so badly victualled that their provisions had gone mouldy before they reached the Pacific. Worse than that, the ventilation below decks was so poor that a fever epidemic struck the crews before they had even crossed the Atlantic, leaving the survivors 'in a very weak and helpless condition, and usually afflicted with fluxes'. Eighty men were so sick they had to be left in Brazil. No proper provision for scurvy had been taken and soon almost every seaman was ill with the disease. In two months 120 men died of scurvy aboard the flagship *Centurion* alone. The men's symptoms included pleurisy, jaundice and ulcers of the kind called 'bullock's liver' by the sailors. The men's gums bled and their teeth fell out, making it impossible for them to chew the hard ship's biscuit which comprised most of their diet. At one stage the sloop *Tryall* had just two officers and three men fit for duty, while on the *Gloucester* only one fit officer remained. Once ashore at Selkirk's Island the men began a slow recovery, 'eating turnips, radishes and scurvy grass'. However, the damage was done and of the 510 crew of the flagship *Centurion* only 130 returned to England.

But how much was Anson to blame for what happened? After all, he was not responsible for the pitiful quality of his crews, many far too feeble for such an onerous voyage. In addition, he was persuaded to employ Dr Ward's famous drop and pill on the sufferers when all else failed. The Admiralty had great faith in Dr Ward, even though on Anson's voyage his treatment actually killed many of the men to whom it was administered, some dying in agony, others vomiting or evacuating their bowels for eight hours at a time until death ensued. In spite of this their Lordships actually equipped each ship in the Channel and West Indian fleets in 1753 with Dr Ward's powders. Soon Ward was a rich man, with a fortune built entirely on his quack remedies. The Admiralty had seen fit to equip Anson's ships with Ward's medicine even though it was well known that scurvy was a disease which could be kept at bay by fresh vegetables and citrus fruit. The crews on Anson's voyage suffered through the stupidity of the Admiralty and through the failure of their commander to employ precautions which had been known about for centuries.

# Roderick Random and Jenkins' Ear

The English author Tobias Smollett undertook some interesting field research for his novel *Roderick Random* by serving as an assistant surgeon in Admiral Vernon's fleet when it attacked the Spanish American port of Cartagena in 1741. Smollett – or, as we shall call him from now on, Random – thus had first-hand experience of one of the most disastrous amphibious operations of the century. Ignoring the evidence from Admiral Hosier's expedition to Porto Bello in 1726 – and presumably not even reading the contemporary poem *Admiral Hosier's Ghost,* which gave a ghastly warning to those who spend too much time in the pestilential Caribbean – the British Admiralty, at the insistence of Vernon – known far and wide as 'the angry admiral' – sent a strong expedition to attack Cartagena and restore British prestige on the Spanish Main. As to why it needed restoring we must refer to a British captain named Robert Jenkins.

In 1739, Jenkins had been asked to attend the House of Commons, bringing with him a nasty looking object – his mummified ear – in a glass bottle. According to the good captain, he had lost this ear at the hands of Spanish privateers, who first half-hanged him and then cut off the ear, bidding him present the bleeding object to his king – George II – with their compliments. This insult was all that the opponents of the government needed to embarrass the 'peace-party' of Sir Robert Walpole. Spanish privateers had long preyed on British merchants in the Caribbean and the time had come to teach the Spaniards a lesson. The House of Commons buzzed with delight and Captain Jenkins' ear became the pretext for war against Spain. On 19 October 1739, hostilities were declared, and as London's bells pealed out, Robert Walpole observed ruefully, 'They may ring their bells now, they will be wringing their hands before long.'

The responsibility for carrying the war into the Caribbean rested with Admiral Edward Vernon, who convinced the British government that a blow against Cartagena would weaken Spain's influence and trade, force her to open her harbours to British traders, and deprive her of Peruvian bullion. To carry out the attack Vernon estimated that he would need some 9,000 British and American troops to capture the city and hold it. In addition, he feared that a combined Franco-Spanish fleet of 30 ships might oppose him in the Caribbean and so he would also require the strongest fleet that could be assembled. But after a long period of peace Vernon might as well have asked for the moon, for the navy was very short of seamen. Although by mid-August 1740 the contingent of 6,000 British troops were ready aboard the transports they were kept in port by shortages of naval personnel. There was no alternative but for General Cathcart, commander of the land forces, to turn over two of his line regiments and 600 of his new marines, to act as sailors for the duration of the voyage. Even this was not enough to get the operation started. Contrary winds kept the soldiers cooped up for six weeks in the crowded vessels, during which time they consumed much of the food intended for the voyage and many developed scurvy. Even though fresh fruit and vegetables were available a stone's-throw away on land, nobody thought to bring it aboard. Before the fleet sailed 60 men had died of scurvy.

It had originally been intended to keep the destination of the fleet secret. Lord Cathcart certainly believed this was so and was astonished when one of his secret orders was reported to him as being the small talk of the coffee-houses in Portsmouth. The national newspapers published details of the fleet's destination as well as a full account of the troops being sent and the strength of the fleet. Any Spanish spy would have found himself redundant.

It was not until November that the fleet eventually left Portsmouth, flying the flag of

Admiral Vernon (1684–1757) portrayed by Thomas Gainsborough. Known as the 'angry admiral',
Vernon proved to be a difficult and uncooperative partner for Brigadier Wentworth during the siege
of Cartagena in 1741.

Admiral Sir Challenor Ogle – over four months after the troops had first gone aboard their transports. In crossing the Atlantic a further 484 men died of smallpox, scurvy, typhus and dysentery, including General Cathcart himself, whose poor condition was exacerbated by too liberal a dosage of Epsom salts. The death of Cathcart was a blow from which the expedition never recovered. His deputy, Brigadier-General Wentworth, was quite incapable of commanding so large a force of men and allowed the naval commanders, notably Admiral Vernon, to dominate him. By the time the fleet reached Jamaica, early in 1741, Wentworth's combined command of 9,000 Anglo-American troops had lost over 600 dead and 1,500 sick.

In spite of heavy losses from scurvy and yellow fever, Vernon refused to be rushed. He feared that if he besieged Cartagena the French might fall on his rear and attack Jamaica. Fortunately for Vernon, the local mosquito was impartial in its attentions, and struck at French sailors as willingly as at their Anglo-Saxon counterparts. The French West Indies Squadron was forced to return to France, with its crews decimated by 'yellow jack'. This was what Vernon was waiting for and he sailed from Jamaica, but only because 37 per cent of Wentworth's soldiers were now manning his ships. On 4 March, the British fleet arrived off Cartagena and prepared to assault the city. Vernon was confident that he could take it; after all, it had been successfully besieged four times in the past: in 1560, 1565, 1586 and – most recently – in 1697, by the French. But, unknown to Vernon, after this last disaster the Spanish had strengthened the city's defences. Far from being helpless, Cartagena was now a tough nut to crack and Vernon's underestimation of Spanish morale was to fatally undermine his mission.

The first target was for Vernon's ships to break into the great harbour in order to land Wentworth's troops. This meant passing through the Boca Chica, which was lined with a series of strong forts. These would have to be destroyed by the guns of the fleet or else captured by a marine landing. On 9 March Admiral Ogle with the *Princess Amelia*, the *Norfolk*, the *Russell* and the *Shrewsbury* began bombarding the two outer forts, St Jago and San Felipe, easily battering them into submission. The following day Wentworth's troops landed on Tierra Bomba. But once ashore Wentworth's men did nothing but dig in and post double and triple sentries everywhere, as if they expected to be attacked from the rear. While Vernon fumed and waited for Wentworth to capture the remaining 'paltry fort', his ships had to lay out at sea – at the mercy of the winds and with some of them losing their anchor cables, cut by the rocky seabed.

To try to speed matters up, Vernon sent in four of his battleships to attack Fort San Luis. What happened next was the clearest indication of the fact that ships cannot silence forts – a lesson that, it would appear, needs to be learned in every fresh generation. After a heavy bombardment the fort remained almost unscathed – though Vernon claimed it had been silenced – while the *Boyne* and the *Hampton Court* were badly damaged and the *Prince Frederick* disabled by enemy fire. In the words of Roderick Random:

> Having cannonaded the fort during the space of four hours, we were all ordered to slip our cables and sheer off; but next day the engagement was renewed and continued from the morning till the afternoon when the enemy's fire from Boca Chica slackened and towards evening was quite silenced. A breach being made on the other side by our land battery, large enough to admit a middle sized baboon, provided he could find means to climb up to it.

Vernon had by now decided that Wentworth was an incompetent and that the operation was doomed. All that remained was to place the blame where it belonged. On 14 April another council of war called off the siege and the troops were re-embarked. But now seamen with long memories began to recount the tale of Admiral Hosier's disastrous expedition. Adverse winds kept the fleet trapped on the pestilential coast for a further ten days and men began to die in droves. When planning the expedition Lord Cathcart had provided hospital ships and surgeons, but he had not imagined losses of this scale. Roderick Random describes in graphic detail the suffering of the men in these dreadful days. In spite of the torrid weather there was little water to go round and the food was unspeakably bad:

> We had languished five weeks on the allowance of a purser's quart *per diem* for each man, in the

torrid zone, where the sun was vertical, and the expense of bodily fluid so great, that a gallon of liquor could scarcely supply the waste of twenty-four hours; especially as our provision consisted of putrid salt beef, to which the sailors gave the name of Irish horse; salt pork of New England, which, though neither fish nor flesh, savoured of both; bread from the same country, every biscuit whereof, like a piece of clock-work, moved by its own internal impulse, occasioned by the myriads of insects that dwelt within it; and butter served out by the gill, that tasted like train-oil thickened with salt.

Relations were so bad between army and navy that Wentworth would not deign to ask Vernon for help, and so hundreds of soldiers suffered neglect while surgeons aboard the men-of-war smoked their pipes and carved mementos of the voyage. In horror the sailors watched the treatment the army doled out to its dead. Instead of wrapping a body in a shroud and weighting the heels before dropping it in the sea, as was naval practice, the soldiers simply heaved it over the side, to be eaten by sharks or pecked at by flocks of seabirds. The air around the fleet – motionless from a lack of wind – was poisoned by the smell of disease and rotting human flesh. By the time the fleet eventually sailed away from Cartagena there were just 1,700 men fit for action out of the original force of 9,000 soldiers, and of the men who had sailed from England under Cathcart over 90 per cent had died of disease.

It had been a disgraceful waste of manpower. As the fleet bore away the mournful remnants of the expedition, Wentworth and Vernon continued the war of words which for them had come to replace the struggle against the enemy. As Random commented:

> The Demon of Discord, with her sooty wings, had breathed her influence upon our counsels; and it might be said of these great men as of Caesar and Pompey, the one could not brook a superior, and the other was impatient of an equal; so that, between the pride of one, and insolence of another, the enterprise miscarried, according to the proverb, 'Between two stools, the backside falls to the ground.'

On his return to London Vernon, of course, had the final word. According to his report the navy had captured forts and struck the Spaniards a heavy blow. By contrast, his silence on the work of the army spoke volumes. When the fleet arrived at Portsmouth, by a curious mischance Wentworth's letters to the War Office were misplaced and delayed, while Vernon's missives arrived at the Admiralty with all haste. It was Vernon's view of the campaign that became the accepted one and Wentworth's merely the apology of an unsuccessful and incompetent officer. As usual it was the men who suffered most from the failures of those sent to lead them, and Admiral Hosier's ghost must have lamented the thousands of British dead and the fact that once again the Admiralty had not heeded its warning.

# CHAPTER 5: ABOVE US THE WAVES

As a weapon essentially of the 20th century, the submarine has had an unparalleled effect on naval warfare. In both world wars German U-boat campaigns came near to defeating Great Britain. And in a sense Britain never really came to terms with what was always considered an 'un-English weapon'.

## K for Catastrophe

The success of German U-boats in the early months of the First World War prompted the British Admiralty to respond by building submarines to a revolutionary design, making them the largest, fastest and most powerful underwater craft in the world. They were revolutionary in that they would be driven by steam engines and would use two funnels. Unfortunately, they also had a record of failure second to none. Unofficially known as the 'suicide club', these 'K' boats were involved in more damage to themselves and other British ships than to the enemy. They became a joke. It was said that one K boat captain telephoned his first lieutenant in the bows saying, 'I say, Number One, my end is diving: what the hell is your end doing?' On the only occasion that one of them actually fired at an enemy ship the torpedo failed to explode.

The idea for the 'K' class originated with the Director of Naval Construction, Sir Eustace Tennyson-d'Eyncourt. It had become apparent to men like Winston Churchill and Admiral Sir John Fisher that by 1914 Britain had been left behind in submarine construction by the Germans and something special was needed to redress the balance. The K ships were certainly special, planned as being three times the size of existing British E class submarines, and fast enough to accompany the Dreadnought battleships on their sweeps. The First Sea Lord wanted a submarine capable of at least 20 knots on the surface, and Tennyson-d'Eyncourt told him that this would have to be driven by steam turbines and carry funnels which could be sealed off when the ship dived.

Not everyone agreed with Fisher that submarines could work effectively on fleet manoeuvres. Commodore Roger Keyes, for one, came to believe the idea absurd. In the battle of the Heligoland Bight the British submarines proved at best a distraction and at worst a serious liability. Three times British submarines mistook British ships for German and tried to torpedo them – a torpedo from one just missing the cruiser *Lowestoft*. Conversely, three British cruisers tried to ram British submarines, mistaking them for U-boats. In Keyes' own words, 'The submarines had proved that they could not be trusted to work in cooperation with surface craft and take care of themselves.' But Fisher was not listening. He continued the search for the fast submarine and by May 1915 he was sure that he had found it. Vickers was ordered to begin work on the K-class, based on d'Eyncourt's original design. Although Fisher was shortly to leave the Admiralty, a total of fourteen steam-driven submarines were ordered before he left.

The K-class submarines were undoubtedly impressive: longer than a football field and heavier – at 2,600 tons – than the latest destroyers. They carried two 4-inch and one 3-inch guns, two 5-foot-high funnels, twin 30-foot periscopes and two tall, retractable wireless aerials.

Admiral Lord Fisher of Kilverstone, G.C.B., O.M. In 1914, as First Sea Lord, 'Jacky' Fisher had been eager to build fast submarines to accompany the Grand Fleet. But the K-class submarines that resulted were some of the least seaworthy vessels ever built for the Royal Navy.

In fact, they carried so much on top that it seemed a miracle that they could dive at all, or resurface. To the professional submariners there seemed to be 'too many damned holes' in the enormous structure, with hatches and vents and funnels, all of which needed to be watertight when submerged. The smallest weakness in one of the seals would spell disaster.

But the Admiralty was rapt. Even before the early models had undergone trials, they had ordered seven more during 1916 at a total cost of £6,000,000. They should have waited, as events were to show. K3 had the honour of testing first. Apart from the fact that her boiler room virtually boiled the men working in it, the heavy sea cracked the windows of the wheelhouse and a British patrol boat opened fire on her, all went quite well. Unfortunately, when K3 tried to dive – with the future King George VI aboard – she went out of control and sank to the bottom of Stokes Bay, with her bows stuck in the mud and her stern rearing high above the water with propellers spinning madly. Happily, no lives were lost and she was shortly refloated. In January 1917, K3 was sent north to join the Grand Fleet at Scapa Flow. In a heavy swell in the North Sea, water entered both funnels, extinguishing the boiler fires and filling the boiler room to a depth of four or five feet. Only a subsidiary diesel engine – which Fisher had insisted should be fitted – got the submarine started again and prevented her from sinking. The warning signs were clear.

The tragic case of the ominously numbered K13 was an early pointer to design faults. On 29 January 1917, Lieutenant-Commander Godfrey Herbert, commanding K13, gave the order to dive in Gaire Loch. The boiler room flooded and the submarine settled on the bottom, just 50 feet below the surface. After a prolonged – and incompetent – rescue operation, Herbert was himself saved but 25 of his crew lost their lives. It should have provided a salutary lesson.

For much of 1917 the Admiralty practised the 'habits of self-deception' on the question of the K boats. Reputations were at stake as well as big contracts, and so the truth would have to be suppressed. Yet in the words of Commander George Bradshaw, the K class 'were looked on with fear and loathing. After all, they murdered many of their officers and crew.' Between January and May 1917 the first thirteen K boats all underwent trials and every one of them experienced trouble. K2, for example, suffered an internal explosion and fire. With no fire extinguishers aboard the submarine had to surface and extinguish the fire with buckets of seawater passed hand to hand. K6 sank on her trials and spent an uneasy time on the bottom before her compressed-air system was repaired and they managed to refloat her; K4 ran aground; K14 developed leaky plates and electrical fires – yet in spite of these failings all were sent north to join the Grand Fleet at Scapa Flow. Even the simplest able seaman could have told their Lordships of the Admiralty that in action a submarine needed to be able to dive in 30 seconds, not five minutes like the K boats. And the 15-20 minutes it took to work up a head of steam meant that the K boats would be 'sitting ducks' for German destroyers.

Once the K boats joined the fleet it was like opening Pandora's box. In June 1917 the 12th Submarine Flotilla – K1, K2, K4, K7 and K8 – took part in an anti-submarine sweep in the North Sea – Operation BB – accompanied by destroyers and conventional submarines. In ten days of operation the British destroyed no U-boats while the Germans sank no fewer than nine British merchantmen under the eyes of the fleet. K7 was once identified as a U-boat and chased and depthcharged by two British destroyers. Escaping by the skin of its teeth, K7 spotted a U-boat and fired a torpedo at point-blank range which hit the German amidships without exploding. The German submarine promptly opened fire on K7 which fired another torpedo and missed. The German then hastily dived – something K7 could not do – and escaped. K2, meanwhile, had been reported lost with all hands. The Fair Isle lighthouse claimed to have seen K2 strike a mine and sink. The Admiralty responded promptly, sending out telegrams to the next of kin. Two days later, in darkness, an unidentified submarine entered Scapa Flow, setting off a general fleet panic. It was, of course, K2. There had been no mine. The lighthouse keepers had merely seen K2 fire one of her 4-inch guns before diving. The fact that the submarine had used the lighthouse as a target was not officially recorded. During the same operation K1 ran aground, her captain escaping censure on the grounds that rats had eaten part of his sea-chart. But there was no happy ending for K1. Later in 1917 she was accidentally rammed by K4 and so badly damaged that she had to be scuttled.

Rear-Admiral Ernest Leir described his experiences with the submarines in this way: 'The only good thing about K boats was that they never engaged the enemy.' Be this as it may, the K boats did undergo one trial by combat, ever afterwards known as the 'battle' of May Island. In December 1917 the K boats were moved from Scapa Flow to Rosyth and Admiral Beatty decided to use them in an important operation which would include battleships, battlecruisers, light cruisers and the two flotillas of type K submarines. On 1 February 1918, Operation E.C.1 took place. Commander Leir – as he then was – in the cruiser *Ithuriel* led the five K boats of the 13th Flotilla along the Firth of Forth, directly in the wake of the battlecruiser *Courageous*, flying the flag of Vice-Admiral Sir Hugh Evan-Thomas. Some five miles behind him came the four battlecruisers of the 2nd Battlecruiser Squadron, and behind them the cruiser *Fearless* leading the four K boats of 12th Flotilla. The night was clear, the sea calm and there seemed little reason to expect trouble – except from the nine K boats present.

Disaster approached in the shape of eight armed trawlers sweeping for mines in the Firth. They operated out of May Island and through a breakdown of communication neither they nor the officers involved in Operation E.C.1 knew of the others' presence. A mist now descended which reduced visibility so that the *Ithuriel* lost contact with the battlecruiser *Courageous* ahead. As *Ithuriel* began to lose direction, chaos ensued among the five K boats. Mine-sweeping trawlers began to appear out of the mist, flashing their navigation lights and baffling the K boat commanders who were trying to follow the stern light of the *Ithuriel*. K14 tried to go hard a'starboard, but her helm jammed for six minutes and her commander had to stop engines to avoid going round in circles. Suddenly, at 19 knots, K22 came crashing into the virtually stationary K14. Lights now flashed out from all directions – the signalman on K14 using an Aldis lamp to call for help. Meanwhile the four huge battlecruisers were bearing down on the scene of the collision, oblivious to the situation ahead. The *Australia* passed by the collision safely, managing to detach a destroyer to investigate, but the last of the big ships – the *Inflexible* – ploughed straight into K22. Ironically, K22 was the renamed K13 which had sunk so tragically in Gaire Loch with the loss of so many lives.

Meanwhile, Leir in the *Ithuriel*, with his remaining K boats, was responding to the appeals for help from K14 and K22. He was now virtually at right angles to the approaching battlecruisers. Although he was able to manoeuvre the cruiser out of harm's way, the sluggish submarines were unsuited to fast movement in any direction except down. In the event, *Australia* and her sisters just managed to scrape past K12 with inches to spare.

Now steaming up the Firth came the cruiser *Fearless*, bringing the other four K boats at their full speed of 21 knots. With a horrible inevitability they joined the confusion ahead. *Fearless* rammed straight into K17, sending her spinning away in a sinking condition. As the *Fearless* reversed her engines, the *Ithuriel* and the K11 were rushing back to the scene of chaos to look for survivors from K14 and K22. Even now the disasters of that early morning were not over. Travelling at full speed K6 rammed into K4 which, for some reason, was unlit and stationary across her path. K4 was cut in half and sank rapidly and K6 narrowly avoided being dragged down with her.

The K boats now faced one more adversary – and the most severe yet. At the tail of the British line were the huge battleships of the 5th Battle Squadron, with their escorting destroyers. While frenzied efforts were made to rescue the survivors of the damaged and sinking K boats, the destroyers escorting the battleships arrived and cut straight through the scene, washing away or cutting to pieces the survivors from K17. Over a hundred men lost their lives that morning.

Keyes had been right in 1914. The verdict of the court of inquiry which followed the disaster was that submarines could not safely work with surface craft. There had been incompetence by individuals but on such a scale that it was impossible ever to get to the bottom of it. The main fault lay with the K boats themselves. As their crew said, 'they were killers'. Strangely, even when the war ended interest in the K boats did not wane. More were built – only to fail. On 20 January 1921, K5 sank with all hands while on exercises. Six months later K15 sank in Portsmouth Harbour. K22 – raised from Gaire Loch in 1916 and damaged at May Island in 1918 – survived to achieve the feat that everybody had expected eventually. Off the west coast of Scotland in 1921 she dived with both funnels still open . . .

---

*'The system of several ships sailing together in a convoy is not recommended in any area where submarine attack is a possibility.'*

**An Admiralty Memorandum on Convoys, 1917**

Their Lordships of the Admiralty were very slow to come to terms with the threat posed by German submarines. It took a younger generation of naval officers, aided by the common sense of politicians like David Lloyd George, to convert the Admiralty to the use of convoys.

---

# L'Entente Cordiale

The British submarine D3, commanded by the Canadian Lieutenant Maitland-Dougall, left Gosport on the afternoon of 7 March 1916 for an anti-submarine patrol in the Channel. She was expected to be at sea for a week. Towards the end of her patrol she encountered an unusual if persistent adversary.

The French airship AT-O took off from Le Havre on the morning of 12 March and headed out along the coast, also looking for German U-boats. It was a misty morning but from 1,600 feet her commander, Lieutenant Sainte Rémy, just made out a vessel heading towards her. Sainte Rémy increased to full speed and tried to identify the mysterious ship – which was a submarine travelling on the surface. According to the Frenchman she carried no signs or distinguishing marks when viewed from above. As the airship passed over the submarine rockets were fired from near the stern of the boat. The French concluded that they were under fire and that the submarine – clearly hostile – was trying to set them ablaze. It does not seem to have occurred to the French crew that the rockets might have been for identification.

The French responded by opening fire on the submarine with their machine gun which caused the rocket firing to stop and the submarine to dive. As it did so, Sainte Rémy dropped two bombs, small 70-pounders, but missed by some distance. As the airship turned the Frenchman dropped four more, hitting the submarine on the conning tower and forcing it back to the surface. As they watched from above the French crew saw the submarine sink back below the waves leaving some figures struggling in the water. They were jubilant – they had sunk a U-boat. Or had they? Sainte Rémy sank down to a mere 60 feet and called out to the four men floundering in the sea. Then, to his horror, he heard their replies – they were British. He threw them lifebelts and hurried to get a ship to come and pick up the survivors, but by the time the French destroyer *Typhone* returned to the scene the men had drowned.

It had been a tragic case of mistaken identity. The signals used for identification by D3 had been quite unknown to the French and although the British crew had clearly painted the correct recognition mark for the period 1 to 15 March on D3's forward hatch, the French seemed quite unaware of its significance. Maitland-Dougall had been quite content to stay on the surface as the airship had approached, having identified her as French. It might have occurred to the French commander that had D3 been a U-boat she would hardly have stayed on the surface long enough for him to hit her with his tiny bombs. And why the French crew regarded the signal rockets as offensive weapons one will never know. Their failure to appreciate what D3 was trying to do caused them to open fire with their guns which left D3 with no option but to try to escape by diving. To the French this was conclusive proof that D3 was German and led to the bombing and the final catastrophe.

---

*'The submarine can only operate by day and in clear weather, and it is practically useless in misty weather.'*

**Admiral Lord Charles Beresford**

Progressive naval thinkers like Sir Percy Scott encountered opposition from traditionalists like Sir Charles Beresford, a brave and charismatic leader but one better suited to an earlier, simpler age.

---

# The *Triton* and the *Oxley*

Within a week of war breaking out in September 1939 the Royal Navy had lost her first submarine, and not even to enemy action at that. It was the by now familiar story of friendly fire – which might otherwise be described as blundering incompetence. There was nothing very friendly about the telegrams which informed the families of the dead that they had been 'lost in action'. It was just a way of shielding the bereaved from the feeling of utter waste which went with the knowledge that one's menfolk had been killed by their own colleagues.

On 9 September, five British submarines, including the *Oxley* – commanded by Lieutenant-Commander Bowerman – and the *Triton* – commanded by Lieutenant-Commander Steel, took up station off the coast of Norway. The submarines were stationed twelve miles apart and each had a sector to patrol, *Oxley* sector 4 and *Triton* sector 5. The two submarines had established good communications earlier in the day. Unfortunately, *Oxley* had begun to lose her bearings and stray into *Triton*'s sector. Just before midnight on 10 September one of *Triton*'s officers sighted an unidentified submarine through his binoculars. He called Steel to the bridge and the crew went to action stations. Steel admits that the thought of it being *Oxley* passed through his mind but he dismissed it as he had been in touch with her that afternoon and had given her *Triton's* position. If it was *Oxley* she was six miles off her station, which was surely impossible.

Steel now took the precaution of locking his armament on the intruder and then signalled a challenge to her. There was no reply, even after another challenge was made. Steel next ordered a signal grenade to be fired and soon three green lights illuminated the scene. Still there was no reply. Steel had done what he could; the submarine must be hostile. At once he ordered two torpedoes to be fired and was gratified to hear an explosion, notifying success. The enemy submarine disappeared, leaving just two survivors swimming towards the *Triton*. One can barely imagine the shock the *Triton* crew experienced when they pulled out of the water Lieutenant-Commander Bowerman of the *Oxley*, along with just one able seaman. The rest of *Oxley's* crew were lost.

Nobody, either at the time or since, blamed Lieutenant-Commander Steel for firing. What baffled everyone was the *Oxley's* failure to respond to any of Steel's signals or requests for identification. The answer was a mixture of misfortune and incompetence. Apparently Bowerman had thought himself two miles inside his own sector at a time when he was in fact four miles inside *Triton's*. He had been called to the bridge when *Triton* fired her signal grenade but when he tried to reply his grenade malfunctioned. His bridge officer, Lieutenant Manley, claimed to have answered *Triton's* challenge, but Bowerman was not convinced that this had been done properly. Before he could put things right his ship was struck by *Triton's* torpedo and he was catapulted into the sea. There was little more to be said. *Triton* had acted correctly throughout and *Oxley* had been lost through bad luck and slack work by her bridge officer. Nobody could have allowed for the malfunctioning of the signal grenade but if Manley had replied initially to *Triton's* challenge the tragedy need never have happened. In wartime nobody gives you a second chance; *Triton* had shot to kill.

## The Admiralty Drags its Feet on Convoys

It was said by Winston Churchill, as First Lord of the Admiralty in 1914, that Sir John Jellicoe, commander-in-chief of the Grand Fleet, was the only man who could have lost the war in an afternoon. The fact that he did not has often been held in his favour. But what has not so often been appreciated is the way in which Jellicoe, as First Sea Lord, came very close to losing the war in a single month – April 1917. Indeed, on Jellicoe's dismissal from the Admiralty in December of that year, the vitriolic Captain Herbert Richmond reflected that 'one obstacle to a successful war is now out of the way'. The problem was that Jellicoe – like so many naval officers of his generation – suffered from 'periscopitis', a morbid and paralyzing fear of submarines.

Popular expectations of an immediate and decisive victory over the German High Seas Fleet in 1914 were based on a misinterpretation of the realities of modern war at sea. Daily newspapers encouraged the British public to expect a 'new Trafalgar', yet in a struggle between powerful industrialized countries victory could not so easily be won. In such a war foreign trade was vital to a country like Britain and so the protection of the sea-lanes became the main task of the navy and the main target for an enemy. In addition, Jellicoe's great Dreadnought fleet

The moment of reckoning comes for a British merchantman as it falls victim to the German U-boat
U-35, April 1917. Germany's strategy of waging unrestricted submarine warfare brought Britain
perilously close to defeat in 1917.

which lurked in its Scottish bases, waiting to spring on the German battlefleet should it emerge from its lair, proved itself surprisingly vulnerable to the previously unconsidered threat of torpedo and mine. The new battleship *Audacious* was destroyed by a mine in the first weeks of the war and the armoured cruisers *Aboukir*, *Hogue* and *Cressy* sunk by a single U-boat in the space of half an hour. As time passed it became apparent that the Germans were not going to play Britain's game and sportingly agree to a trial of strength in the North Sea; they had no intention of playing Villeneuve to Jellicoe's Nelson. Instead they would use the weapons of the weaker party – commerce raiding by surface craft and by submarines. Before 1914 British naval thinkers had rejected the possibility of widespread U-boat action, Churchill even claiming that such warfare was not suitable for civilized powers. But the old civilities were gone and international law was about to be flouted in a way that Churchill and the Admiralty would have believed 'unthinkable' in 1913.

At the outbreak of war in 1914 Germany had planned to rely on her surface raiders – like the cruiser *Emden* – to strike at British commerce. But the Royal Navy had cleared the seas of all of these within months and Admiral Tirpitz was forced to fall back on his small submarine fleet of perhaps 20 operational craft. To his surprise these were immensely successful and sank some 40 ships in the first ten weeks of hostilities. But the sinking of the great liner *Lusitania* on 7 May 1915 – with a consequent loss of over a thousand lives, including Americans – was a propaganda disaster for the Germans and threatened to alienate the United States and bring her into the war against Germany. The result was that Tirpitz ordered a reduction in U-boat activity against merchant shipping. At this stage the Admiralty – which had developed anti-submarine weapons like nets, depth charges and underwater acoustics – became complacent, believing that the Germans would not dare to return to an unrestricted U-boat campaign. But they were wrong. The immense losses suffered by Germany on the Western Front during 1916 and the effect of Britain's tight naval blockade convinced her leaders that the war could only be won by a return to unrestricted U-boat attacks on British shipping, regardless of America's reaction.

On 1 February 1917 Tirpitz announced an unrestricted U-boat campaign around the coasts of Britain. The Germans now had 154 U-boats, bigger and with a greater range than ever before. These were ocean-going submarines which could operate in the North Atlantic and strike at ships crossing from the United States to Europe. Shipping losses rose sharply. During February 1917 86 ships were lost, in March 103 and in April 155. These figures were so disastrous that they suggested that unless the U-boat threat could be overcome Britain would be defeated within months. Nearly a million tons of merchant shipping had been lost in a single month and this could not be replaced. Despondency ruled the Admiralty. Jellicoe, the First Sea Lord, saw no answer and expected Britain to be forced to the negotiating table. For the first time in Britain's long history, her army needed to win the war before her navy lost it. But there was a solution, an ancient standby used by the Admiralty in almost every previous war and yet overlooked on this occasion: the convoy.

The short-sightedness of Britain's naval heads in 1916 and 1917 almost defies belief. They were still committed to a 'find and kill' policy towards U-boats, employing over 3,000 vessels to hunt them down and in the last six months of 1916 achieving just fifteen 'kills'. It was an exercise in futility, particularly as the hunters were so ill-equipped. In July 1917, in the face of a demand by escort vessels for a weekly supply of 500 depth charges, the Admiralty could supply just 140. During the farcical 'Second Battle of Beachy Head' in September 1916 three German U-boats were unsuccessfully hunted for seven days by 49 destroyers, 48 torpedo boats, 7 'Q' ships and 468 armed auxiliaries; the U-boats escaped, having sunk a further 30 merchantmen. There had to be a simpler way to solve the problem but the ailing and deeply depressed hypochondriac that Sir John Jellicoe had become after his long vigil at Scapa Flow could not see it. In Jellicoe's own words, 'There was no single way of defeating the U-boat.' As far as he was concerned Britain might as well give up. When men like Richmond and R.G.H. Henderson had the temerity to whisper 'convoys' in his hearing he dolefully told them that convoys would merely concentrate more ships together to be sunk by U-boats. In any case, merchant skippers were too undisciplined and slack to stay together and convoys would involve the use of too many escorts. As it happened, Jellicoe did not know his job. Even while he spoke convoys were operating successfully from Harwich to the Hook of Holland, and from France to the Welsh coalfields. Richmond was quite outspoken in his criticism of the First Sea Lord: 'Having missed two chances of destroying the German Fleet he is busy ruining the country by not taking steps to defeat the submarine.' But Jellicoe was not the only culprit. Senior Admiralty opinion can be judged by this extract from an Admiralty pamphlet issued in January 1917:

> The system of several ships sailing together in a convoy is not recommended in any area where submarine attack is a possibility. It is evident that the larger the number of ships forming the convoy, the greater is the chance of a submarine being able to attack successfully, the greater the difficulty of the escort in preventing such an attack.

But as naval historian John Winton has pointed out:

> It would be difficult to find, even in the long record of Admiralty bureaucracy, a more stupid document and one which more pigheadedly ignored all the lessons of past naval history . . . Nor was it the product of a single deranged mind. As far as can be judged, it represented collective opinion in the Admiralty at the time.

The head of the Anti-Submarine Division – Rear-Admiral Duff – kept the Admiralty supplied with statistics concerning the struggle against the U-boat and according to his figures the losses that were taking place were by no means as serious as had been suggested. It was he who informed their Lordships that every week there were some 5,000 inward and outward ship movements, so many indeed that there was no possibility whatsoever of providing anti-submarines escorts. But Duff's figures were profoundly wrong. His total included daily movements by ferries, small coasters and short-haul trading vessels, none of which need concern a convoy planner. What was even worse was that Duff was claiming that weekly shipping losses of 40 or so merchantmen formed just a tiny proportion of total sailings. But when Captain Richmond and Commander Henderson queried these figures they discovered that they were wrong – fantastically wrong. The correct weekly sailing figure for merchant ships was just 130 vessels, easily within the capability of the navy to escort. Also – and this was a truly shocking revelation – the shipping losses of 40 out of 130 weekly meant that well over a quarter of all vessels leaving Britain were being sunk by U-boats. These figures meant only one thing – imminent defeat for Great Britain. The news was conveyed to Prime Minister Lloyd George through Maurice Hankey, secretary to the War Cabinet. Lloyd George was astounded: 'What an amazing miscalculation. The blunder on which their policy was based was an arithmetical mix-up which would not have been perpetrated by an ordinary clerk in a shipping office.' This brooked no delay and Lloyd George at once informed Jellicoe and Duff that they had better come up with a solution or heads would roll. Within days the Admiralty underwent a remarkable conversion, albeit an unwilling one. Jellicoe told the prime minister that he now believed there was 'sufficient reason for believing that we can accept the many disadvantages of large convoys with the certainty of great reduction in our present losses'.

Convoys were introduced, and not a moment too soon. In July and August of 1917 only 5 out of 800 ships sailing in convoys were sunk by U-boat attack. Even so Jellicoe and Duff continued to drag their feet, claiming that convoys should be employed only for homeward-bound ships. From now on the only ships sunk were those outward bound. Again Lloyd George had to wave his big stick. Duff was forced to convoy outward bound ships as well – not, apparently, for their safety but to give them 'practice' at travelling with escorts. The prime minister's patience snapped and Jellicoe was dismissed as First Sea Lord in December 1917. His health had been poor for some time and his pessimism was damaging to the younger men around him.

Jellicoe's blunder over convoys was one of the greatest mistakes of the whole First World War. His failure to accept evidence which conflicted with his own preconceptions, based as these were on bogus figures, cost the country three million tons of merchant shipping and brought Britain closer to defeat than any of the German offensives in France ever did. Faced by the submarine threat – an enemy he could not understand – Sir John Jellicoe was reduced to a level of inertia in which he abandoned the struggle and could see only defeat.

# Torpedoes Away

In the early hours of 14 October 1939, at the British naval base at Scapa Flow, the battleship *Royal Oak* lay calmly at anchor. Few of her crew heard the strange grazing sound as a German torpedo scraped her anchor chain, and those that did discounted it. Invisible in the moonless dark, but feeling horribly exposed on the surface and in the midst of the entire British Home Fleet, German U-boat U-47, commanded by Lieutenant Günther Prien, was having a bad time. The tremendous shadow of the battleship seemed to tower over him and yet at point-blank range Prien had just missed with each of his four forward torpedoes. Showing remarkable calm Prien swung the U-boat round and fired his single stern torpedo. This time there surely could be no doubt. But again the impossible happened and there was no sound. Of the five torpedoes he had fired four had been duds, and the fifth had gone wildly off course and merely scraped the big ship's anchor chain. What on earth was going on? With all his torpedo tubes empty Prien faced the choice of either reloading – a dangerous and time-consuming operation – or making his escape. Showing great courage he reloaded and with his next two torpedoes he sent the *Royal Oak* to the bottom, with the loss of 833 British sailors. Prien returned to a hero's welcome in Germany, but already questions were being asked about the effectiveness of German torpedoes.

There had been earlier signs of trouble. On 14 September, U-39 had broken through a destroyer screen and had fired two torpedoes ( G-7a-type with magnetic detonators) at the British aircraft carrier *Ark Royal* from just 800 yards. This type of torpedo did not need to strike the target but was designed to explode once it came into contact with the ship's own magnetic field. Lieutenant Gerhard Glattes was exuberant at the thought of eliminating such an important target so early in the war. Suddenly, through his periscope he saw both torpedoes explode, 100 yards from the carrier. Alerted by the tracks of compressed-air bubbles leading from the explosions, three British destroyers pounced on U-39 before it could escape and forced it to the surface. Glattes and his crew were taken prisoner. Just six days later a similar fate befell U-27. Admiral Dönitz was fortunate that the commanders of these two submarines were taken alive as they were able to smuggle out of their British POW camp reports that their

A U-boat on patrol during the Second World War. In the early years of the war German U-boats were equipped with torpedoes so deficient that many important British ships escaped destruction.

torpedoes were detonating prematurely. The news came as a shock to the German Admiralty which believed that in the magnetic detonator it had a thoroughly reliable weapon. Yet in spite of evidence to the contrary the Germans were painfully slow to react.

Just two weeks after Prien's successful action in Scapa Flow, U-56, commanded by Lieutenant Wilhelm Zahn, was presented with one of the most important targets of the war. Whereas the *Royal Oak* had been an old and unmodernized First World War battleship, the *Nelson* was the flagship of the British Home Fleet and one of its strongest warships. Furthermore, on the morning of 30 October, a conference was taking place aboard *Nelson* attended by the First Lord of the Admiralty, Winston Churchill, the First Sea Lord, Sir Dudley Pound, and the Commander-in-Chief Home Fleet, Sir Charles Forbes – quite a haul for a U-boat captain. Unknown to these dignitaries, U-56 had just launched three torpedoes at the battleship, prior to diving. Inside the U-boat Zahn and his crew waited impatiently for the explosions which would signal success. Instead the crew heard two clanging noises as metal hit metal. There were no explosions. The torpedoes had simply bumped into the battleship and sunk to the bottom of the North Sea. As the realization spread through the U-boat the disappointment was overwhelming. At risk of their lives they had penetrated the British destroyer screen and had struck the enemy flagship – but with dud torpedoes. It all seemed pointless. 'Deep dejection' overwhelmed Zahn and his crew so that, on their return to Germany, Admiral Dönitz was forced to take them off further U-boat duties.

What had begun as a trickle now became a flood. Dönitz found himself deluged in reports of dud torpedoes from returning U-boat commanders. U-25 fired four duds in a row at the beginning of November, while U-46 fired seven torpedoes into a convoy of ships without achieving a single hit. In despair Dönitz wrote, 'The torpedo inspectors have fallen down on their job. At least 30 per cent of all torpedoes are duds!'

Certainly German torpedoes were by now far more technically complex than those used in the First World War, when detonation took place on contact with the vessel's hull. A new percussion pistol had been introduced in 1928 by the Torpedo Experimental Institute. But the greatest failure was with the MZ pistol (magnetically operated detonating device) which utilized the magnetism of a target's hull and exploded underneath the vessel rather than on contact with its side. The German torpedo experts had overlooked the fact that a vessel's magnetic earth field varied according to its position on the globe. The further north the target ship was – and much of the naval struggle between Britain and Germany took place in the seas north of Scotland – the stronger was the influence of the Earth's magnetism on the 'magnetic pistol' of the torpedo. The result was that during the Norwegian campaign in 1940 torpedoes were often detonated prematurely before getting anywhere near their target. Another reason for the failure of the MZ at this time was the 'magnetic storms' associated with powerful sunspots.

The Germans were not alone in their use of magnetic pistols. The British had experienced similar problems, and so had designed their torpedoes to act on both 'contact' and 'magnetic' pistols. If one failed the other might succeed. Germany's inability to adapt to these technical problems cost Admiral Dönitz and his U-boat commanders dear in the first year of the war. U-25 fired three torpedoes at a British cruiser but all exploded before reaching her. U-46 and U-48 fired torpedoes at the battleship *Warspite* during the Norwegian campaign, but again they misfired.

Matters reached a head on 15 April when Prien, hero of Scapa Flow, encountered a British troop convoy off Narvik. U-47 followed the British ships until they anchored in Bygden Fjord and Prien found himself surrounded by four immense targets of three troopships and a cruiser. Switching his magnetic pistols to percussion detonators Prien fired four torpedoes at point-blank range. No hits were achieved. Controlling his temper with difficulty, Prien reloaded, checking every detail personally. Again he fired four torpedoes, again every one missed! One did explode, far away from the targets against the rocky shoreline of the fjord. On his return to Germany Prien presented a report which forced the German Admiralty to act.

Dönitz summoned the torpedo inspector, Rear-Admiral Oskar Kummetz, to account for this appalling record of failure. Kummetz had only just returned from Norway himself where, while travelling in the cruiser *Blücher*, he had been torpedoed – ironically by a Norwegian fort – and forced to swim to the shore before being rescued. Under questioning, Kummetz replied that he did not know why the torpedoes were failing. He had not been in the job long and had been unable to carry out tests on the new torpedoes because the Baltic was frozen. It was now revealed to Dönitz that the torpedoes currently being used by German submarines had *never* actually been tested at all. When tests were subsequently carried out the torpedoes were shown to run nearly ten feet deeper than their design specification. This being the case, neither the percussion pistol nor the magnetic one had any chance of working. Dönitz had no alternative but to recall all his U-boats. As he said, 'It is my belief that never before in military history has a force been sent into battle with such a useless weapon.'

The truth was that the deficiencies of their torpedoes had been known to the German torpedo specialists for some time. During the Spanish Civil War German ships had experienced continual failures with torpedoes – which exploded prematurely, failed to run straight and often sank before reaching the target – but nothing had been done about it. The head of the

115

TVA (Torpedo Test Institute), Oskar Wehr, an officer as arrogant as he was complacent, failed to accept any kind of criticism, claiming that it only served to depress the man at the front who had to use the weapons. His decision to reject the critical reports condemned German U-boats to a campaign of futility during the first year of the war and saved innumerable British ships from destruction.

---

*'A submarine cannot stay any length of time under water, because it must frequently come into harbour to replenish its electric batteries.'*

**Admiral Lord Charles Beresford**

Before the outbreak of the First World War in 1914 Sir Percy Scott predicted the widespread use of submarines by Germany, but his warnings went unheeded as 'experts' like Admiral Beresford tried to ridicule the submarine threat.

---

# The Q-Ship

The introduction of Q-ships – merchantmen with concealed guns – made a big initial impact on the fight against U-boats. But after a period of success, German skippers became increasingly suspicious of merchant ships which seemed too confident, so that by the end of the war their successes were few and difficult to achieve. The Q-ship *Cymric* had been a schooner prior to being converted, and on 15 October 1918 she was cruising off the coast of Yorkshire. She had already had one piece of excitement that day when she had almost fired on one of the infamous K boats, as it lay basking in the sun. Robbed of her kill, *Cymric* sailed on, doubly determined to make her mark. A second submarine was sighted, the crew went to action stations, but again there was the frustration that it was 'one of ours'.

Meanwhile the British submarine J6, commanded by Lieutenant-Commander Geoffrey Warburton, was on patrol in the same area. Because the 'J' class submarines slightly resembled U-boats, the crews always took great pains to keep the huge J6 painted on the conning tower bright and clean. But this time fate was against them. By a most curious chance something was hanging from the conning tower which provided a second upright on the 'J' turning it into a 'U'. Thus to all intents and purposes U-6 was blithely sailing about on the surface when it encountered *Cymric*.

J6 slowly approached the schooner, but unknown to the submarine crew the Q-ship's gunners were waiting their chance. Keen eyes aboard the *Cymric* noted a limp ensign flying from the submarine's flagpole, but they took no notice of that – they had been fooled by false colours in the past.

Suddenly *Cymric* broke out the white ensign, dropped her disguise and opened fire on J6. The submarine never had a chance. An officer on J6 raised a rifle to fire an identification signal but it was blown from his hand and the signal was never sent. The Q-ship's 4-inch gun scored an immediate hit, while on the submarine an officer was waving something which resembled a large white tablecloth. Before *Cymric* could fire again the submarine drifted into a fog-bank. But as she was swallowed up in the gloom J6's signaller managed to flash out the word 'Help'.

The Q-ship was still not sure what to make of the mystery submarine and followed her into the fog. There she found J6 sinking, with men jumping over the side and being collected in a small boat. As some survivors reached *Cymric* their hatbands displayed the words 'HM Submarines' and the truth at last dawned on the Q-ship's crew. It was a sickening moment for all concerned. Only fifteen of the submarine's crew survived their ordeal. The subsequent court of inquiry absolved the Q-ship from blame and recorded the incident as a 'hazard of war'. Ironically, it appears that the J6 suspected *Cymric* of being a German Q-ship and was suspicious of her from the start. In an amazing display of camaraderie the survivors from J6 stood and saluted the captain of the schooner – a man who had earned two D.S.O.s and two D.S.C.s – as he left the courtroom.

# CHAPTER 6: THAT SINKING FEELING

Nobody thanks the captain who comes back after he has lost his ship. And yet all too often he is not to blame when disaster comes. Sometimes faulty design consigns his vessel to 'Davy Jones' Locker', but more often it is the effects of wind and tide, and the elemental power of the sea, that overcomes man's puny attempts to impose himself on the ocean. The sea tolerates until it loses its patience, and then . . .

## The White Ship

The loss of King Henry I's vessel known as the White Ship may be regarded as one of the most disastrous shipwrecks in English history. It cost the life of Henry's son and heir, William, and paved the way for a disputed succession on the king's death. It was also an avoidable disaster, as William of Malmesbury tells us in his *Gesta Regum Anglorum*.

On 25 November 1120, Henry I's son, William, ordered a ship to be made ready to follow his father, who had already set out from Barfleur in France to return to England. William was only 17 and urged on by a crowd of his friends, all of them drunk, he prepared to set out in the royal yacht – known as the White Ship – even though the weather was bad and the seas rough. The sailors were far too drunk to do their jobs properly and boasted to the prince that they would overtake the king's vessel as theirs was the best ship afloat. In darkness the group of revellers launched the ship and crammed on sail to try to catch the king's ship, but nobody was navigating properly and the ship ran onto rocks not far from the shore. The more they tried to push themselves off the rocks the more the waves smashed them against their jagged points. The sea now broke over the ship, sweeping men overboard. A single small boat was launched and the young prince taken aboard, to be rowed back to the shore. But his bastard sister, the Countess of Perche, was still aboard and called on him to return and rescue her. Touched with pity the prince returned to the stricken vessel and tried to take off his sister but so many people forced their way into the boat that it capsized and all were drowned. Just one rough sailor – some say a butcher – survived to reach the shore and he was able to describe to the king the tragic end of the White Ship and the death of the prince. It is said that Henry I 'never smiled again'.

## The Loss of the *Mary Rose*

The loss of the Tudor warship *Mary Rose* on 19 July 1545 was an event made even more poignant by the fact that it occurred inside Portsmouth Harbour under the eyes of both King Henry VIII and of Lady Mary Carew, wife of the admiral, Sir George Carew. Furthermore, Sir George's last recorded words may give us a clue to the disaster that befell the English flagship. As his uncle, Sir Gawen Carew, commanding the *Matthew Gonson*, called to his

The reason for the loss of the warship the *Mary Rose*, pride of Henry VIII's fleet, in July 1545, remains something of a mystery. One possible explanation is that the weight of her heavily armed crew caused the ship to heel over and capsize.

nephew to ask what was amiss with the *Mary Rose*, which was beginning to heel, he heard Sir George call back as if in despair, 'I have the sort of knaves I cannot rule', desperate words for any ship's captain even at the best of times. But at the moment of going into battle against a French invasion fleet they suggest indiscipline of a kind that should have been avoided.

The clinker-built carrack *Mary Rose*, along with her 'sister ship' *Peter Pomegranate*, was built for the young King Henry VIII and was probably launched in the late summer of 1511. Within a year she was in action against the French near Brest where she was the flagship of Sir Edward Howard, 'chief capteyn and admyrall of the flete'. Her success in that battle, where she engaged the French flagship, the *Grand Luise*, caused her to be called 'the noblest ship of sayle and grett shipp at this hour that I trow be in Christendom'. Her manoeuvrability was one of her great strengths and at this stage there can be no suggestion other than that she was a thoroughly seaworthy vessel. Henry VIII certainly thought so, and it was as a scaled-up version of the *Mary Rose* that the *Henri Grace à Dieu* [the *Great Harry*] was built.

In 1536, the *Mary Rose* and the *Great Harry* were both rebuilt in the carvel-style in the dockyards at Portsmouth. The *Mary Rose* was increased in size from 600 to 700 tons, with her crew raised to some 415 men. She was rearmed with the latest bronze muzzle-loading guns and thereafter carried 91 cannon, 50 handguns and 250 longbows, as well as pikes and bills for her infantrymen. In spite of her alterations, the *Mary Rose* continued to have the enormously tall and ornate castles fore and aft which were such a feature of English ships of the period, and such a threat to their stability.

In July 1545 the French King Francis I launched an invasion fleet of 235 ships and 30,000 men against England, commanded by the Admiral of France, Claude d'Annebault. From the start fortune appeared to favour the English. On 6 July, d'Annebault held a great state dinner aboard his flagship, the 800-ton *Carraquon*. While the ship was crowded with court ladies and dignitaries the cooks had an accident with the ovens, setting fire to the vessel. Within minutes the whole ship was ablaze and guns and powder exploded, killing almost everyone aboard. D'Annebault survived the fire and transferred his flag to another huge carrack, *La Maitresse*, but it ran aground while attempting to leave harbour. Undeterred, D'Annebault continued in the wounded vessel, only for it to capsize off the Isle of Wight. D'Annebault, bearing a charmed life, was rescued by one of his galleys and had to seek a third flagship.

Meanwhile, the *Mary Rose* was leading the port division of the English fleet out of Portsmouth Harbour to meet the French, while Viscount Lisle in the *Great Harry* led the starboard division. Significantly, the chroniclers report that half the mariners in the *Mary Rose* were so experienced that they were fit to be shipmasters in their own right. And it may be that the old adage that 'too many cooks spoil the broth' explains what happened next. As Carew's flagship made its way across Portsmouth Harbour, passing Southsea Castle, onlookers there noticed that she seemed to be in trouble. She looked to be overloaded and her lower gun ports were perilously close to the water. In addition, although the day was relatively calm, there seemed to be confusion in raising the sails and the ship was handling badly. Carew's uncle, Sir Gawen, commanding the *Matthew Gonson*, asked his own master what he thought was happening on the *Mary Rose* and was told that if she kept heeling like that she would soon turn over. This alarmed Sir Gawen and he called out to his nephew only to receive the desperate reply quoted above. Clearly the *Mary Rose* was out of control and neither its captain – Roger Grenville – nor the admiral seemed able to put matters right. Then, in the words of the Spanish ambassador, 'she [the *Mary Rose*] heeled over with the wind, the water entered by the lowest row of gunports which had been left open after firing. All the 500 men on board were drowned save about 25 or 30 servants, sailors and the like.' The French tried later to claim that she had been sunk by gunfire but there was absolutely no truth in this.

We will never know what had really happened on the *Mary Rose*, nor understand Sir George Carew's last desperate words. Clearly, with the ship going into battle, she was very heavily loaded. There may indeed have been as many as 700 men aboard when she sank, hundreds of them soldiers – some heavily armoured – and the crowded conditions aboard must have made it difficult for the sailors to go about their normal tasks. With the tremendous extra weight of so many men with their weapons any heeling might have become serious as the crew lost their footing and fell towards the side which was sinking. Guns may have broken loose and added their weight so that soon water would begin to enter by the open gun ports. Once this happened the ship was doomed. The armoured men would sink like stones, while hundreds more aboard would be hit by falling spars or trapped beneath decks.

Stated simply, the ship was far too heavily loaded and had lost stability. Its commanders – Grenville and Carew – appear to have lost control of their crew, who mismanaged the hoisting of the sails. The additional weight of armoured men and heavily shotted guns proved fatal once the ship began to heel and, with the excessively tall forecastle and aftcastle of the *Mary Rose*, this was always going to be a danger. That in the heat of the crisis Carew failed to govern his men can only be surmised. Indiscipline aboard – through caste or rank – may be guessed at, for it was an age when gentlemen would not deign to haul on ropes with mariners. It was the task of the common seamen to take the gentlemen soldiers close enough to the enemy ships so that warfare could be conducted as if on land. In the end the *Mary Rose* may have been a victim of that singularly English preoccupation – social status.

# The Loss of the *Vasa*

On a beautiful summer's evening in August 1628, many of the inhabitants of Stockholm had come down to the city harbour to watch the *Vasa*, Sweden's latest and most magnificent warship, begin her maiden voyage. The ship was packed with service and civic dignitaries, including fleet commander Jonsson, as well as the wives and children of the crew. For the first part of the journey, along Skeppsbron, the *Vasa* was 'warped' by her crew, but after reaching Stadsgarden her master, Captain Söfring, ordered the anchors drawn in and the sails raised – the *Vasa* was in her element at last. She fired two guns to signal that she was about to depart.

At first there was only a light breeze to fill her sails and so she moved slowly, then as she sailed beyond the cover of the cliffs at Söder a stronger gust of wind hit her, making her heel slightly before righting herself. All around her a small flotilla of sailing and rowing boats, bedecked with flags and packed with well-wishers, tried to keep pace with her. A sudden swift breeze now filled her sails and she heeled alarmingly, forcing Söfring to bellow through his speaking-trumpet for the men in the rigging to cast loose the topsails. But it was not enough. Another gust of wind hit the *Vasa* and she heeled over so far that the sea gushed in through her open gun-ports. Not far from Beckholmen she capsized and slipped quickly under the water, carrying with her some three or four hundred people – women and children as well as her crewmen. The fleet commander – Hans Jonsson – died with the *Vasa*, though the ship's captain made a remarkable escape after being underwater for some minutes.

The loss of the *Vasa* was a blow to the whole nation. With the Thirty Years War raging across the Baltic in Germany it was clear that Sweden could be drawn into the fighting at any moment. The *Vasa* had been a vital element in Sweden's seapower and her loss could not easily be made good. It is not surprising then that a howl of popular outrage demanded to know who was responsible for the catastrophe. Clearly mistakes had been made and those responsible must pay. Without delay an inquiry was set up by the Council of the Realm and the *Vasa*'s captain and her builder were dragged before the court, presided over by Admiral Carl Carlsson Gyllenhielm. The hunt was on for a scapegoat to allay public discontent with the government. But this was easier said than done. It soon became apparent that the ship's crew and her captain had done nothing unusual and that in their opinion the fault resided in the design of the vessel. The captain explained under cross-examination that he had never had confidence in the *Vasa* and believed that she would capsize once her sails were raised. He told the court that her superstructure was far too bulky and that she was 'heavier over than under'. Gyllenhielm was clearly astonished at this line of argument and tried to insist that it was the captain's responsibility to report such misgivings. The captain absolved himself by blaming the builder, who had said that if he had known that she was top-heavy he would have increased her ballast. How could he do that, asked the captain, when the gun ports were just three and a half feet above the water. Any lower and the ship would have capsized in any sea other than a flat calm. It was Jöran Matsson, the master of the *Vasa*, who gave the real clue to the disaster. When asked if he had felt the ship to be top heavy he revealed that Admiral Fleming had been told as much weeks before. A 'capsizing test' had been held in which 30 of the crew had run from side to side of the ship to see how much she heeled. The results were so alarming that Fleming had stopped the test to prevent her heeling right over. Matsson continued by adding that the *Vasa* was too narrow-bottomed and was bound to capsize whatever the weather and however much ballast was added. When he had told the admiral this Fleming had replied, 'The builder has built ships before. You don't need to worry like that.'

The builder, Hein Jacobsson, was now called. When questioned on the narrow build of the

*Vasa* he was able to point out that he had not laid the keel. He had followed the blueprint of the original builder – Master Henrik – who had died the previous year. Henrik had discussed the new ship's dimensions with none other than the king himself. Far from being narrow-bottomed the *Vasa* was, in fact, one foot five inches broader than originally planned. The court asked why the superstructure had been so large but Jacobsson was able to point out that the *Vasa* had been modelled on a French ship built in Holland which was, to the best of his knowledge, still afloat. Moreover, the *Vasa* was no narrower in the beam than another of the king's ships – the *Kronan* – and she was a sturdy ship, which had given good service.

The court faced a difficult choice. Clearly there had been mistakes in the design of the *Vasa* but when the problems of instability had been drawn to the attention of Admiral Fleming, Gyllenhielm's right-hand man, he had dismissed them airily, relying entirely on the technical skill of the builder rather than the empirical evidence of the sailors – the men who had to turn a thing of lines and angles into a ship of war, capable of facing an enemy broadside or surviving a storm intact. Fleming would not do as a scapegoat for he could easily point out that the designs originated with the king himself. If there had been mistakes they had been passed by Gustavus Adolphus, famed 'Lion of the North', and as scapegoats go he was too strong a prey even for predatory public opinion. The loss of the *Vasa* had been inevitable from the moment that Gustavus Adolphus and Master Henrik had completed their flawed blueprint.

# D'Estrées the Navigator

On the night of 11 May 1678, the French Admiral Jean d'Estrées, commanding a large French armada, achieved an extraordinary 'first' in naval history by running the entire fleet aground on the Aves Islands, near Curaçao. D'Estrées was not the sort of man to listen to his subordinates and his haughtiness was to be his undoing. As a navigator he had severe limitations but he was not prepared to admit them nor to seek advice from any man more knowledgeable than himself. His method of approaching Curaçao was bizarre in the extreme. He simply followed a latitude and then when he thought he had gone far enough he turned south. This hit and miss method, unfortunately, was definitely more 'hit' than 'miss'. Instead of reaching Curaçao he ran his ships aground on some reefs, responding far too slowly to a warning gun fired by one of the accompanying buccaneer ships. Twelve vessels – including seven ships of the line – were wrecked on the rocks and the best that could be done was to take off their crews. Some of the other vessels were able to be refloated but the loss of so many fine warships should have led to the admiral's dismissal. Instead, he was promoted by the king. Colbert, the minister of marine, was left with the job of rescuing what he could from the wreckage. By dint of enormous effort an old captain named Forant managed to save 364 cannon and 3,000 shot from the wrecked fleet.

# Admiral Hovenden Walker at Quebec

It is usually a mistake to select a military commander for any reason other than military skill, yet in the early 18th century a man's political affiliation was frequently used as a better guide to his ability than any other. This was especially true of Admiral Hovenden Walker – a good

Tory, and a close friend of the politician then in the ascendant, Henry St. John (later first Viscount Bolingbroke). And though Walker had risen to flag rank through his own efforts rather than through his contacts, he was not noted for his ability or his initiative, so that his appointment to command the expedition to Canada in 1711 came as something of a surprise to his contemporaries.

The idea of an expedition to capture Quebec from the French was St. John's own and he went to great lengths to maintain secrecy. One of his measures was uniquely bizarre. In an attempt to convince the French that Walker's fleet was bound for the Mediterranean, St. John ordered the ships to be loaded with just three months' provisions instead of the eight that would really be needed for a transatlantic expedition. Whether the French were taken in we do not know. What is certain, however, is that Walker's fleet set off pitifully short of food and every other necessity and found it impossible to re-provision in the ports of New England. St. John's idiocy shows the dangers of political interference in the planning of naval expeditions. In any case, London and Plymouth – where the fleet was assembling – were teeming with French spies. It would have been a miracle if the French did not know Walker's real destination, as it was the talk of the coffee houses and taverns. The only tight secrecy was that maintained between St. John and the navy commissioners, which resulted in many essentials being left behind when the ships sailed. St. John's greatest coup in the field of espionage appears to have been to deceive Admiral Sir John Leake, the First Commissioner of the Admiralty. It was another of St. John's tricks to send two vessels – the 80-gun *Humber* and *Devonshire* – with the fleet to begin with, only for them to suddenly turn back to the amazement of everyone, including Admiral Walker, who was not in on the secret.

In 1709 the much-loved Admiral Sir Clowdesley Shovell, flying his flag in the *Association*, lost his way off the Isles of Scilly and ran his ships aground. His body was later recovered by wreckers and buried in Westminster Abbey.

The fleet – which was now as thoroughly bemused as any that had ever left England's shores – eventually sailed at the beginning of May 1711 and arrived in New England on 25 June. With Walker's fleet was a force of 5,300 soldiers and marines, commanded by Brigadier-General John Hill, which camped at Noddle's Island in Boston Bay. However, the American colonists were not prepared for so large an expedition to arrive without proper provisions. The price of food rose sharply and soon relations between the British and the Americans were strained. It was not until September that the British were able to obtain a further three months' supply of food to supplement their already meagre rations. And to the scourge of famine was now added the even greater problem of desertion. The sailors, notably, jumped ship and merged into the local population in the hope of finding a better life in the American colonies. Walker was forced to try to find crews for his ships by pressing colonial fishermen. But his biggest problem – which was to contribute in no small way to the failure of the expedition – was to find pilots who knew how to navigate the St. Lawrence River. Far from locating a supply of willing local pilots Walker found that the Bostonians seemed determined not to help him. Again he had to resort to force, with local sheriffs hunting down men who had refused to serve. Walker even found to his cost that the man chosen to be the chief pilot of the fleet – Captain Cyprian Southack – had never been further up the St. Lawrence than the Sept Isles at the mouth and was not keen to go any further. Even the famous Captain Bonner of Boston – reputed to be the best pilot on the river – had only ever taken a sloop up river and did not like the idea of taking responsibility for a man-of-war. Incredibly Walker had to fall back on a Frenchman he had picked up in Plymouth! The colonists were highly suspicious of this man and Colonel Samuel Vetch referred to him as 'an ignorant, pretending, idle, drunken Fellow [who] is come on no good Design'. This shook Walker's confidence and he next tried to bribe a captured Frenchman, Captain Paradis, of the sloop *Neptune*. Paradis was offered a small fortune if he would navigate the fleet to Quebec. He agreed and sailed in Walker's flagship, the 80-gun *Edgar*. A further problem was that no two maps or charts of the St. Lawrence agreed with each other. When old seamen who had sailed on Phips' expedition of 1690 were consulted all they could do was recount terrifying stories of the problems that were to be faced – fogs, shoals, currents, tides and storms.

By this stage Walker was beginning to lose his nerve and now decided not to risk his large 80-gun ships. On 30 July with just nine warships, two bomb vessels and the 60 transports and tenders carrying the troops, he left Boston Harbour. In pleasant weather he reached the mouth of the St Lawrence and then decided to entrust the navigation to Colonel Vetch in the frigate *Despatch*. Vetch was an unusual choice, being both a soldier and a landsman rather than a seaman, yet he started well and seemed to be living up to his boast of being the best pilot in the fleet. Vetch had already begun to doubt his admiral's qualities as either a leader or a sailor and he was determined not to see the fleet handed over to the traitorous Frenchman, Paradis.

Trouble really began when Walker asked Vetch to transfer to the tiny frigate *Sapphire*, which the colonel refused to do as he did not want to move all his baggage. Walker reluctantly accepted this excuse but told Vetch to await his signal the following day to lead the fleet up river. Vetch claimed that no signal was made by Walker and so he chose to follow rather than lead the other ships. He later claimed that had he led the fleet, as he expected to do, the disaster which occurred would have been prevented. But Vetch appears to have been a very slippery fellow. When asked after the disaster why he had told the admiral that he was the best pilot available, he promptly denied it and said that he 'could undergo nothing that related to Sea Affairs'. He had only been willing to go up a river in a small craft to check for difficulties. Either there had been a misunderstanding between himself and Walker or else Vetch was a liar.

By 13 August Paradis seemed to have taken charge of the navigation with Walker's approval. However, the fleet found it immensely difficult to enter the river past the island of Anticosti because of alternate contrary winds and fogs. On 23 August there were intermittent breaks in the fog but no sight of land and Paradis advised Walker to allow his ships to drift on a south-west current. But at that time Walker was nowhere near where he thought he was. Because of an easterly wind the fleet was quite close to the northern shore of the St Lawrence and when a report was brought to him – as he was preparing for bed – that flashes of white spray had been sighted, indicating that they were near a shoal or reef, he reached the catastrophic conclusion that they were near the south shore. Had this been true it would not have presented much of a problem as he would have had clear water to the west. With this in mind he ordered the fleet to wear and bring to on the other tack. In the event this was a fatal order. The admiral's slumbers were soon disturbed by a young army officer named Goddard, who brought the dreadful news that there were breakers to leeward of the flagship. Walker called Goddard a young idiot and tried to get to sleep again, but Goddard returned and demanded that he come on deck. There were now breakers all around. Walker awoke with a shock. Above he could hear running feet and the sounds of panic. The whole fleet was on the north shore, some already aground. How on earth they could have reached this parlous state without any of the lookouts raising the alarm is just one of many unanswered questions.

Walker's flagship, along with several of the other men-of-war, managed to raise sail and stand off into the mid-channel, though others had to anchor in terrifying proximity to the rocks. Eight of the transports were already aground and breaking up, their crews' desperate cries for help echoing in the darkness. In all around one thousand soldiers and sailors were lost that night. The gale which had been blowing the fleet towards the shore abated just in time, for otherwise every ship would have been lost.

The next two days must have seemed a hell to Walker. Instead of moving up river towards Quebec, he spent his time sailing to and fro trying to rescue what he could from the wreckage of the expedition. He called a council of war which simply served to confirm his verdict that the operation would have to be called off. The search for scapegoats was already apparent in the council's resolution: 'It is our unanimous Opinion that by reason of the Ignorance of the Pilots aboard the Men of War, it is wholly impracticable to go up the River of St Lawrence so far as Quebec.' Both Walker and General Hill were keen to return to England but the admiral was particularly anxious about the sort of reception he would receive there. In the event, a few days after they had reached home, while Walker was in London, his flagship, the *Edgar*, blew up with the loss of her entire crew and most of his charts and journals.

Walker's reception was far better than he dared expect. After all, he was a stout Tory and with St John still in the ascendant, there was little to be gained from turning the admiral into a scapegoat. Instead the blame was attributed to the colonists, whose treachery, it was claimed, lay at the root of the disaster. But Walker was living on borrowed time. It would only take a shift in political power for the Whigs to demand a full account of his part in the debacle. In March 1715 the day came that he must have been dreading. In spite of his reasonable plea that most of his papers had been lost in the *Edgar* he was ordered to produce a full report for the Admiralty. He was to be punished less for his blunders than for his politics. A month later his half pay was stopped and his name was struck off the list of admirals: he was condemned without a hearing. In 1720 Walker published his account of the expedition and in the introduction made it clear that he saw himself as a victim rather than the perpetrator of his own destruction:

The Expedition to Canada has made as great a Noise in London, almost as if the Fate of all Britain had depended upon it . . . And perhaps, had I had the Misfortune of being lost among the Rocks of Scilly with some of the capital ships of the Fleet; instead of being buried at the Publick Charge in Westminster Abby, certain Great Men would have advised my being Interred under the Gallows; so malignant seems their Rage against me.

In his reference to a misfortune among the 'Rocks of Scilly' Walker is reminding his readers of the loss of the much-loved Sir Clowdesley Shovell in the *Association*. Compared to Shovell's miscalculation Walker's crime may seem very minor. Yet Shovell was a great seaman who did not owe his popularity to party faction. And Shovell had the fortune to go down with his ship.

# The Loss of the *Royal George*

In August 1782 the *Royal George* was one of only three 100-gun three-deck ships-of-the-line in the Royal Navy. Along with her sisters *Victory* and *Britannia* she was one of the flagships of a British expedition assembling at Portsmouth to relieve Gibraltar, then under siege by the Spaniards. She carried the flag of one of the most able naval commanders of his time, Richard Kempenfeldt, known to all as 'the brains of the Navy'. But on 29 August, just two days before the fleet was due to sail, and with the entire British force gathered around her in a calm sea off Southsea, the *Royal George* suddenly sank, with the loss of between eight and nine hundred lives, including that of the admiral. So sudden was the event that it is reported that a local lady, writing a letter to one of her friends, gazed out of her window at the fleet peacefully at anchor and marked the great man-of-war, with its admiral's pennant hardly rippled by the wind, before looking down at her paper and completing a sentence. When she looked back out to sea, the *Royal George* had gone, and the peaceful scene was all confusion. How could it have happened?

The *Royal George* had been launched in 1756 and at that time was the largest warship ever built for the Royal Navy. It had taken some 3,840 trees from 110 acres of forest to build her at a cost of £65,274. In her 26 years of service she had been 'active' for just ten of them and had been laid up for fifteen years between 1762 and 1777. She had been present at the battle of Quiberon Bay and had achieved the unusual feat of sinking the 70-gun French ship *Superbe* with a single broadside. Yet even while she was on the active list the *Royal George* spent just 59 months at sea, the rest in harbour with her hull prey to the shipworm, which could bore holes up to a foot in length in the planks of wooden ships.

On 29 August 1782 the *Royal George* was swarming with visitors – mainly women and children – and may have been signalling the traditional 'wedding garland', by which it was permissible for women to visit their menfolk aboard prior to some long voyage. With shore leave forbidden – desertion was a constant headache so close to embarkation – it would have stretched discipline to its limits to deny the men this final celebration. As well as the 300 women, 'some of the most depraved characters', there were also moneylenders pursuing bad debts and tinkers and hucksters selling their wares. Below decks in the great man-of-war it must have more closely resembled Gin Lane in Hogarth's print than a flagship of the Royal Navy. While these revels were taking place the *Royal George* had been heeled over to port to allow a repair to take place to her copper-sheathed hull – the replacement of a water-cock – a normal procedure while in harbour but very unusual so soon before departure and while the ship was so heavily loaded with provisions and the extra weight of so many visitors. The heeling had been achieved by transferring all the guns from one side to the other, again a perfectly normal

Divers examine the wreck of the *Royal George*. The ship was lost off Southsea in 1782 owing to the negligence of her crew, who overloaded her when she was heeled over under repair.

way of achieving the angle required but only safe if the lower-deck gun ports were securely closed and plugged. But in this instance the ports, close to the sea by virtue of the ship's heel, had not been closed at all and were being used to receive extra cargo. To add to the confusion the three warrant officers who should have been most concerned with the progress of this work – the master, the gunner and the boatswain – were all ashore, in spite of leave having being cancelled. A perfectly avoidable tragedy was imminent.

Ordinary Seaman James Ingram witnessed what happened next. At just after 9 am, a lighter carrying rum came alongside the *Royal George*. She was lashed to the warship and Ingram and others were ordered to clear her. Some sailors jumped aboard the lighter and began passing the heavy rum casks through the gun ports to avoid hauling them all the way up onto deck. No one suspected danger, although water was beginning to slop in through the ports. Ominously it was noticed that rats and mice were beginning to scuttle clear. The weight of the rum casks, stacked against the larboard side of the ship, and the weight of the sea which came through the gun ports brought the latter right down to the level of the choppy water, then at the height of the flood. The carpenter – now thoroughly alarmed – ran to the quarterdeck to warn the Lieutenant of the Watch, Monins Hollingbery, but this officer dismissed him 'with a flea in his ear'. The carpenter returned a few minutes later and demanded that the officer right the ship for it was flooding. Hollingbery, known as an 'irascible fellow', replied, 'Damme, Sir, if you can manage the ship better than I can you had better take command.' Hollingbery ordered a drummer to beat 'Right Ship' but the boy never got started for at that moment the ship began to capsize. Ingram was one of the few survivors. Neither the captain nor many of his officers were even aware that their ship was in danger.

Captain Waghorn – who, like Ingram and Hollingbery, survived the disaster – later faced a court-martial. In view of the obvious human errors involved it is nothing less than amazing to read the findings of the court:

> It appears to the Court that the ship was not overheeled . . . that the Captain, Officers and Ship's Company used every exertion to right the ship as soon as the alarm was given of her settling; and the Court is of the opinion, from the short space of time between the alarm being given and the sinking of the ship, that some material part of her frame gave way, which can only be accounted for by the general state of the decay of her timbers . . . The Captain, Officers and Ship's Company are acquitted of all blame.

This verdict was, of course, nothing more than a whitewash. There never was any evidence that her hull had collapsed. This was merely a fashionable theory advanced to conceal the extent of human incompetence present on the day of the disaster. After all, no wreck has the right of reply. The explanation – a relatively simple one – was that the *Royal George* had been overheeled and that the water entering through the gun ports increased the angle of heeling until the ship lost stability and capsized. And for this the captain, Martin Waghorn, must take much of the blame. Why was it decided to heel a heavily laden man-of-war for such a trivial reason? Furthermore, once the decision was taken Waghorn should have ensured that the gun ports were secured. Even more surprising was the decision (perhaps not his) to allow further heavy cargo to be taken aboard through these gun ports when they were so close to a rising tide. It was a failure in seamanship by many men, yet as every captain knew the buck finally stopped with him. Although acquitted by the court-martial Waghorn was placed on half-pay and remained a captain until his death in 1787.

# The Loss of HMS *Captain*

The transition from wooden warships to ironclads was not achieved without a great struggle on the part of traditionalists of the 'wood floats, iron sinks' school. But even they were eventually forced into silence by the progress made by France, Britain's most formidable naval opponent, in the field of ironclad warships. The launching of the *Gloire* in 1859 forced the British Admiralty to begin a serious reappraisal of the future of two hitherto fundamentals of naval warfare: sail power and broadside armament. By 1866 the hybrid wooden-ironclads had been consigned to the dustbin of history and the way was open for a brilliant, young inventor, Captain Cowper Phipps Coles, to press the claims of the low freeboard turret-ship over the broadside and box-battery armaments then in favour. But in doing so he met the resistance of the Chief Constructor for the Admiralty, E.J. Reed, who had designed a new ironclad for the

Admiralty named the *Monarch*. Determined to prove that he could do better Coles, with the assistance of Messrs Laird of Birkenhead, began work on a privately built turret-ship to be known as the *Captain*. It would be the first and only battleship ever privately designed and built for the Royal Navy. Reed condemned Coles as an amateur who had got all his sums wrong, but Coles received enormous public support and even, it is said, the favour of the Royal Family. Everyone, it seemed, wanted to see the Admiralty with egg on its face. Coles, in fact, had received encouragement for his revolving gun turret designs from none other person than Prince Albert. After the death of the Prince Consort, Queen Victoria showed her continuing support for the young inventor by according him the ultimate accolade – a plaster bust of Albert.

Coles' notion of a turret ship was relatively simple, if revolutionary. In place of a mass of smooth-bore guns along a broadside, he claimed that a far more destructive effect could be achieved by just four heavily rifled guns mounted on a turntable, which enabled them to fire to all points of the compass. It was simple in theory – 'Turn the gun not the ship'. Once the *Captain* was completed Reed, although praising its lines, denounced it as the work of 'an amateur architect and a commercial builder', and predicted that it would capsize owing to its instability. Yet public and press were behind Coles all the way and very much wanted to see him succeed. Doubts were swept aside. Even the First Lord of the Admiralty, Hugh Childers, put his political weight behind Coles and his new ship. As a result, the *Captain*, when completed, was widely acknowledged as the finest fighting ship in the fleet. She was 320 feet long, had a beam of 53 feet and a draught of 25 feet 9 inches. In contrast to Reed's *Monarch*, which had a freeboard of 14 feet, the *Captain*, as designed by Coles was to have just 8 feet 6 inches, and due to a subsequent error in fact only drew 6 feet 8 inches. This was dangerously little and the manufacturers, Laird, were so concerned that they asked the Admiralty to test her stability by inclining her. These tests were carried out and – perhaps surprisingly – the results were satisfactory. Armed with four 25-ton guns in two heavily armoured turrets she also carried one funnel and three tripod masts, giving her more sailpower and equal steampower to Reed's *Monarch*. But if the truth be told she was dangerously top heavy.

And yet for a while all went well. In May 1871 she tested her stability by firing her guns during a heavy gale in the Bay of Biscay and again she came through with flying colours. Admiral Symonds noted, 'She is a most formidable vessel and could, I believe, by her superior armament, destroy all the broadside ships of the squadron in detail.' Coles, himself, wrote, 'She walks the water like a thing of life.' The third time she went to sea, in September, Coles himself travelled with her across the Bay of Biscay. He was keen that the commander-in-chief of the Channel Fleet – Admiral Milne – should spend a night aboard the *Captain* but the admiral wisely refused. Towards midnight on 6 September the barometer began to drop sharply signifying dirty weather. The *Captain* was somewhat astern of Milne's flagship, the *Lord Warden*, and as the wind rose she began heeling to starboard. The weather now closed in, with sheeting rain, and the *Lord Warden* lost sight of the *Captain*'s red bow light. Two hours later the wind lessened, the clouds parted and in the moonlight the *Lord Warden* could see that the *Captain* was no longer where she had been last observed. As dawn broke it was clear that the *Captain* was missing, presumed sunk. Milne's ships began to search for survivors but found only wreckage.

It is only through the reports of the few men who did survive that we can piece together the last moments of the *Captain*. Apparently just after midnight the ship lurched and Captain Burgoyne asked to know the angle of heel, only to be told in rapid succession, '18 degrees! 23 degrees! 28 degrees!' The ship was now on her beam ends and began to capsize, 'trembling with every blow which the short, jumping seas, white with foam, struck her'. In the boiler

HMS *Captain* was the brainchild of the brilliant inventor Captain Cowper Phipps Coles. She embodied the latest thinking in turret design but proved fatally unstable at sea.

room the crew suffered a double agony: first the furnace doors broke, showering them with burning coals; then, when the sea poured in onto the coals it boiled and steamed, scalding and skinning them alive. None of these men managed to reach the upper decks. Just eighteen men escaped in a launch and came ashore at Finisterre, Captain Burgoyne having refused the chance to join them for fear of swamping their flimsy vessel.

A court-martial was held to determine responsibility for the disaster that cost the lives of 500 men, including Burgoyne and Captain Coles. Amongst technical evidence presented it was revealed that the *Captain*'s masts were so robust that her sails did not blow away as on other vessels in high winds, but acted as wind traps to add to her instability. In addition, the *Captain* had the narrowest hull built before the *Dreadnought* in 1906 and was equipped with the most extensive sailing rig ever installed in a British ironclad: a sure formula for disaster, as Reed had always predicted. The court's verdict was a formality: that the ship had been too unstable for use at sea and might only have continued as a coastal defence vessel. She was top heavy and her masts and sails only added to the danger. It had been a mistake to build her and she had only been constructed 'in deference to public opinion' and 'in opposition to the views and opinions of the Controller of the Navy and his department'. The court's message was a case of 'I told you so' aimed at presumptuous private designers who might in future seek to challenge the navy's monopoly in ship design. But the First Lord, Hugh Childers, struck back at Reed, accusing him of dereliction of duty in not informing him of his reservations about the *Captain*'s stability. This was hardly ethical in view of Reed's known criticism of Coles' design, but Childers was a politician and he needed a scapegoat. Ironically, the struggle between Coles and Reed finally ended in a draw. The *Captain* had indeed been a failure, as Reed claimed, 'a disastrous dead-end in naval architecture'. Yet not everything was lost. Within twelve months Reed's newest ironclad – the mastless *Devastation* – was launched. In every way she was Reed's design except one: her turrets were pure Cowper Coles and the Admiralty acknowledged this in paying heavy royalties to his widow for use of the design.

# The Loss of the *Vanguard*

The 1st Reserve Squadron, under the command of Vice-Admiral Sir Walter Tarleton, left Portland on 29 July 1875 for exercises off the coast of Ireland. Tarleton was flying his flag in the *Warrior*, Britain's first iron battleship, and with him were three other ironclad battleships, *Hector*, *Vanguard* and *Iron Duke*, travelling at 8 knots in two divisions. On board the *Vanguard*, leading the port division of Tarleton's squadron, Lieutenant William Hathorn had just relieved Captain Richard Dawkins, who had gone below to his cabin. There seemed to be no cause for alarm. At almost exactly the same time Captain Henry Hickley of the *Iron Duke*, second ship in the port column, also went below, leaving an officer of the watch. Both captains – Dawkins and Hickley – had been on deck for many hours and both were tired. Suddenly a thick fog descended and visibility was reduced to less than the length of one of the battleships. Each of the ships was travelling at twice the rate permitted in fog and they would obviously have to reduce speed; but how to do it safely? There had been no signal from the admiral to reduce speed, but there again no signal could have been seen. Dawkins returned to deck and discussed with Hathorn the correct signal with the steam-whistle for altering speed. They decided to sound the ship's pennants and reduced speed to 6 and then 5 knots. Dawkins was not sure of the correct signal and needed time to check the signals book. But before he could do anything he received an emergency report of a sailing ship 'right ahead'. This placed Dawkins in an impossible position. If he continued on his current heading he would hit the sailing ship, if he stopped he would be rammed by the *Iron Duke*, and if he swung away in either direction anything might happen.

Dawkins decided to stop and to swing slightly to port to allow the other ship to pass. He could hear Tarleton on the starboard bow sounding his pennants but as far as he could tell, *Iron Duke* had made no signal at all. He placed look-outs all round the ship but it was difficult to pull up such a large vessel quickly. As she slowed the worst happened: the *Iron Duke*, apparently steaming at undiminished speed, drove straight into her from behind. In fact, the *Iron Duke* had turned slightly to port to avoid the possibility of running into the *Vanguard*, only to find that she had done the same.

Dawkins had only been on deck seven minutes but in that time his ship had been fatally damaged and he sounded his whistle continuously, calling for help. The *Iron Duke* quickly lowered her boats to help rescue the crew of the stricken ship. But was the *Vanguard* sinking? Chief Engineer Robert Brown reported that she was, in spite of the watertight doors being closed, but Dawkins was not prepared to give in so easily. While his crew was taken off he struggled to save his ship by his own efforts but was eventually forced to leave – the last to go – leaving just one casualty behind, his pet dog.

A court-martial was held on 10 September but its members seemed still to inhabit a world of wooden ships and Nelsonian tactics. Their understanding of the problems of ironclads was minimal. Dawkins came in for most criticism for not having saved the ship rather than for saving the entire crew. The court was entirely unsympathetic to the captain's dilemma and decided that he was travelling too fast, had left the deck at the wrong time, and had slowed down without correctly informing the *Iron Duke*. The court also believed that Dawkins should have got his pumps working and saved his vessel. The court concluded by blaming Dawkins for showing lack of judgment and neglect of duty in saving his men and losing his ship. The only redeeming feature, according to the Admiralty, was that the *Iron Duke* had actually succeeded in doing what it had been built to do – sink a battleship. After the court-martial an anonymous ditty was composed which contained these pertinent comments:

> Run into and sunk by another tin junk,
> T'was very good sport d'ye see.
> 'For it clearly showed what a fine ram she had got'
> Said the Lords of the Admiraltee.

> 'In steering' says he, 'to avoid a big smash
> I used common sense d'ye see.'
> 'We know nothing at all about that at Whitehall'
> Said the Lords of the Admiraltee.

> For the Adm'rals all who just sit at Whitehall
> Should know about ships d'ye see.
> We must clear out those frauds who proclaim themselves Lords
> From out of the Adm'raltee.

# The Loss of the *Grosser Kurfürst*

In 1878 the German imperial navy had a reputation in Britain probably slightly less than that of the Swiss, and the unfortunate disaster which took place on 31 May 1878, on a beautifully clear day off the Kent coast, tended to confirm the suspicion that the Germans could not navigate a toy duck in a bath.

On that Friday afternoon a group of spectators stood on the cliffs watching a squadron of three German ironclad battleships, under the command of Admiral von Batsch, travelling slowly by in two columns. They had left Wilhelmshaven on 6 May and were on a training cruise to Plymouth. Von Batsch's flagship, the *König Wilhelm*, was leading the port division and behind her came the *Preussen*. The starboard division consisted of the single ironclad *Grosser Kurfürst*. As the German warships sailed by the onlookers could see that two small sailing ships were crossing their bows, forcing the *Grosser Kurfürst* to swing to starboard to pass under their sterns. The *König Wilhelm*, in trying to avoid the same vessels, now made a terrible mistake. The inexperienced crew at her helm – a young petty officer and six raw recruits – got confused and when ordered to 'starboard the helm' did the precise opposite, causing the flagship to ram the *Grosser Kurfürst*, 'ripping off the armour plates like the skin of an orange and sweeping away the quarter boats like strips of paper'. The wretched von Batsch was in his cabin when the disaster took place and by the time he got on deck the stricken ironclad was sinking, with the loss of 284 men of her crew of nearly 500, in spite of the efforts of rescue craft from nearby Sandgate.

# PART II

# THE BATTLE OF DREPANA (250 BC)

Although Napoleon claimed that every French soldier carried a marshal's baton in his knapsack, it has been relatively rare for a common seaman to reach the dizzy heights of command – rare but not unknown. What is unknown is for the reverse to happen and for an admiral to want to abandon command for the pleasures of drill as in the case of the Roman admiral, Claudius Pulcher, who – in the words of Polybius: 'owing to his predilections as a drill-master' – positioned himself at the rear of the Roman fleet advancing towards the harbour of Drepana in 250 BC 'in order to hustle laggards'. Hoping to surprise the Carthaginian fleet there, Pulcher lost all capacity to 'lead' his ships with the result that he was unable to react to events as they unfolded. Pulcher's decision – as eccentric as Persano's at Lissa (see p. 154) – was fatal to Roman chances in the battle.

The Carthaginian admiral, Adherbal, sighted the leading Roman ships as they approached the harbour and did the only thing he could. He ordered his fleet out to sea, so that they would not be trapped without being able to manoeuvre in the narrow spaces of the harbour. The Carthaginian ships made a rush for the open sea, arriving in disorder, but they were saved by the fact that the Romans were in even more confusion. With their admiral a mile behind, and the enemy fleeing from the harbour, what were the leading ships to do now? The van of the Roman line had been told to enter the harbour. Without any counter orders they did just that, ship following ship until they were as crowded together as the Carthaginians had been. When word reached Pulcher that the van was entering the harbour, he immediately sent a fast ship forward to tell them to come out again. But with the centre of the Roman line now pushing their way into the harbour and the van trying to force their way out again there was unutterable confusion, with many ships ramming into each other and snapping off their banks of oars. Roman morale, which had never been high, literally sank beneath the waves before they had even engaged an enemy ship. Pulcher's decision to lead from the rear

Roman and Carthaginian galleys at close quarters. At the battle of Drepana the Roman commander Claudius Pulcher attempted to direct events from the rear. In the confusion that ensued the Romans suffered a humiliating defeat at the hands of their Carthaginian foes.

had created one of history's great log-jams. The battle was lost already.

The Roman captains desperately tried to form up in battle line. With some ships still in the harbour, and all of the others in the shallow waters along the shore, the Carthaginians attacked. As Adherbal bore down on them some Roman ships ran aground, while others could not manoeuvre because their oars had been destroyed in the earlier confusion. Some 93 Roman galleys were sunk or taken, and only the 27 ships of the rear with Pulcher in command managed to escape. As many as 20,000 Roman soldiers and sailors were lost in this catastrophic display of ineptitude by Claudius Pulcher, for which he was severely punished on his return to Rome.

# THE BATTLE OF DAMME (1213)

King John of England may not be famous for getting along with his barons, or for governing the country wisely in the absence of his brother, Richard I, but when it came to naval affairs John was in his element. In his wars with King Philip Augustus of France he gave the English their first victory at sea over an enemy that took a lot of convincing that *La Manche* was in fact the English Channel.

In 1213 King Philip had assembled a vast fleet to invade England. In fact, it was not so much a fleet as a collection of everything that floated on the coast facing England, and he prepared to fill it with a large army. But before he could set out for England news reached Philip that his vassal, the Count of Flanders, had revolted and he decided to invade his lands rather than those of the English. This was a big mistake, as it turned out. Without a second thought he ordered his fleet to proceed to Damme, the seaport of Bruges, where it soon became apparent that there was not enough room in the harbour for so many ships. His commanders carelessly anchored some ships outside the harbour and beached the rest. Their crews then went ashore to indulge in a little rape and pillage, leaving no guards to protect the ships.

Meanwhile, the English, commanded by John's able deputy William Longsword, Earl of Salisbury, approached Damme with a force of ships scarcely a third as strong as the French. But with the French fleet

unprotected it was not long before Longsword's English and Flemish troops had captured the French ships and burned them in their hundreds. It was a victory as absolute as any in naval history. The returning French king found nothing but charcoal and the few ships the English had not had time to burn. 'The French know little about the ways of the sea,' the king reflected, and angrily he burned the rest of his ships himself.

# THE BATTLE OF SOUTH FORELAND (1217)

The battle fought in the Channel on St Bartholomew's Day 1217 established two important 'truths' of naval warfare: one was that the fleet which gained the weather gauge and had the wind in their favour had a winning advantage in the days of sail and two, that however terrifying his reputation, the pirate will always be mastered by the true sailor.

The death of King John in 1216 united England once again in support of his nine-year-old son, Henry, and against his French rival Prince Louis. But the French were not prepared to surrender their foothold in England and in August 1217 a French fleet of between 200 and 300 ships crossed the Channel bringing troops and supplies for the French prince. Many of the ships were merchantmen, and they were led by the renegade and pirate, Eustace the Monk. When Eustace's ships were sighted off Dover the governor of the town, Hubert de Burgh, an able man who hated the French pirate with a blazing intensity after his sacking of nearby Folkestone, put to sea with a small force of 30 or so vessels, including sixteen large cogs.

When Hubert drew into sight of the French they mocked the size of his squadron, laughing and boasting that they would soon string up the English from their rigging. But the French were surprised to see that the English were avoiding them and seemed to be heading instead towards Calais. In fact, Hubert was manoeuvring to gain the weather gauge, which would give him a decisive advantage in the coming battle. He could choose when and where to attack, while Eustace could do no more than be carried by the wind. The arrogance and complacency of the Monk and his followers was about to be punished. Outnumbered probably by five to one, Hubert began by attacking the rear of the

French fleet, knowing that the centre and van could not come back to its aid. Using the wind to blow powdered quicklime into the faces of the French, Hubert's knights were irresistible. The English ships moved relentlessly through the French fleet, killing as they went. In panic, Eustace hid below decks and disguised himself to try to evade capture. But he was too well known and too many bitter men had a score to settle with him. His head was cut off and stuck on a pike, while his body was unceremoniously tipped overboard. What followed was a massacre. Without a leader the French crews panicked, many jumping overboard to avoid a crueller death. Eventually, it is said, just fifteen French ships returned to Calais, while those captured were towed triumphantly into Dover. The battle had been a lesson in seamanship.

## THE BATTLE OF SLUYS (1340)

Medieval sea battles were rarely fought out of sight of land and resembled land battles fought on water. But this view does scant justice to the skills of some medieval seamen, notably those from the Italian city-states of Venice, Genoa and Pisa. The English were relatively backward in the maritime arts, though in 1340 – at the start of the Hundred Years War – the English King Edward III was able to assemble a fleet of some 200 ships, filled with soldiers, sailors and archers drawn particularly from the southern counties and the seven Cinque Ports. With this powerful array he gave battle to the French King Philip near the town of Sluys on the coast of Flanders, on 24 June. Although naval tactics were relatively primitive at this time, common sense was always an advantage, and the lack of sense shown by the French commanders and their Genoese mercenaries – who should have known better – contributed to their catastrophic defeat.

The French king had given command of the fleet to two of his bravest knights, the Sieur de Kiriet and the Sieur de Bahuchet, the former probably a Breton and as such likely to be a good sailor. With the two knights was a very experienced sailor, the Genoese Admiral Barbavera, who commanded a squadron of his own

ships. Barbavera pressed for an active response to the English; he argued in favour of weighing anchor and setting out to sea where superior French numbers and size of ship would be an advantage. But the two French knights seemed to have lost their nerve and insisted on fighting on the defensive, staying at anchor in shallow water and lashing their ships together so that the three French divisions were drawn into a single unit. They were convinced that this would make it difficult for the English to board their ships, except at the narrow prow. This was a terrible mistake as it took away from the French all manoeuvrability. The ships in the right and centre, with their thousands of soldiers and crossbowmen, had to stand doing nothing while the English sailed round their left flank and concentrated all their weight on this alone. Barbavera fumed in his trap on the right while the English archers shot down the French knights in their hundreds. The Genoese crossbowmen – as would happen six years later at Crécy – were outshot by the English, five arrows to one dart. With wind and tide in their favour, the English were able to choose where to attack while the French could only stand and wait.

The French left was hinged on the large carrack, the *Great Christopher*, taken from the English in an earlier skirmish and here King Edward's knights made their strongest attacks. Once the English archers had cleared the decks of the foremost ships they were able to occupy the rigging and crows' nests of the French ships and rain death on the trapped French soldiers on the right and in the centre. There was no escape and thousands of French died by drowning rather than face the arrows. Soon the entire left and centre of the French fleet was captured and their crews driven overboard. Only Barbavera, cutting himself free, escaped with a few of his ships. The battle of Sluys gave England control of the Channel and ruled out any immediate threat of a French invasion.

It had been a stunning victory for the weaker fleet which had adopted positive tactics against a passive enemy. It is said 30,000 Frenchmen died – an exaggeration – but probably not by too much. There was no escape at sea, particularly for those in armour. So great was the French defeat that it is said none dared tell the French king. Eventually his jester revealed all with a curious quip: the French must have been braver than the English, for they jumped into the sea by scores, while the islanders stayed in their ships.

The battle of Sluys could be described as a land battle fought at sea. Massed English archers gave notice of the threat they would pose at Crécy and Poitiers by defeating a Franco-Genoese fleet off the coast of Flanders. Victory gave England control of the English Channel.

# THE BATTLE OF NEGROPONT
## (1470)

Command of a fleet in battle is not a job for amateurs and rarely has this been more clearly demonstrated than during the Turkish attack on the Venetian colony of Negropont. To lead a relieving fleet the Venetian authorities appointed Nicolò Canale, 'a man of letters rather than a fighter' and 'a learned man readier to read books rather to direct the affairs of the sea'. As a leading citizen of Venice Canale was prepared to do his best but he lacked both the experience and the necessary toughness. To make matters worse he was also sent against an enemy five times as strong as himself.

Canale left Venice in July 1470 with a fleet of just 53 galleys, and 18 smaller ships, a force quite inadequate to the task he was being set. He sailed on to Crete and then to the island of Euboea, off the eastern coast of Greece. The Venetian defenders of Negropont had put up a strong resistance for three weeks before Canale's arrival, but when the Venetian commander saw the huge size of the Turkish fleet, as well as the quality of its ships, he lost his nerve completely and withdrew to Samothrace and sent appeals to Venice for more help. All that was forthcoming were some indulgences from the Pope: his men could now die with their sins absolved. Canale was not reassured. But the Turkish troops besieging the city were entirely dependent on a pontoon bridge connecting the city to the mainland. If this could be severed the attack would soon fail.

At the urgings of his captains Canale dipped a toe into the world of naval combat. He edged his squadron, with both the wind and the tide in his favour, towards the bridge. Everything pointed to a sudden and decisive strike against the pontoon, just as the Hungarian leader Hunyadi had done the year before to a Turkish force besieging Belgrade. But the water was too cold and Canale removed his toe: in full view of the city walls, with the defenders urging them on, the Venetian fleet withdrew. The tide began to turn and the chance was lost.

With their confidence in Canale broken the Venetian crews began to squabble amongst themselves and mutiny broke out. There was no point in waiting to watch the city fall and Canale ordered a return to Venice. The defenders of Negropont knew they had been abandoned and the next day the Turks burst into the city and massacred the inhabitants. The governor,

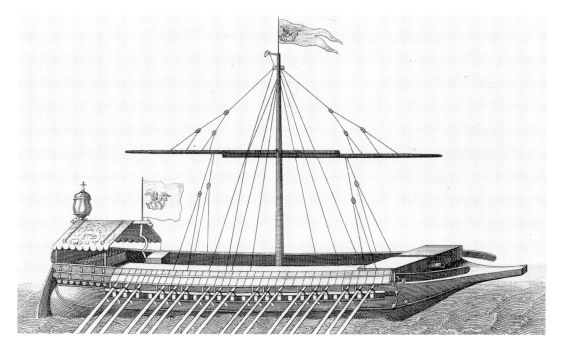

The Venetian galleys of the 15th century were splendid craft, but Venetian admirals rarely rose to the occasion when confronting Turkish opponents.

Paolo Erizzo, was persuaded to surrender on the understanding that he would keep his head. The Turkish Sultan cut him in half at the waist.

When Canale reached Venice he was accused of abandoning Negropont and was put on trial. Yet what did the Venetian authorities expect when they picked such a man? Was he a coward or was he just over-cautious? It is a moot point. Canale surrendered himself to his fate, saying, 'I am here to obey, do with me as you please.' At his trial Canale was found guilty on all charges, particularly that of failing to break the Turkish pontoon when his fleet had the advantage of the wind and were making 15 knots towards it. Nearly three hundred years later a British admiral would be executed for far less (see p. 35), yet Canale escaped with banishment for life to Porto Guaro – just 30 miles away – a small fine and the loss of his rank of captain-general. One imagines, as he returned to his books, that Nicolò Canale was relieved.

## THE BATTLE OF SAPIENZA (1499)

With the advent of Turkish naval power in the eastern Mediterranean the fortunes of Venice declined. In 1500 a Turkish official told the Venetian ambassador, 'Tell the Signoria that they have done with wedding the sea; it is our turn now.' After the disaster at Sapienza the previous year who could deny it?

In 1499 the 65-year-old Antonio Grimani was elected to command the Venetian fleet which would be sent against the Turks. Stirred by recent setbacks the Venetians made a big effort to assemble the best fleet possible, calling up vessels from Candia, Corfu and Dalmatia, and even pressing the city's gondoliers into service with the galleys. Yet behind this warlike preparation there was an air of uncertainty. Grimani was far too old for command and his enormous wealth had enabled him to secure the position of captain-general by a donation of 16,000 ducats to the state. Yet when Grimani tried to ascertain whether he was to seek an engagement with the Turks or to act defensively there was no one to tell him. Thus the fleet sailed without precise instructions and with an elderly leader unsure of his role.

Grimani's fleet of perhaps 170 galleys encountered the Turkish fleet – numerically slightly stronger – under the command of Borrak Rais at Porto Longo, on the island of Sapienza, off the west coast of Greece. He immediately called a council of war and determined to attack the enemy but when this took place everything went wrong. Grimani's orders were chaotic and his commanders would not cooperate with him. Grimani now proved himself to be not only a blunderer but a coward as well, staying well out of the fighting. Some Venetian galleys never even joined the action and there were cries for their captains to be hanged as traitors.

The Venetians withdrew and dropped anchor. They had not suffered very heavy losses and they began to discuss what to do next. Grimani, swaggering boldly to conceal the terrible fright he had just had at being in action, ordered his crews to kill their captains the next day if they did not follow his orders. It was not a very reassuring message when the admiral is the biggest coward of them all. Before the fight could be renewed Grimani was reinforced by four French galleys, which it was hoped would inspire the whole fleet. On the second day of the battle Grimani's orders were so strange that nobody could believe them. Out of a total of 170 galleys at his disposal he sent just two large ones – one Venetian and one French – to take on the entire Turkish fleet. Miraculously, after a furious defence against swarms of Turkish ships, the galleys withdrew unharmed, though what had been achieved nobody seemed to know. Grimani continued to have trouble enforcing his authority on the other captains. 'Through lack of love for Christ and our country, lack of courage, lack of discipline, and lack of reputation', the Venetians were wasting their chances of an important victory.

On 25 August Grimani ordered a further attack on the Turks. At first the Venetians fought well and captured some of the enemy vessels. But then the love of loot overcame the sailors and many stopped fighting to seize what they could from the captured vessels. While disorder broke out in the Venetian fleet the Turks counterattacked, recaptured their lost vessels and won the battle. The French, in disgust at the Venetian leadership, deserted and sailed off to Rhodes. In spite of the courage of individual captains the Venetian fleet was rife with discontent. Grimani had no option but to return home, leaving the Turks to capture Lepanto, the prime aim of their expedition.

Popular fury was widespread at the news and Grimani was brought back to Venice in chains. The mob howled for his blood, particularly as he had secretly been buying support so that he might be Doge. To accusations that he was a coward he rightly pointed out that his instructions had been imprecise and that he had done what he could with poor material. Surprisingly enough he was supported by his officers – among whom were many who should have been on trial with Grimani for cowardice. Found guilty of 'weakness and irresolution', the admiral was banished to the island of Cherso, another victim of an absurd selection procedure.

## THE BATTLE OF DJERBA (1560)

'Vacillating' and 'cowardly' are the two words that best describe Gian Andrea Doria, commander of the Christian fleet at Djerba in 1560. If ever a commander failed his men it was Doria and yet his capacity to survive setbacks that would have broken a better man indicate a strength of purpose that was truly astounding. Eleven years later at Lepanto he was still entrusted with a major command by Don John of Austria – the right wing of the Christian fleet – which Doria completely mishandled, allowing the Turks under Ulugh Ali to fall on the Christian centre.

Command of the Spanish expedition of 1560 – designed to strike at Turkish strongholds on the North African coast – had originally been allocated to the 93-year-old Genoese admiral, Andrea Doria, but he was too ill to go to sea and handed over responsibility to his 20-year-old great-nephew, Gian Andrea. It is indicative of the awe in which the old man was still held that so many experienced captains agreed to sail under the leadership of a callow youth. It is sad to relate that Gian Andrea possessed none of the positive qualities of his great-uncle, yet all and more of his negative ones, for the elder Doria was as Machiavellian as any Medici or Sforza.

The fleet that would sail under Gian Andrea was not large, consisting of about 50 galleys and some 60 or so sailing vessels which carried the 5,000 German, Italian and Spanish troops, with their siege train. For once the Spaniards had taken the Turks by surprise and there was no strong Ottoman presence in the western Mediterranean so, to start with at least, Gian Andrea had things to himself. But vacillation was his undoing. Doria could not decide whether to make a strike at Tripoli and two priceless weeks were wasted in making a decision. Eventually the choice fell on Djerba, and a landing took place on 7 March. But the Christians had already advertised their presence too widely. Doria's ships had had a brush with two Turkish galleys under Ulugh Ali and had allowed them to escape, carrying the news all the way to Constantinople. From that point onwards the Christians were living on borrowed time.

Meanwhile, the Spanish troops had captured Djerba and had begun the construction of a fort which they proposed to garrison and hold. It took nearly two months to complete the structure, during which time the main Turkish fleet under Piali Pasa was racing across the Mediterranean to intercept them. Just as the work on land was completed and some of the troops were being re-embarked on the ships, a frigate sailed into harbour with the alarming news that a large Turkish fleet – in fact, only 86 galleys, but enough – was almost upon them.

A disgraceful scene now followed. The German mercenary troops claimed that their contracts did not cover garrison duty and they insisted on being taken aboard the ships first. It took nearly 24 hours of squabbling and wrangling before the question of precedence was settled and Doria decided to re-embark the whole army. But before he could do so the Turks appeared. If the Christian commanders had kept their heads the Turks could have been held off. All that was needed was for a line of the best Spanish galleys to go out to meet the Turks and hold them out at sea while the troops were taken aboard. But this needed leadership and Doria was past being able to exercise any. He was thinking only of saving his own skin. In great disorder the entire Christian fleet weighed anchor and jostled each other trying to get out of the harbour to escape. When he saw his own way blocked Doria ran his flagship aground, disembarked and rode off into the interior.

Piali Pasa, seeing the extraordinary sight of a fleet behaving like a maddened crowd pursued by an unseen terror, raised his sails and headed into them, capturing or destroying ship after ship with scarcely any resistance. The Christian losses were very heavy. Some 30 galleys were taken or sunk, including the *capitanas* of the Pope, Sicily, Monaco and Terranova. Others followed Doria, running themselves aground and taking refuge in the fort. The one bright point in a dismal day was the heroic display by the galleon from Cigala which drove off eighteen Turkish galleys including Piali Pasa's flagship.

The scene now shifted to the land where a large Turkish force landed and began to besiege the fort. Gian Andrea Doria, with certain gentlemen of his entourage, escaped in a fast sailing frigate before the final catastrophe, when the garrison was forced to surrender from lack of water. The defeat was a shattering one for Spain, made more so by the poor resistance put up by her crews. Not until Don John's victory at Lepanto in 1571 was Christian pride restored in the western Mediterranean.

# THE DUTCH IN THE MEDWAY
## (1667)

During the Second Dutch War, 1665-7, the Dutch Admiral de Ruyter achieved the important feat of sailing up the River Medway, capturing the largest English warship of her day, the *Royal Charles*, and destroying numerous other ships, as well as ravaging the dockyards at Chatham. It was one of the most humiliating naval disasters in English history, due, to a large extent, to the incompetence of King Charles II and the Admiralty. Unlike the many other naval setbacks in this book, the Dutch raid in the Medway is not even redeemed, from the English point of view, by the courage of the common sailors. In every way the Dutch raid was an indictment of administrative incompetence, popular hysteria, and rank cowardice.

The English had been given many advance warnings of the possibility of the very raid that the Dutch carried out. Sir William Monson had tried to warn the king of the vulnerability of the defences on the Medway but his warnings were simply ignored. In 1660 the garrison at Upnor Castle on the banks of the Medway had been just 30 men. After Monson's warning the garrison was removed altogether because there was not enough money to pay even that many men. At Sheerness the authorities could not find enough men to build a fort at the entrance to the Medway. So low were the wages and so poor the conditions that nobody would work there. Although a chain had been manufactured to act

The Dutch admiral Michael Adriaanszoon de Ruyter (1607–76). De Ruyter's raid on the Medway in June 1667, during which the English flagship the *Royal Charles* was captured and then taken back to Holland, was one of the most humiliating episodes in British naval history.

as a boom across the Medway, two ships – the *Matthias* and the *Charles V* – had to be on permanent station to protect it and these could not be properly crewed, for the Admiralty had not enough money to pay the seamen. At the Chatham dockyards the workers were in a state of mutiny, again over the non-payment of wages. Sailors were deserting the navy in droves to work on merchant vessels, complaining that they had

to use half their wages to bribe the navy paymasters to give them the rest. More men were brought in to replace the missing sailors but these were generally of poor quality, as one observer wrote, 'Poor silly lads and raw country fellows.'

Before the Dutch were prepared to risk the difficult passage of the Thames and Medway they needed to be certain they would not be trapped on the many sandbanks and mudflats. What they needed were Englishmen with special knowledge of the area who would be willing to serve the Dutch for a big reward. Sad to relate there were many such men, including English seamen. One man, Robert Holland, had served as a captain during the Commonwealth and, embittered by his lack of prospects under Charles II, he readily turned traitor and was in the forefront of the Dutch operation. To support the fleet a force of some 4,000 Dutch soldiers were to be conveyed in transports under the command of another English renegade, Colonel Thomas Dolman.

On 4 June the Dutch fleet of perhaps 80 ships set sail for the Thames estuary, their aim being to capture or destroy the English men-of-war stationed in the Medway. What preparations had the English made to repel the invaders? The answer is virtually none. There had been warnings from a number of sources yet the complacency of the king and his court was astonishing. Charles II believed that the Dutch would never dare to do such a thing as invade English territory and that his ally, Louis XIV of France, would certainly prevent them. Rather than strengthening the fleet against the Dutch threat the Lord High Admiral, the Duke of York, had actually decided to make cuts in the size of the navy. Those ships in service were also to be reduced to skeleton crews to save money. The king's Secretary of State, Lord Arlington, smugly told the king that all the Dutch preparations were mere 'bravado' and that like themselves the Dutch could not afford to fight a war.

In spite of England's belief that it was all bravado, the Dutch reached the North Foreland and anchored, prior to holding a council of war aboard de Ruyter's flagship, the *Zeven Provincien*. Even when reports reached London that the Dutch were at the mouth of the Thames, the government refused to take the threat seriously. For three days no action was taken to prepare for an attack. On the very date that the Dutch anchored, Samuel Pepys reports:

> Captain Perriman brings us word how the *Happy Returne*'s crew below in the Hope, ordered to carry the Portugal Embassador to Holland (and the Embassador, I think, on board) refuse to go till paid; and by their example two or three more ships are in a mutiny: which is a sad consideration while so many of the enemy's ships are at this day triumphing in the sea.

It was not until 10 June that the English began to respond and then it was only with blind panic. In Gravesend the local population simply fled from their homes leaving 'not twelve men' behind to defend the town. At Sheerness the English man-of-war *Unity* fired a single broadside at the approaching Dutch before fleeing up the Medway. At the Sheerness Fort two men were killed, whereupon the whole garrison except for seven abandoned their positions and ran off. The remaining seven, made suddenly aware of the value of discretion, soon followed.

The following day the Duke of Albemarle arrived at Chatham but what he found was not to his liking:

> I found scarce twelve of eight hundred men which were then in the king's pay, in his Majesty's yards; and these so distracted with fear that I could have little or no service from them . . . I went to visit the chain, which was the next thing to be fortified for the security of the river, where I found no works for the defence of it. I then immediately set soldiers to work for the raising two batteries, for there was no other men to be got; and when I had employed them in it, I found it very difficult to get tools, for Commissioner Pett would not furnish us with above thirty till, by breaking open the stores, we found more . . .

Albemarle's efforts were to be in vain. The Dutch Captain Jan van Brakel in the *Vrede* offered to take two fireships against the chain and break it. To do so he would have to overcome the resistance of the *Unity*. In the event that turned out to be very little. So dispirited were the English sailors that they had to be kept aboard by force. While van Brakel captured the *Unity*, the fireship *Pro Patria* pressed hard against the chain, which either broke or sank. The way was now open for the Dutch ships to break into the upper reaches of the Medway, destroying the *Charles V* and the *Matthias* as they went. Their main target was the *Royal Charles*, greatest ship in the English fleet, which was lying unprotected and which was abandoned without a fight. Albemarle, who was desperately trying to organize some defences, now put himself at the head of some pikemen, ready to make a 'do or die' attempt to save the flagship, but his friends persuaded him not to throw away his life and he withdrew with the rest. On the *Royal Charles* the only sign of fighting was between the Dutch commanders who had taken her and wanted the honour of the prize.

Opposite the Chatham dockyards the Dutch battleships engaged the guns of Upnor Castle, while their fireships burned first the *Loyal London* and then the *Royal Oak* and *Royal James*. The courage of the Dutch crews seemed to be in inverse proportion to the cowardice of the English, who abandoned every ship and position as the Dutch reached them. The only exception to this shameful episode was the example set by Captain Archibald Douglas with his Scots, who occupied the *Royal Oak* and fought aboard her until she burned away and sank, Douglas dying in the terrible conflagration.

Showing consummate skill the Dutch returned down the Medway with their prizes, drawing praise even from the English for their navigation. In London, Pepys tells us, hundreds of people besieged the banks trying to withdraw all their money for fear that the Dutch would come up the Thames and take the capital. And everywhere in London the search went on for scapegoats. The chief culprit, of course, was the king himself, who had allowed his navy to fall into such a disgraceful state. Seamen's wives marched up and down outside the home of the old chancellor, Clarendon, shouting, 'This comes of your not paying our husbands.' A more realistic target was Commissioner Peter Pett, who was specifically in charge of Chatham Dockyards. The Duke of Albemarle blamed Pett for the lack of defences on the Medway and accused him of refusing to release the best wood when the duke was trying to build his defensive batteries. But it was pointless blaming individuals. In 1667, the people of London were recovering from the Great Plague and the Great Fire, and the Dutch attack seemed further confirmation that something worse could always happen. Their courage was in their boots and so they ran when they met the invaders. Ironically, it was peace that the Dutch wanted, not further war. They had delivered a painful lesson to English arrogance and brought the English government to their senses. The Second Dutch War ended a few months later with the Peace of Breda. Pepys records that people were pleased to see the war ended but they were also ashamed.

## THE BATTLE OF OLAND (1676)

During the war between Sweden and the alliance of Denmark and Holland, much of the fighting took place on the Baltic Sea. What advantage the Swedes enjoyed in numbers and quality of ships they undoubtedly surrendered through the incompetence of their inexperienced admirals. A single incident from the early part of the war illustrates how naval disasters are just as often man-made as due to the action of the elements.

On 6 September 1675 the Swedish Admiral Stenbock put to sea with a large fleet of 66 ships,

including the mighty *Krona*, whose 128 guns made her one of the strongest ships afloat. But appearances can be deceptive. The Swedish fleet was at a low ebb and the voyage consisted of a series of mishaps. To start with, the two flagships, *Krona* and *Svärd*, took eight hours to weigh anchor. While the rest of the fleet waited, the *Jupiter* collided with the *Postiljon*, forcing the latter to return for repairs. A few days later the *Krona* lost her anchor. Stenbock lowered another anchor, while he looked for the first, but forgot that he had ordered the rest of the fleet to sail and had not cancelled the order. The fleet put out to sea and stayed there all day wondering where the commander had got to. A gale began to blow and the *Elefant* collided with the *Merkurius*, and then later on with the *Drake*, dismasting both of them. Other ships were wrecked and the *Jupiter*, without any orders, sailed home on its own initiative. Unfortunately it lost its anchor and was blown out to sea just as the rest of the fleet were returning. The voyage had been unanimously cancelled.

But if the Swedish fleet was such a threat to itself what would happen when it encountered the combined Danish-Dutch fleet, commanded as it was by the formidable Martin Tromp? The answer came when the two fleets met at the battle of Oland on 1 June 1676. The Swedish fleet, now commanded by Admiral Creutz, consisted of 26 battleships and 12 frigates with 2,184 guns, against the Allied fleet under Tromp of 25 battleships, 10 frigates and 1,727 guns. The advantage appeared to lie with the Swedes but their commander, Creutz, had never commanded a fleet before, whereas Tromp was a legend in his lifetime.

The battle began in earnest when Tromp's flagship, the *Christianus V*, engaged Creutz's flagship, the huge *Krona*. The Swedish ship had its lower gun ports open and was battering away at a Danish fireship, when Admiral Uggla – commanding the Swedish van – fired a gun forward to recall his advanced ships. Creutz, in the *Krona*, mistook this signal for a gun fired aft – the signal to go about. Furiously shouting, 'Where the deuce is Uggla going?', Creutz ordered the rest of the fleet to tack. But his seamanship let him down disastrously. His fleet had been sailing with the wind abaft the beam, whereas on the starboard tack he would be close hauled. The open gun ports would then, of course, be on the lee side. With the Swedish ships carrying full sail Creutz should have shortened his sail or closed the gun ports. He did neither and the consequences were all too predictable. The *Krona* heeled alarmingly and the gun ports went under water. It was now too late to do anything to save the great ship and another gust of wind turned her on her side. Before she could sink flames burst out of the magazine followed by a terrible explosion which tore the ship to pieces. The *Krona* sank with over 800 of her crew, including the commander.

Uggla could only watch in horror for few moments before it was his turn. The fleet was now in chaos, with some going one way and some another. Uggla's flagship, the *Svärd*, lost her mainmast and was disabled; the *Venus* lost her topmast, the *Merkurius* was badly holed below the water line. The battle was turning into a rout. Uggla managed to set fire to Tromp's ship but the flames were soon brought under control, and the Swedish admiral had to strike his colours to the Dutch commander. But just as Tromp moved up to take his prize a Dutch fireship intervened and set the *Svärd* alight, causing her to blow up with the loss of over 600 of her crew including Uggla.

Both Swedish flagships had therefore disappeared in spectacular fashion, but there was still a third disaster to come for the Swedes. At the sight of *Svärd*'s fate most of the Swedish ships simply panicked and fled. But in the chaos a third great Swedish ship – the *Apple* – ran aground on a reef and was wrecked. The battle thus ended in a total defeat for the Swedes who had lost their three greatest ships, along with five others. Creutz's failure as an admiral had contributed much to the disaster, yet morale within the Swedish fleet had been low before he took up his command and so the blame is not his alone. The results of the battle were serious as the Danish and Dutch allies now had complete control of the Baltic Sea.

# THE BATTLE OF BEACHY HEAD
## (1690)

The Carthaginians had a nasty way of dealing with commanders who failed: they crucified them. In Revolutionary France they used the guillotine. The British have been known to shoot failed admirals – Byng, for example (see p. 35) – but most often they give them a chance to explain themselves at a court-martial. Such was the fate that awaited Admiral Arthur Herbert, Lord Torrington, after his return from the battle of Beachy Head in 1690. First lodged in the Tower, Torrington was accused of 'high crimes' and later court-martialled

at Sheerness. His fellow admirals acquitted him of all charges. Yet in some ways he was very fortunate. Although an intensely brave man Torrington had failed to carry out his direct orders, not by disobediently forcing an action with the enemy when required to desist, but rather by allowing his head to rule his heart and by fighting tamely for fear of suffering irreversible losses. There was logic in what Torrington did, literally to preserve a 'fleet in being', but his orders had been to fight and that is what he did not do. What was worse, his Dutch allies did fight and took most of the casualties. They were aggrieved at their English allies and felt that Torrington had abandoned them to the French.

After William of Orange's invasion of England in 1688 the English navy found itself stretched as rarely before. Although there was the usual need to patrol the Channel to watch the main French fleet at Brest, an additional strong squadron had to be sent to the Mediterranean under Vice-Admiral Henry Killigrew. A further force then had to be found to escort to Spain a princess whom the king there had married by proxy, which onerous task fell to Lord Russell, while Sir Clowdesley Shovel had to convoy King William himself to Carrickfergus in Ireland. This had the effect of diminishing English naval strength in the Channel to such a degree that the French decided to exploit the situation. Admiral Tourville, with 68 men-of-war – and flying his flag in the magnificent new 104-gun *Soleil Royal* – came out into the Channel to challenge the English commander Torrington, and his Dutch ally, Cornelis Evertson, who had between them just 56 ships-of-the-line. With such an advantage the French were certain that they could defeat the English or drive them back into harbour. Either way, the Channel would be open for France to undertake a successful invasion in support of the exiled Catholic King James II.

In view of the superiority of the enemy, and believing that he should preserve his ships to face a possible invasion, Torrington would have preferred to avoid fighting Tourville at such an obvious disadvantage. But in the absence of King William, the Queen sent firm orders to her commander that he must fight the French, whatever the odds. Torrington was clearly dismayed by such a peremptory order to engage – which bore the stamp of his political opponents Nottingham and Russell – and reacted in the worst possible way. He accepted the letter of the law but not its spirit. Thus he would fight, because the Queen bade him do it, but he would fight faintly and seek to disengage as the opportunity arose.

On 30 June Tourville's French fleet was passing Beachy Head and Torrington, flying his flag in the 100-gun *Royal Sovereign* – now nearly 50 years old – gained the weather gauge of him and came down upon him in order of battle. In his van was the Dutch squadron of 22 ships under Admiral Evertson and it was this force which had most of the fighting, at different times facing as many as three separate French divisions and a host of ships under Château-Renault, de Nesmond and Tourville himself, and being badly mauled. The English centre commanded by Torrington kept at a greater distance – up to 500 metres – from the French centre and here the fighting was less intense, but the English rear under Rear-Admiral Delavall, who was disconcerted by Torrington's apparent passivity, came to grips with the French rear commanded by D'Estrées at close range.

The battle was entirely in the French favour and the Anglo-Dutch fleet was facing overwhelming defeat. However, as darkness fell Torrington cleverly anchored his ships and the French drifted past them, unable to regain the wind and return to finish them off. Torrington had averted a disaster but there was no way in which he could disguise a defeat. The English admiral managed to get his ships back into the Thames but not without losses. The English 70-gun *Anne* had to be beached at Winchelsea, where she was later burned. The Dutch lost the *Utrecht* in the battle, and three more ships-of-the-line in the escape. As many as ten smaller vessels were lost and most of the Dutch and some of the English men-of-war had sustained very heavy damage. Dutch casualties had been considerable including two rear-admirals killed. England's allies were convinced that Torrington had abandoned them in the battle and, in spite of his acquittal at court-martial, King William could never bring himself to forgive the man who had deserted his countrymen.

## BENBOW'S LAST FIGHT (1702)

The story of Admiral Benbow's last fight with the French in 1702 is one of the most famous in the annals of the Royal Navy, preserved in legend and in song. It is famous not only for the virtually unsupported struggle that Benbow's flagship, the *Breda*, made against four and sometimes five French men-of-war, but also for

Admiral John Benbow (1653–1702) won renown as a fighting admiral for his many tussles with the French in the English Channel in the 1690s. His daring attempt to pursue the retreating French in the Caribbean in 1702, which was defied by his own captains, has become part of British naval folklore.

the most disgraceful cowardice exhibited by the captains of the other vessels in Benbow's command.

At the outbreak of the War of the Spanish Succession in Europe, Vice-Admiral John Benbow, commanding a British squadron at Port Royal in Jamaica, set out to intercept a similar force under the French Admiral Ducasse. On 19 August the two squadrons, the English being somewhat the stronger, sighted each other off Santa Marta, near the Gulf of Venezuela, and a complex six-day action began.

Benbow sighted six French ships – four of them battleships mounting between 60 and 70 guns – steering to the westward and seeking to avoid battle. He immediately gave chase, ordering Captain Richard Kirkby in the *Defiance* to take the lead, followed by the

*Pendennis*, the *Windsor*, the flagship *Breda*, the *Greenwich*, the *Ruby* and finally the *Falmouth*. But Kirkby was very slow to move up and Benbow noticed that as soon as the *Defiance* and the *Windsor* – under Captain Constable – received fire from the French they immediately pulled away out of range. This was the start of nearly a week of agony for Benbow, an officer who had risen the hard way and was renowned in the navy for his rough tongue and his fighting spirit.

The first day's fighting – what there was of it – was between the rear French vessels and Kirkby and Constable, the most cowardly of the British commanders. Kirkby was already unpopular on his ship, the *Defiance*, and during the brief exchange of fire the wounded coxswain of that vessel denounced his captain as a coward. When warned to watch his mouth by an officer many of the ship's gunners joined in, condemning Kirkby for taking the French shots and not fighting back.

For the second day Benbow decided to lead by example. He placed his flagship, the *Breda*, at the head of the British line, and hoisted signal for the *Defiance* and *Windsor* to back him up. He was wasting his time. Only the *Ruby*, smallest of his ships, supported him in action against Ducasse's vessels, while the rest of the squadron stayed three or four miles away and watched. Benbow's desperate signals to the *Defiance* to come up were simply ignored.

On the third day, the *Breda* and the *Ruby* again bore the brunt of the fighting. Benbow managed to shatter one of the French ships with his guns but the gallant *Ruby*, assailed by three heavy ships in turn, came in for heavy punishment and the admiral was finally forced to tow her out of the fight, and order her to return to Port Royal. The *Defiance* and the *Windsor* were in range of the French several times during the day but fired not a single shot. Kirkby's excuse for not firing was that he was not apparently 'within point-blank range of the sternmost' of the French ships. The boatswain of the *Defiance* told Kirkby that the admiral was signalling from the *Breda* for him to join the line of battle, whereupon Kirkby told him 'to hold his tongue' otherwise 'he would run his sword into him'. The gunners apparently cried out 'they had as good throw the guns overboard as stand by them'.

On the fourth day the rearmost ship of the line, the *Falmouth*, seeing the cowardice of the other captains, pushed up to join Benbow in the van, while Kirkby and Constable stayed some distance off as if waiting to see the admiral destroyed by the enemy. Meanwhile Captain Cooper Wade of the *Greenwich* had joined the

others in their virtual mutiny, answering Benbow when he asked why he was sailing away that his ship would not answer its helm.

On the fifth day there was no fighting but Benbow continued his relentless pursuit of the French squadron, this time accompanied only by the *Falmouth*, and with the rest of his ships trailing along behind. But in the early hours of the sixth day the *Breda* came up with the French ships and a fierce battle ensued. After an hour's fighting a chainshot shattered Benbow's right leg but he insisted on conducting the battle until by the first light of dawn he could see that the *Breda* had badly damaged another one of the French 70-gun ships, which was helpless in the water. This seemed to attract the *Defiance* and the *Windsor*, which came up and started firing into the wreck. However, when the courageous French crew fired back the *Defiance* drew out of range, to the great disgust of her crew. Seeing that the *Breda* was unsupported three other French ships returned and took their shattered comrade in tow and so Benbow was robbed of his prize.

By this stage the admiral had lost all patience and sent messages to each of his captains to say that he was amazed at their behaviour. This prompted Captain Kirkby to come aboard the flagship and tell Benbow that he was sorry to see him injured but he had brought it on himself. The squadron was exhausted after the six-day battle and was far too weak to engage the French successfully. Benbow offered to listen to the rest of the captains and they joined Kirkby on the *Breda*. All six captains signed a resolution against fighting further on the grounds that they were short of men, out of ammunition, were suffering from disabled guns and rigging, lacked wind to catch the French and that the enemy was stronger than they were. Benbow was beside himself with rage, saying that in future he would only dare to go to sea with his relations around him as he could trust nobody else. This put an end to the battle as Benbow knew that if he continued to fight the French alone, sooner or later he would be sunk or taken prisoner to no good purpose. For the moment the captains, led by Kirkby and Constable, had won.

Such cowardice was not unique by any means but on such a scale it was quite remarkable. Apparently on the few occasions that they had been engaged with the enemy the captains had shown extraordinary pusillanimity. A lieutenant on the *Greenwich* reported that Captain Wade had been so frightened that he had said, 'If any of the enemy's ships boarded us we should be immediately taken for he was not prepared to defend himself.' The lieutenant suggested that Wade go below and bolt down the hatches, whereupon the captain complained that his windows had not been planked up and the French might come through there. Meanwhile, the boatswain on the *Defiance* reported that Kirkby hid behind the mizzen mast when there was any firing, or lay prone on the deck.

Benbow returned to Port Royal in Jamaica and immediately instigated court-martial proceedings against the captains for cowardice, disobedience and neglect of duty. His leg had been amputated and he was a dying man, but he was determined to see justice done or else 'nobody is ever safe to head any party if not stood by'. The court was presided over by Admiral Whetstone and there could be little doubt about the verdict on Kirkby and Constable, who were both found guilty and sentenced to be shot; Hudson of the *Pendennis* would have shared their fate but died before the trial and Cooper Wade of the *Greenwich* escaped with his life but was dismissed the service and imprisoned. Fogg of the *Breda* and Vincent of the *Falmouth* were able to prove that they had only signed Kirkby's resolution for fear that the others would desert the squadron and leave them alone to fight the French. Benbow himself spoke in their defence and both were exonerated. The admiral never lived to see the end of the trial, dying on 4 November 1702 from the wound he suffered in the battle. If anything could have lifted the 'melancholy' which afflicted him in his last days it may have been the letter from his erstwhile foe, Admiral Ducasse. The Frenchman wrote to congratulate Benbow on his courageous fight and to say, 'I had no hope but to have supped in your cabin. As for your cowardly captains, hang them, for, by Heaven, they deserve it.' Such sentiments give another meaning to the phrase 'a band of brothers'.

# THE BATTLE OF TOULON (1744)

In 1742 Admiral Thomas Matthews was given the command of England's Mediterranean Fleet, a far from easy office in which he was likely to face not only the the fleet of Spain, with whom England was at war, but possibly France as well. It was more than ever essential that he should mould a tight command but this would depend a lot on the relationship he developed with his subordinate commanders. In fact, Matthews was a poor

choice for a number of reasons. In the first place, at 65 he was really too old for such onerous duty and, in spite of being a brave and capable officer in his younger days he had spent a long period ashore, spending the years from 1724 to 1736 running his own estates and the following six as commissioner of Chatham Dockyard. In addition he was plagued by a urinary complaint – the gravel – which made him extremely ill-tempered and intolerant, so much so that the Italians nicknamed him *Il Furibondo*. In a phrase, he was no longer really fit for active service. Although nobody would have questioned his courage or his strategic appreciation, there had to be severe doubts about his health and his capacity to get on with his subordinates.

Matters would have been easier if Matthews had not had as his second-in-command Vice-Admiral Richard Lestock, just three years his junior in age, and by no means his junior in ability, experience and seamanship. Lestock had enjoyed a fine career and had played a notable part in Admiral Vernon's expedition to Cartagena in 1740. Unfortunately, Lestock and Matthews had met before, and they hated each other. While Lestock had commanded a squadron in the Medway, Matthews had been in charge of Chatham Dockyard. It may have been a case of the pot calling the kettle black, but Matthews insisted that Lestock – who suffered severely from gout – was physically unfit for an active command. To make matters worse, prior to Matthews' arrival in the Mediterranean, Lestock had been in acting command of the Mediterranean Fleet and was convinced that he could do a better job than Matthews. When he failed to get the command, it may be that Lestock determined to ruin Matthews, though we have no certain evidence of this. We may be better advised to let the events speak for themselves.

On his arrival at Villefranche, where the English fleet was anchored, Matthews got off on the wrong foot by insulting Lestock in front of visiting Piedmontese dignitaries. He then sent Lestock with a small squadron to watch the French at Toulon, while he involved himself with Piedmontese politics to the disapproval of his rear-admiral, William Rowley, who hardly ever saw his commander and was never consulted when tactics were being discussed.

On 8 February 1744, the Franco-Spanish fleet sailed from Toulon, while the English fleet – just 20 miles down the road at Villefranche – also prepared to sail. With battle imminent Lestock visited Matthews on board the fleet flagship, the *Namur*, to ask whether the commander had any orders for him. Matthews – incredibly – replied that he had no orders for him, observed what a cold evening it was and curtly wished him good night. At his later court-martial Matthews claimed that his behaviour 'arose out of pure regard for the Vice-Admiral's state of health'. That Lestock must have left the flagship in a fury hardly needs mentioning. But how would he react tomorrow if battle should be joined?

The following day Matthews formed up his fleet with Rowley in the van in the *Barfleur*, himself commanding the centre in the *Namur* with Lestock leading the rear in the *Neptune*. Both the Franco-Spanish and the British fleets had 29 ships-of-the-line but Lestock's behaviour was soon to give the enemy a substantial superiority. When Matthews came up with the Franco-Spanish ships he had advantage of the wind. Rowley's van came into action against the French centre commanded by the 78-year-old Admiral de Court de la Bruyère, while Matthews himself attacked the Spanish rear under Don José Navarro. This left the French van unopposed, while the English rear under Lestock remained several miles behind the action. Lestock was actually working to rule, using as his justification the Rules of Engagement which forbade him to break the line to engage because the line-of-battle signal was still flying from the *Namur*. He was taking advantage of a technical excuse to abandon Matthews at whatever cost to his country.

Meanwhile, the fighting was intense and as Matthews closed on the Spanish admiral he expected the rest of his fleet to form up in a new line based on him. But few of the English captains – apart from Edward Hawke in the *Berwick* – took any notice. While four of the Spanish ships pounded the *Namur* and one of its supporters, the *Marlborough*, Hawke achieved the heroic feat of forcing the Spanish ship *Poder* to strike her colours. But elsewhere, some eleven English captains chose to conform to the original line of battle, and did not enter the fight.

The French admiral now signalled for his van to come about and put the English van under a double fire, which forced Matthews to order his fleet to go about as well. With his flagship and the *Marlborough* severely damaged, Matthews had no alternative but to make his way to Minorca, while the Spaniards headed for Cartagena and the French for Toulon. It had been a hard-fought action, with heavy casualties, but with no advantage to either side. In fact the recriminations afterwards were almost more bloody than the battle itself. The Spaniards complained that the French had not supported them – an odd assertion in view of de Court's skilful performance – and the old admiral was

sacrificed to his new allies by being dismissed. Once the English reached Minorca Matthews ordered Lestock to strike his flag and return home: Lestock replied that nothing would please him more. The two old gentlemen now began a battle of words which made the battle of Toulon seem like a tea party. Matthews followed Lestock to England and the battle was fought and refought inside and outside the House of Commons, and later in courts-martial which both admirals demanded. The battle of Toulon was remarkable in being the occasion for a further eleven courts-martial of captains, most in Lestock's rear division. Sir John Norris – the 90-year-old Admiral of the Fleet – suffered the disgrace of his son failing to turn up for court-martial and staying abroad.

The courts-martial of the two chief protagonists were awaited with great anticipation by the general populace. Two admirals – one of them John Byng – and fourteen captains sat in judgment on Admirals Matthews and Lestock. But Lestock, an MP and a cunning litigant, appears to have suborned witnesses and tampered with ships' logs, so that while he was found not guilty, Matthews never really had a chance. Matthews was condemned and cashiered for having endangered his fleet by engaging in battle before his vice-admiral – Lestock – could come to his aid, and for breaking the line of battle to engage the enemy. It was an outrageous decision in every way. However unpleasant Matthews was as a person, he had undoubtedly carried the fight to the enemy and personally risked himself and his flagship in the action. Lestock, on the other hand, had played the renegade traitor. However much excuse there might be for Lestock in personal terms – through his illness and the insults heaped on him by Matthews which must have embittered his mind – one cannot justify his treachery, which might have resulted in a major defeat for king and country, and the unnecessary death of many innocent English sailors. Yet Lestock did not live long to enjoy his triumph; within three years he was dead from 'gout of the stomach'.

# THE ARMADA OF 1779

While the War of American Independence has rightly drawn the attention of most historians of the period away from what was happening in Europe, events of a potentially vital – if ultimately sterile – nature were taking place in the English Channel. The French and Spanish, balked so often in the past, were attempting nothing less than a full-scale invasion of England. Taking advantage of Britain's commitments across the Atlantic – with one British fleet in American waters and another under Rodney in the West Indies – the French and Spanish assembled a combined fleet which out-numbered available British strength by two to one. Furthermore, they had timed their expedition with great skill, for political schism in Britain had left her vulnerable as never before. Yet the great invasion plan failed and ever since has earned just a footnote in the history of the war with the American colonies, becoming known as 'The Other Armada'.

The French plan to invade England was relatively simple, if any combined operation in conjunction with the Spaniards as allies can ever be called simple. Two armies – of 20,000 soldiers each – were assembled on the coast of France, complete with their transports: one at St Malo and the other at Le Havre. The Comte d'Orvilliers would sail with the main French fleet from Toulon and rendezvous with the Spanish fleet under the elderly Don Luis de Córdoba, before sailing into the Channel and taking command of it, if necessary by defeating the British Home Fleet. Once command of the seas had been achieved the transports would sail from their home ports and occupy Portsmouth and the Isle of Wight, preparatory to marching on London. It sounded eminently possible and yet the French were overlooking the vagaries of wind, tide and weather, as well as their even more unpredictable allies.

The plan was to be set in motion in May 1779 but one delay after another meant that d'Orvilliers could not sail until early June. And when at last the fleet set off his ships sailed undermanned and under-provisioned. To add to his problems, the standard of his officers and men was very poor. To increase the number of senior officers many unsuitable junior ones had been rapidly promoted, while to fill their places involved scouring the ranks of common seamen. It was said that 'the ignorance and inexperience of three quarters of the officers on board the fleet was so great that there were ships in which neither the captain nor any other officer knew how to take a bearing'. The seamen had not been found from the mercantile marine or the fishing fleets, but instead from hospitals or prisons. Speed had been so vital that corners had been cut in preparation.

D'Orvilliers first sailed to Corunna where he had agreed to meet the Spanish ships. However, quixotically, the Spaniards expressed complete surprise at his arrival and took a further six weeks to make the rendezvous. They then claimed to know nothing of the French plans, which had been laid out carefully for them some months before. Another week passed as the French tried to devise signals which would allow the Spaniards – too proud to accept orders from French-men – to take orders only from other Spaniards. During the negotiations the Spanish constantly pressed for a change of plan and a descent on Gibraltar instead. The French commander – at his wits' end – eventually devised a formula for dividing his fleet into three squadrons, each of nine French and six Spanish ships, while retaining a 'corps of observation' of sixteen Spanish ships, all under the Spanish admiral, thereby giving him in effect a separate command. With 66 ships-of-the-line and a swarm of frigates and smaller craft the Franco-Spanish Armada seemed a very strong one, and far outnumbered the battleships that the British could employ in the Channel – 40 at the most.

But the two months delay in coordinating the fleets had done more damage to them than any engagement with the enemy. The French ships had been at sea since June and had already used up a large part of their food and water. Moreover, the poor living conditions aboard the French ships had encouraged the spread of disease; first scurvy, then smallpox and finally 'putrid fever'. D'Orvilliers' own son died in his arms and this loss seemed to fill him with such depression that he was a broken man from then onwards. As he wrote:

Blackness overwhelms me . . . What a wonderful opportunity is slipping from our grasp. England, without resources or allies was on the point of being taught a lesson; success seemed within our grasp; at last we could hope to humiliate our proud rival but the elements are arming themselves against us and staying the stroke of our vengeance.

It was August before the Armada eventually entered the Channel and now it felt the full fury of the August gales. So many French seamen were sick that there were often too few to operate the ships effectively, let alone man the guns if a battle took place. Daily, d'Orvilliers received chilling tales of disease, death and short provisions from his captains. All he could do was to send begging letters by despatch boat to the Minister of Marine, asking for more supplies and, especially, more men. Yet these were never forthcoming. After all, there had not been enough sailors to man the ships in the first place.

The Franco-Spanish ships managed to reach Ply-mouth and then, to their frustration, found themselves blown back all the way into the Atlantic. It was like a game of 'snakes and ladders' in which d'Orvilliers had an unerring knack of finding the snakes. So frustrated were the French by this time that they abandoned their original plan, which was to seize Portsmouth, in favour of taking Plymouth and occupying Cornwall, where they would winter prior to an assault on London in the Spring. It was a mad plan. The French underestimated the severe weather they would meet off Cornwall. D'Orvilliers battled his way back to Plymouth but was then driven back into the Atlantic again. At the end of August the French decided to lie off the Isles of Scilly and try to ambush the British fleet, if it should pass.

Meanwhile, the British fleet was having problems of its own. After the great days of Hawke, Anson, Boscawen and others, the navy was at a very low ebb. There were men of ability like Lord Howe, but they often refused commands, and the Admiralty under Lord Sandwich was as inefficient as in the days of Nottingham and Buckingham in the early 17th century. Moreover, the service was in schism, rent by the dispute between Admiral Keppel and Admiral Palliser over the conduct of the battle of Ushant the year before. A joke then popular spoke of the two contending parties as Montagus (the family name of Lord Sandwich) and the Capulets (Keppelites). As one serving officer wrote:

> The navy is torn to pieces by dissension. Officers scarcely ever see each other except when on duty. Nor have they any longer access to the tables of their superiors, as formerly when an Anson or a Boscawen, a Hawke, a Saunders, a Keppel commanded the fleets of England. Then all was cordiality, ardour and affection. The commanders took a pride in teaching the inferior orders their professional duties. Now party, disunion, mutual jealousy and want of confidence are universal.

When Keppel resigned his command of the Channel Fleet in March 1779 the government had found it difficult to get a worthy successor. Keppel's friends Howe and Mann both refused the job, as they despised Lord Sandwich. Eventually the government was saved from an embarrassing situation when the sick, elderly and far from inspired Vice-Admiral Sir Charles Hardy – then governor of Greenwich Hospital – offered to take on the job. Hardy would have been an even more dreadful candidate had the king not been able to persuade the very able Richard Kempenfelt to act as flag captain to Hardy aboard the new three-decker *Victory*.

The British fleet eventually formed up in three divisions: the van commanded by Vice-Admiral Darby in the 100-gun *Britannia*; Hardy in the centre, flying his

flag in the *Victory*; and Rear-Admiral Digby in the 90-gun *Prince George* took the rear. A fourth flag officer, Sir John Lockhart, flew his flag in the 100-gun *Royal George*. Present with Hardy were two stars of the next generation, Captains Jervis and Duncan.

Thus equipped, Sir Charles Hardy left harbour at the Isle of Wight on 16 June, with 30 battleships and eight frigates, a force approximately as strong as the French fleet alone but far inferior to the combined Franco-Spanish fleet it expected to have to face. In the next two months Hardy was to be reinforced by only an extra eight ships of the line. And so he faced an awkward decision: whether to adopt a masterly and watchful policy or straightaway give battle to the enemy, as the king demanded in resounding words, 'It was the vigour of mind shown by Queen Elizabeth and her subjects, added to the assistance of divine Providence, that saved this island when it was attacked by the Spaniards.' This may have sounded well but it did not reflect current realities. In the days of Drake or Hawkins it would have been inconceivable that seamen like Howe and Mann would refuse to serve their sovereign for party reasons. Hardy's advisers were divided – some for fighting and some for withdrawing. Sir Thomas Pye claimed that if nine British three-deckers got amongst the enemy they would be enough in themselves to break up any allied fleet, occasioning 'anarchy and confusion' among ships of different nations. But Comptroller Middleton – later the peerless Lord Barham – argued that it was better to play for time, allowing disease and the elements to work their will on the enemy, as well as the natural dissension between allies. It might not be necessary to fight at all and certainly not until Hardy had been reinforced with every possible ship. So desperate did things get that the heroic Captain MacBride offered to man and lead the old and rotten three-decker *Blenheim*, which had been condemned as unfit for service.

And now began a game of 'blind man's buff' in the Channel. As the Franco-Spanish fleet went one way, the British seemed to be going another. D'Orvilliers reached Plymouth; Hardy was at the Scilly Isles. The Admiralty's instructions to Hardy had left to him the final decision of fight or flight, and the elderly admiral was clearly feeling the weight of responsibility. The advantage of retreat – a Fabian retreat – began to assume more attractive proportions in his mind. If he withdrew up the Channel he would draw the enemy fleet further and further away from its base at Brest. Hardy therefore decided to pull back at least as far as Spithead, with the Franco-Spanish fleet forced to follow him. It could be seen as masterly, but it could also be seen as cowardly.

As has been pointed out since, Hardy obviously believed that he held the future of his country in his charge and that a wrong decision might have been irreparable. Like Jellicoe at Jutland, in Churchill's famous words, he could have lost the war in an afternoon. Yet the sight of a British fleet retreating before an enemy was anathema to the fighting traditions of the Royal Navy. Some writers since have considered Hardy's withdrawal one of the most disgraceful occurrences in Britain's naval history, with ships like the *Royal George* – Hawke's flagship at Quiberon Bay – and the *Victory* – Nelson's flagship at Trafalgar – misused by a tired old incompetent. Events seemed to prove Hardy right. Yet, had he but known it, the weakened state of the enemy fleet offered an easy victory for the taking. The well-manned and provisioned British fleet, however deficient in numbers, would have found few if any of the French and Spanish ships able to fully man their guns and return other than token resistance. But Hardy was no Nelson. It is impossible to believe that the latter would not have scattered the invasion fleet, revealing it for what it was – a nightmare grown to great proportions because it fed on men's fears. Had Hardy fought d'Orvilliers in the Channel there could realistically only have been one result – a shattering defeat for the allies.

On 3 September d'Orvilliers gave up and returned to Brest, landing 8,000 sick men from his ships. Depressed at the loss of his son and finding himself the scapegoat of a failed operation, he resigned from the navy. If the admiral was to blame it was because he failed to impose himself sufficiently on both his friends and his enemies. The Spaniards had been very difficult allies and had contributed a great deal to the disaster, notably by delaying the operation so that the good early summer weather was lost. And the French administrators had failed to support a fleet which was operating in French waters. They should have been able to provide more supplies and men as the need arose. Yet ultimately the plan was probably impossible. The French might have secured a landing somewhere on the south coast of England but they could never have maintained their troops there. Once the British regained control of the Channel the invasion force would have been cut off and forced to surrender. The operation was grandiose because it was planned by men who had no sense of reality. France was a state approaching bankruptcy, on a downward spiral that would lead to revolution. Such military extravaganzas were merely the products of men out of touch with political realities and engaging, like desperate and inveterate gamblers, in ever more fanciful ways of spending the nation's wealth. Perhaps d'Orvilliers deserved more from history's verdict and Hardy less: the former tried too hard and lost, the latter tried hardly at all and won. They were both incompetent in their way, but history is always on the side of the winners.

## THE BATTLE OF NAVARINO (1827)

Vice-Admiral Sir Edward Codrington, K.C.B., had been one of Nelson's 'band of brothers'. He had commanded the battleship *Orion* at Trafalgar in 1805 and had laid her alongside the 74-gun French ship *Intrépide* and made her his prize. Then, showing his warm-hearted nature, he wrote to his wife in England and asked her to provide for the needs of his prisoner, the French Commodore Cyprian Infernet. Codrington was a hard-fighting sailor, pugnacious but intensely human. He knew nothing of the complexities of a diplomatic system which now placed him alongside his lifelong enemies the French as allies rather than combatants. He was a man to command fleets but not a man to command and subdue a nature which saw things in black and white rather than diplomatic grey. As such he was a man ill-equipped to be plunged into the baffling morass known to the 19th century as the 'Eastern Question'.

The Greek War of Independence had flared up in 1821 and at first the Greeks were successful in repelling the troops of their Turkish masters. However, when the Sultan at Constantinople summoned help from his vassal, Mehemet Ali of Egypt, the Greeks faced a new threat from Mehemet's son, Ibrahim Pasha, and the army and navy of Egypt. The Greek fight for freedom had struck a chord in the minds and hearts of many Europeans and help flooded in from many countries, notably from Britain – from whence the able Sir Thomas Cochrane (a seasoned mercenary who had played a leading part in the South American wars of independence) took command of the embryonic Greek navy. Tsar Nicholas I of Russia saw an opportunity to help the Greeks and at the same time to weaken Russia's traditional enemies, the Turks. But Britain and France had ambivalent attitudes towards the Turks. On one hand they wished to see the Greeks win their independence, on the other they did not want to see

Ottoman Turkey so weakened that Russia gained control of Constantinople and commanded the straits between the Black Sea and the Mediterranean. Thus while Britain and France were prepared to cooperate with Russia in preventing Ibrahim Pasha destroying the Greeks, Britain insisted on walking a diplomatic tightrope which involved making certain that the Turks and their Egyptian vassals were not dangerously weakened. It was a task for a skilled diplomat – it was not a task for Sir Edward Codrington, courageous fighting admiral but as subtle as a 32-pounder passing through a ship's rigging.

In 1827 Britain, France and Russia signed the Treaty of London whereby they agreed among other things to enforce an armistice between the belligerents in the Greco-Turkish War. Codrington, commanding the British Mediterranean Fleet and flying his flag in the 84-gun *Asia*, was told that the Greeks had agreed to an armistice but the Turks had not. It was therefore his task, along with a Russian squadron under Rear-Admiral Count Heiden and a French squadron commanded by Rear-Admiral Henri de Rigny, to prevent the Turks and Egyptians from using their powerful fleet against the Greeks. There was no men-

tion in his orders of using force, though Codrington assumed that this ultimate threat was available to him if necessary. He therefore approached the harbour of Navarino in Messenia, where the Turco-Egyptian fleet was anchored. It was a strong fleet, of 89 ships carrying 2,240 heavy guns – more than twice as many guns as the combined British, French and Russian fleets.

When they arrived outside the harbour, a messenger was sent by the Egyptian commander, Ibrahim Pasha, to Codrington's flagship with the news that Lord Cochrane had made an attack on Patras, in the Gulf of Corinth, thereby breaking the armistice. The Egyptian leader asked permission to sail against the Greeks, but Codrington returned a vehement negative. He had come to preserve peace not to connive at its rupture. The messenger returned with his answer and the Allies assumed all was well. However, the next day, 2 October, a message came from the frigate *Dartmouth*, which had been guarding the entrance to Navarino Bay: a part of the Sultan's fleet was preparing to leave harbour to fight Cochrane. Codrington acted quickly, intercepting this Turkish force and driving it back towards the bay. Two days later, the *Dartmouth* reported that the Turks were again trying to break out.

A view of the battle of Navarino, 20 October 1827. Admiral Codrington's victory over the Turco-Egyptian fleet won him the enduring gratitude of the Greek nation, but a stern reprimand from the British Admiralty.

This convinced Codrington and his fellow admirals that they could not trust the Turks. To make matters worse, when Ibrahim Pasha disembarked the troops that were to have been taken to fight Cochrane at Patras, the men carried out an orgy of rape and pillage on the local Greek population. Codrington could not accept this and told Ibrahim Pasha that he would have to enter Navarino Bay in order to supervise the good behaviour of the Sultan's fleet.

On 20 October, Codrington led the Allied fleet into the bay, where they found the Turco-Egyptian fleet drawn up in a huge semi-circle. The British admiral issued strict orders to all the Allied ships:

> No gun is to be fired from the combined fleet without a signal being made for that purpose, unless shot be fired from any of the Turkish ships; in which case the ships so firing are to be destroyed immediately . . . In case of a regular battle ensuing, and creating any of that confusion which must naturally arise from it, it is to be observed that, in the words of Nelson, 'No Captain can do very wrong who places his ship alongside that of an enemy.'

This was splendid, fighting talk but was it quite appropriate? And did Codrington really believe that the ships of five nations could stay crowded together in a small harbour without some problems arising? The situation was so tense that had a gun been fired by mistake then a general fight was certain to begin. Was this really what Codrington's political masters wanted? The last thing they had intended was for him to 'play the Russian game' and help wipe out the Turkish Fleet, which alone might have prevented the Russians reaching Constantinople and the Bosphorus.

As the Allied ships entered the harbour a small boat brought Codrington a message from Ibrahim Pasha, asking him to retire from the harbour as he had not been given permission to enter. Codrington was the wrong man with whom to adopt that tone and he replied, 'I am come not to receive orders, but to give them; and, if any shot be fired at the Allied fleet, the Turkish fleet shall be destroyed.' This was blunt – if rather high-handed. Codrington's mission, after all, had been to persuade the warring parties to accept an armistice, not to destroy one of them. And the intention of the Allied commanders could be clearly seen by the fact that their ships were entering the bay all cleared for action – as provocative a gesture as possible.

It was no great surprise when firing broke out. It was a misunderstanding, of course, but no less deadly for that. The British frigate *Dartmouth* sent a boat to ask some Turkish fireships to move further away from where she was anchored. The Turks, assuming that the boat contained a boarding party, opened fire on it, killing an officer and wounding some of the men. The frigate returned a 'defensive' fire, which was then taken up by a nearby French man-of-war. Up until now only muskets had been used, until suddenly the Turks fired their cannons at the French flagship, the *Sirène*, and firing became general. Codrington manifested no great disappointment at the failure of his diplomacy and seemed much happier pouring the fire of the *Asia* into the Turkish flagship. Soon the whole bay was shrouded in smoke, partly made up of Egyptian and Turkish vessels burning and sinking under the Allied fire, and also of the Muslim crews burning their own vessels to avoid capture. The battle was no contest due to the superiority of the discipline and gunnery of the Allied crews. Turkish and Egyptian losses were enormous, as high as 60 ships sunk or burned, with at least 6,000 dead and 4,000 wounded. Allied losses were quite heavy: of the British, 75 were killed and 197 wounded; the Russians lost 59 killed and 137 wounded; the French had 40 killed and 141 wounded. No Allied vessel was lost though many of them suffered some damage.

The Allied admirals congratulated themselves on a thoroughly good victory and sent Ibrahim the following not very reassuring message:

> As the squadrons of the Allied Powers did not enter Navarino with an hostile intention, but only to renew to the Commanders of the Turkish fleet propositions which were to the advantage of the Grand Signior himself, it is not our intention to destroy what ships of the Ottoman navy may yet remain, now that so signal a vengeance has been taken for the first cannon-shot which has been ventured to be fired on the Allied flags.

This statement has an unpleasantly smug feel about it. Perhaps Codrington would not have felt so happy if he had known that the British, French and Russian ambassadors were at that moment apologizing to the Sultan in Constantinople for this 'untoward event'. The speed of diplomatic events left Codrington baffled. Rather than being ruined by the battle, Ibrahim Pasha, the wily son of a cunning father, used it as the first step in the liberation of Egypt from Turkish rule. In Cairo Mehemet Ali was secretly delighted. It must have taken Codrington's breath away.

Count Heiden and Admiral de Rigny were showered with honours by their grateful governments – de Rigny was ennobled and became Minister of Marine. But poor Codrington was quickly made to understand that his triumph at Navarino had indeed been an 'untoward event', and he was criticized for his rash, useless and impolitic behaviour. Vice-Admiral Sir John

Gore was sent out to meet Codrington with a whole list of questions for the commander to answer in explaining his actions. In the House of Commons Codrington was denounced as disobedient to his orders and it began to look as if he were being prepared, like Byng a century before, as a political sacrifice by an unpopular government, or as a peace offering to the Ottoman Sultan. Ironically, it was not until 1851 – the year of his death – that Codrington received justice, but not from his own people. In that year the Greek Chamber of Deputies recorded their thanks to him and decreed that his illustrious name, surmounted by a wreath of laurels, should be carved on tablets and stand forever in the parliament building of an independent Greece.

---

*'Their Lordships felt it their bounden duty to discourage to the utmost of their ability the use of steam vessels, as they considered that the introduction of steam was calculated to strike a fatal blow at the naval supremacy of the Empire.'*

**Lord Melville, First Lord of the Admiralty, 1828**

During the 19th century the admiralty tried to obstruct all technological improvements in shipbuilding and design. They believed that by doing so they could cling on to the advantage won by Nelson at Trafalgar. The result was that many technical innovations were made by designers in France, Italy or the United States and Britain was left trailing – dangerously – behind.

---

## THE BATTLE OF LISSA (1866)

When war broke out between Italy and Austria in 1866 command of the new Italian navy was given to Admiral Count Carlo Pellion di Persano. It cannot be said that he was pleased to be so honoured. At 60 years of age, and having successfully masqueraded as a naval officer for nearly a generation, he was not happy to be asked to risk his reputation in the autumn of his years. For a few months in 1862 he had been the Minister of Marine and though his tenure of office had been short he had used his time wisely, promoting himself twice. And in a country so short of naval heroes that they honoured the treacherous 16th-century Genoese Captain Andrea Doria and his cowardly nephew Gian (see p. 139) as great admirals, Persano was widely regarded as the 'only' worthwhile admiral Italy had and a natural choice to lead his country in wartime.

What the Italians lacked in leadership they tried to make up for with material. Since 1860 the newly united kingdom had devoted £12 million to building as fine an ironclad fleet as any in the world. Unfortunately Italy had been short-changed. Two large armoured ships – *Re d'Italia* and *Re di Portogallo* – had been built at great cost in the United States. Heavily gunned and strongly armoured, they gave every impression of being fine ships. In truth, however, the armour plating had been imposed on green wood and they were structurally unsound. What was worse, at least from the point of view of their crew, was that the Americans had dumped filth and refuse inside their frames, which rotted and made them unendurably foul ships in which to sail. As if this was not bad enough the two ships were both unseaworthy, lacking buoyancy and being very slow to manoeuvre.

Admiral Persano had a child-like affection for the armoured ram *Affondatore* – which he regarded almost as his own private yacht. Built in England, to better specifications than the armoured cruisers, she was otherwise a grotesque creation with a ram 26 feet long projecting from her bows, making her a very bad seaboat. She was too heavily weighed down by her armour and her guns to steer at all well. Yet in spite of every defect the whole of Italy shared Persano's predilection for this 'Cyrano' of a warship.

The Italians had two other armoured rams – *Terribile* and *Formidabile* – which failed entirely to live up to their names. To complete the ironclad fleet, Persano had at his disposal five broadside armoured ships and two gunboats. As a second division, the Italian fleet was accompanied to battle by a large number of wooden frigates, some of which were steam powered. On paper the Italian fleet seemed impressive. But appearances were deceptive. The quality of officer training was derisory and the technical skills of the sailors quite unsuited to modern naval warfare. The gunners, in particular, were raw recruits who betrayed their lack of discipline in the heat of battle, while the marine engineers – many of whom had been British and who had refused to serve in wartime – failed to get the best out of their modern ships.

Persano may have been a charlatan but he was no fool. He knew the weaknesses of a fleet which had been built entirely for prestige rather than use. Even though the Austrians had a fleet scarcely half as strong in modern ships and guns as his own, Persano declared, 'I fear we shall go down.' As a result he tried to avoid fighting and made every excuse for delay. Italian politicians, who had seen such vast sums paid out in building the fleet, soon lost patience with him. At his later impeachment in the Italian Senate it was said of him,

> Persano's acts in one continued series, exhibit a true repugnance to taking any decisive step. Now he talks of waiting for steel shot; now he wants to transfer guns from one ship to another; now it is gun-carriages which are lacking; now ammunition for his Armstrong guns; now swift scouts; now store-ships; now doctors; now nurses; now engineers; now lieutenants; now speaking tubes; now pilots; now marines; and when he has the fleet in perfect order, for such was the opinion of all, and when he might with success have attacked the Austrians, he runs back to port to wait for the *Affondatore*.

Persano's only response to such criticism was to plead with the prime minister: 'This fleet is not ready for war. Help me, I earnestly entreat you.' His obsession with the *Affondatore* was such that he felt he dare not act until she had returned from Gibraltar. Yet even without the ram he held an overwhelming supremacy over the Austrians, conditional on one deficiency alone – a total absence of martial spirit.

Rear-Admiral Baron Wilhelm von Tegetthof, commander of the Austrian fleet, was as unlike Persano as it was possible to be. While his seamanship might not have earned him the command of even a frigate in the British navy his courage and leadership were redolent

Rear-Admiral Wilhelm von Tegetthof of the Austrian navy, victor over the Italians at Lissa. Nelson would have recognized in him a kindred spirit.

of an earlier age. Like Don John of Austria at Lepanto, Tegetthof bestrode the stage like a titan. Under his inspiring command he moulded the motley array of Austrian warships into a formidable force. Outmanned and outgunned in every way the Austrian fleet under Tegetthof was never outfought. Even though his best ships, the ironclads *Ferdinand Maximilian* and *Habsburg*, had to put to sea without their main Krupp guns – detained by the Prussians for the duration of the war – and replaced by old muzzle-loaders, their engines were in prime condition. If he could not shoot at the enemy, Tegetthof was determined to come to close quarters and ram him. Where other Austrian ships lacked armour Tegetthof made sure his ships were protected with anchor chains, railway rails and stout planking. He intended to fight even though outnumbered 2 to 1 in ships, 2 to 1 in guns, 3 to 1 in tonnage and nearly 3 to

1 in engine horsepower. Ironically, over 800 of the men serving in his fleet were Venetian, inhabitants of that part of Italy which was still under Austrian control. Yet these Italians fought for Tegetthof in a way in which their compatriots would not fight for Persano. Never were the personalities of two naval leaders so vital to the outcome of a battle.

On 27 June Tegetthof went looking for Persano. He found him at anchor in the port of Ancona. For three hours the Austrians cruised up and down, inviting the much more powerful Italians to come out and fight. Persano later claimed that he was hoping 'to entice the hostile fleet to offer battle, and to annihilate it if it makes the attempt'. But this was an odd interpretation of events as Persano stayed in harbour until the Austrians lost patience and sailed off. Then he sailed out with four ironclads and headed in the opposite direction. A week passed and Persano telegraphed the Minister of Marine: 'Anxious to fight; I entreat you to send at once the *Affondatore.*' The minister replied urging him to sweep the Austrians from the seas like 'a second Tromp'. Another week passed and Persano telegraphed: 'Want two or three more days.' But the government was losing patience with him and sent him a strong despatch:

> Would you tell the people, the people who in their mad vanity believe their sailors are best in the world – that in spite of the twelve millions we have added to their debt, the squadron that we have collected is one incapable of facing the enemy? We should be stoned. And who has ever heard the Austrian fleet mentioned except with contempt?

The press added their weight, screeching at Persano: 'Do something; fight the Austrians; land on their coast; attack Lissa – only move.' Hysteria now replaced inertia. Persano received a direct order from the Minister of Marine: 'Go out of harbour with your fleet; leave behind any ships which want guns.' Persano sullenly led his ships out into the Adriatic, steamed up and down for a while without attempting to find the Austrians and bring them to battle, and then returned to Ancona. Not once had he discussed plans with his commanders, for the simple reason that he had no plans. Morale in the fleet sank and captains squabbled with each other in the absence of any guiding hand. Persano was simply out of his depth. And now the king intervened, ordering Persano 'to attempt against the hostile fortresses or fleet what operations may be thought convenient to obtain a success'. It was royally put but the message was clear: find the enemy and fight him. In panic, Persano decided he had better attack the island of Lissa – about which he knew next to nothing and had no maps.

Lissa was a fortified Austrian island in the Adriatic, 130 miles south of the Italian base at Ancona and 30 miles from the Dalmatian coast. Sparsely populated, it held a garrison of nearly 2,000 Austrian soldiers and had strong batteries of guns situated high above the sea. Silencing these guns would present a very difficult task for naval forces as their own armament, designed for ship-to-ship encounters, might lack the elevation necessary. It would be vitally important for a landing of troops and marines to be made so that the island batteries could be captured by ground troops. Naturally, Persano gave far too little thought to how he would go about subduing the defences of Lissa.

On 16 July Persano's fleet – still short of his beloved *Affondatore* – put to sea and headed for Lissa. It was divided into four divisions: the van was led by Rear-Admiral Vacca in the *Carignano*; the centre by Persano himself in the *Re d'Italia*; the rear by Captain Riboti in the *Re di Portogallo*; and the reserve by Vice-Admiral Albini. Incredibly, Persano had taken no coal with him besides what his ships had in their bunkers – enough for just four days at sea. Furthermore, having no idea of the strength of the garrison on Lissa, he had taken just 1,500 soldiers and marines with the fleet. Arriving at the island the following day, and without making any effort to locate Tegetthof's fleet, Persano divided up his own squadron, sending Vacca with three ironclads to bombard Comisa in the west, Albini with his wooden ships to attack Porto Manego in the south, while he himself with the rest of the fleet attacked Porto San Giorgio in the north. It was a formula for disaster. If the Austrians took him unawares his disparate forces would be destroyed. In fact, the Austrians on Lissa had telegraphed Tegetthof with details of the Italian fleet before the attack began. Undismayed by the fact that the Italian ships were flying either English or French flags to confuse them, the Austrian telegraphers drolly wired Tegetthof, 'Fierce cannonade from Italian ships: no casualties.' It was enough for Tegetthof and he set off at full speed from Pola, 175 miles north of Lissa. Surely Persano had ample time to take the island. The Austrians could not arrive for many hours. But the Italian cannonade was anything but fierce. In fact, Albini simply refused to attack Porto Manego on the grounds that it was too dangerous a task. This news staggered Persano who had only given Albini the job because he had thought it was easy. He therefore ordered Albini to land troops instead. Albini, however, took no notice and simply steamed up and down the southern coast of Lissa, contributing nothing to the battle.

As night fell Persano pulled back his ships, allowing the Austrians to reform. He had cut the telegraphic wire from Lissa but not before Tegetthof had sent a reply to the garrison: 'Hold out till the fleet can come to you.' When he heard of this message Persano claimed it was simply a ruse and made no preparations for the arrival of the Austrian fleet. At daybreak the sight that met Persano's eyes must have filled him with joy: at last the *Affondatore* had arrived. But not everything was good news. The *Formidabile* had received a pounding from the shore batteries and asked permission to return to Ancona, while Admiral Albini was refusing to land any troops as he said the surf was too dangerous. Persano, only a few miles away, noted that the sea was calm and 'there was not the faintest oscillation on board his flagship'. He now summoned his captains to a council of war. What would they do if the Austrian fleet came? 'Sink them with our rams,' was the universal cry. Yet no ship had been positioned to give early warning of the Austrian fleet's arrival. The Italian ironclads were in no sort of order when one of the Italian sailing boats signalled to Persano, 'Suspected vessels in sight.' The inevitable had happened and Persano had been caught unawares.

Tegetthof, flying his flag in the *Ferdinand Maximilian*, now bore down on the Italians like a storm at sea. With his watchword, 'Rush on the enemy and sink him', the Austrian was precisely the sort of commander to exploit the chaos in the Italian fleet. Short of guns as he was, Tegetthof had ordered his gunners to concentrate their fire on particular portions of the Italian ships to maximize the effect. His aim was to fight at close quarters and he formed his ships into three wedge formations, each of seven ships, with his strongest ships at the head and the other ironclads on each wing. His weaker, wooden ships were grouped for protection behind the ironclads.

When he saw Tegetthof bearing down on him Persano panicked. In the space of a few minutes he issued so many orders that everyone was totally confused. Albini was ordered to abandon the disembarkation of troops and bring his ships into action behind the ironclads. True to form Albini claimed he had not received the signal and did nothing. In the confusion Persano formed up his ships in line abreast, but facing in the wrong direction. To add to the chaos two Italian ships signalled that their engines were malfunctioning, while the *Formidabile* headed off towards Ancona, claiming she was too weak to fight but showing a

remarkably clean pair of heels. At last Persano achieved his intention of forming a line abreast. Then, suddenly, he changed his mind and ordered his fleet to form line ahead. Ships were swinging this way and that in the utmost chaos as the Austrian fleet came within firing range.

At the head of the Italian line were Vacca's three ironclads, but Persano's own division had fallen so far behind that an enormous gap developed. It hardly needed the 'Nelson touch' for Tegetthof to see where to break the Italian line. But in case of doubt Persano made it easier for him by making what must be one of the most extraordinary decisions in the history of sea warfare. At the moment of battle, with his flag flying from the *Re d'Italia*, Persano decided to transfer to 'a faster, handier' ship, his beloved *Affondatore*. Ordering the flagship to stop engines he boarded his launch and was taken to the armoured ram, a vessel almost without rigging so that he would be unable to communicate with the rest of the fleet by flag signals. From now on the captains of the Italian fleet, spread out across thirteen miles of sea, would have no idea where their commander was. Once aboard the *Affondatore* Persano began to race impotently up and down the Italian line, removed from command by his own decision. After the battle he tried to explain his action:

> I perceived the convenience of taking up my position outside the line in an ironclad of great speed, to be able to dash into the heat of battle, or carefully to convey the necessary orders to the different parts of the squadron and direct their movements according to necessity.

The only people who believed him were those who doubted his sanity.

The wretched engineers of the *Re d'Italia* hardly had time to restart the ship's engines and their launch was unable to return from the *Affondatore* before Tegetthof's wedge of ships – painted black for identification – burst through the Italian line. While Albini's wooden vessels, armed with 420 guns, refused to join the fight the Austrian ironclads pulverized the unfortunate *Re d'Italia*. Determined to make use of his ram Tegetthof, behaving like a 'beau sabreur' in a cavalry encounter on land, literally 'charged' what he took to be Persano's flagship. With its captain, Sterneck, halfway up the rigging and peering through the smoke to help him navigate, the *Ferdinand Maximilian*, steaming at full speed, rammed straight into the *Re d'Italia*, ripping a huge hole in her side. The Italian ship was doomed. Yet at this late stage the crew showed courage that would have shamed men like Persano and Albini. Captain Faa di Bruno, declar-

The Austrian victory at Lissa in July 1866 – the first clash between ironclad steam fleets – was a triumph for courage and seamanship over overwhelming numbers.

ing that the captain should perish with his ship, put a pistol to his head and killed himself, while the chief gunner fired a last shot even as the ship slipped beneath the waves. Unfortunately as the Austrians tried to rescue the survivors from the *Re d'Italia* they were fired on by other Italian ships and forced to abandon them. The heroic Sterneck, clinging to the rigging by one hand, next tried to ram the *Palestro* and came so close to the Italian ship that an Austrian sailor was able to tear down the Italian flag as the *Ferdinand Maximilian* scraped by.

At close range and in the confusion the Italians had surrendered all the advantages they had possessed in manpower and gunnery. The Italian gunners – many of them raw recruits – raked the wooden-walled *Kaiser* from close range only to find that they had forgotten to load any shells. Meanwhile, Persano in the *Affondatore* continued to appear and disappear from the action like an uninvited guest at a party. First he headed straight towards the *Kaiser*, intent on ramming her, then lost his nerve and ordered the *Affondatore* to swerve away. Later he had another chance, and even got as far as ordering his men to lie flat upon the deck because of the

expected impact. But he was a poseur not a fighter and again veered away. Braver souls paid a higher price that day. Persano managed one further fatuous signal, 'The admiral informs the fleet that the ship which does not fight is not at its post.' Fortunately few of the Italians seemed to have noticed it.

Tegetthof now forced his way through to Lissa and found to his joy that the Austrian flag was still flying. He formed up his ironclads again, waiting to see if Persano would renew the contest. The fighting had shown that the Italian armoured ships were immune to his guns and that only ramming was likely to be successful. And he knew that under a more forceful commander the Italians must have succeeded in wrecking his ships. Yet Persano had no stomach for the fight and as night fell he ordered his battered fleet to return to Ancona. That night the *Palestro*, which had been in the thick of the fight and had been set on fire at one stage, blew up. Her captain had flooded the magazine to save her but had overlooked a store of shells carelessly left on deck. Refusing to abandon his vessel he died along with over 200 of her crew.

Persano, meanwhile, was still looking for his exflagship, *Re d'Italia*. She was far more comfortable than *Affondatore* for cruising and he wanted to reboard her for the return journey to Ancona. To his extreme irritation he was informed that she had been sunk, taking with her to the bottom some 400 of her crew. Petulantly Persano now took out his frustrations on the *Affondatore*, accounting for his dismal performance by claiming that she was an awkward ship and too difficult to handle. Ironically, on the return journey to Ancona the *Affondatore* sank in a storm.

Italian losses of three ironclads and over 600 men killed were heavy when compared to the Austrian casualties of just 38 killed and 138 wounded. The Italian gunnery had been risible; no shells had penetrated the Austrian armour and few of Tegetthof's ironclads were even seriously dented. Only the wooden ship *Kaiser* – which had been in the thick of a battle against ironclads – had suffered much material damage. Yet the spirit of the *Kaiser* stood in stark contrast with the cowardice of Albini and his wooden ships, which simply refused to join the battle. The Italian defeat was the result not so much of faulty leadership as an absolute absence of command. Persano's few interventions in the action caused only confusion and throughout the Italian fleet fought as a series of individual ships, perfect strangers one to another.

Persano was 'an admiral of words rather than action' and only put to sea when forced by political and popular pressure. Devoid of moral courage he even tried to blame this shocking defeat on his subordinates. On returning to Ancona he initially spread the word that he had won a great victory, sinking three Austrian ships. However, a swift count indicated that the *Re d'Italia*, *Affondatore* and *Palestro* had failed to reach harbour. How had they fared in the battle? When the truth began to leak out Persano changed his tune and said that it had still been victory but a hard-won triumph. Even this did not last long. Persano next tried to claim that he had been in the thick of the fighting throughout and that the *Affondatore* had suffered grievously at the hands of the Austrian gunners.

When the truth was finally revealed the fury of the Italian people knew no bounds. Not only was Persano a coward but he was a liar as well. Tried by the Senate on charges of incapacity, negligence, disobedience, cowardice and treason, Persano was very fortunate to escape with his life. He was found guilty of incapacity, negligence and disobedience, and stripped of his rank. Albini, rightly, suffered a similar humiliation, though

when one considers the fate of Admiral Byng, one can only reflect on how lucky both these Italian admirals were.

## THE BATTLE OF MANILA BAY (1898)

The incident which sparked war between the United States and Spain in 1898 was the mysterious loss of the American battleship *Maine* in an explosion in Havana Harbour. Although modern research has shown that the destruction of the *Maine* had absolutely nothing to do with the Spanish government, it was seen as a convenient *casus belli* and President McKinley declared war on Spain on 21 April 1898. Americans saw it as a 'splendid little war', but for the Spaniards the war was anything but splendid. It is doubtful if any country has ever entered a war with as little enthusiasm as did Spain in 1898. The lengthy struggle against the rebels in Cuba made the idea of war against the United States immensely unpopular in Spain itself. It is probable that Spain's decision to fight was based more on archaic notions of 'honour' than realistic strategy. As America's ambassador to Spain said, 'They know Cuba is lost but they will seek honorable defeat in war.'

The Spanish government was quite aware that they had neither the army nor the navy to fight the United States. The navy was particularly weak, consisting of just four armoured cruisers, twelve old unprotected cruisers, five torpedo boats, three destroyers and some small gunboats, and even this diminutive force had to be split between the Caribbean and the Pacific. Nor were all of these units operational anyway, as there was a shortage of trained sailors. Some of the Spanish ships had too few crew members to put to sea. Shortages of coal and munitions meant that fleet manoeuvres were almost unknown and gunnery practice unheard of. In Spain's primitive colonial ports there were no dockyard facilities so that ships damaged in action could not be repaired. But worst of all, Spain's admirals were imbued with a deep sense of despair and thought only in terms of personal honour and of limiting their own casualties; the idea of victory was simply dismissed as impossible. At Manila, in the Philippines, where the Americans would strike their first blow, the fleet of Admiral Montojo consisted of what the Americans

Commodore Dewey during the battle of Manila Bay, 1 May 1898, when his guns destroyed a force of Spanish ships in the course of a single morning's engagement. The one-sided encounter contributed to ultimate US victory in the Spanish–American War and made Dewey a national hero.

described as 'old tubs not warships'.

While the Spaniards were a prey to defeatism, the Americans faced the challenge of war with energy. Commodore Dewey took over command of the US Asiatic Fleet stationed at Hong Kong in January 1898, and immediately began preparations for an attack on the Philippines. He placed his ships on war footing and drilled his men so that when the time came for action – and Dewey was certain that it could not long be postponed – everything would go smoothly. Once the cruiser *Baltimore* had arrived from Honolulu with ammunition he was able to bring his entire fleet up to 60 per cent of maximum. When the American ships left harbour on 24 April they were saluted by the crews of the British ships stationed there, who wished them well, but as Dewey later remembered: 'In the Hong Kong Club it was not possible to get bets, even at heavy odds, that our expedition would be a success.'

Awaiting the Americans was Spanish Admiral Montojo y Pasarón with 25 vessels. Few of them were fit to stand in line of battle against Dewey's powerful quartet of cruisers. Montojo's six cruisers were all smaller than Dewey's smallest, several of them had iron hulls and one, the *Castilla*, was made of wood. In both heavy guns and light weapons the Americans had an advantage; the Spanish did not even have any warheads for their torpedoes. Dewey's ships were simply larger, faster and more modern. Montojo's only possible advantage was that in any battle fought within Manila Bay, he could fight with the support of heavy shore-based guns. In the event, however, he chose not to do this.

Although the Spanish at Manila knew that Dewey was coming and how strong he was, they made no preparations to meet him. Even after news was received that the Americans had been sighted on 30 April, Montojo insisted on celebrating the birthday of one of his officers in the admiral's house in Manila. Officers from throughout the fleet came to the party. Some returned to their ships, inebriated, after the battle had already started; others, hung-over until the next morning, missed the action altogether.

When the American fleet reached Manila Bay Dewey first sent the *Boston* to Subic Bay, where he thought Montojo would be. In fact, Montojo had considered going there and had even sent orders for the harbour to be fortified. To his chagrin he found out that his orders had been ignored and none of the work had been carried out. When Dewey heard that Montojo was not at Subic Bay he called his captains aboard the flagship – the *Olympia* – and made plans for a battle to be fought

inside Manila Bay. Dewey had little up-to-date information about the shore defences in the bay and around Manila city itself, and presumed they would be formidable. He therefore decided to enter the bay under cover of night, hoping to slip by the shore batteries unnoticed. Just before midnight, with all lights extinguished, the American ships passed silently under the Spanish guns. At one moment sparks from the furnace of one of the American ships shot into the air, causing a trigger-happy Spaniard to fire aimlessly into the sea, but otherwise the Americans encountered no resistance. Spanish soldiers on the island of Corregidor later said that the American ships had been clearly visible but that their officers had given no orders to open fire with their 8-inch guns.

In fact Spanish defeatism was to be Dewey's biggest ally in the battle ahead. Montojo was so certain of defeat that he had taken two extraordinary decisions. First he had anchored his fleet at Cavite rather than under the guns of Manila's fortifications in case stray American shells fell in the city causing unnecessary civilian casualties. As a humanitarian gesture it was admirable but as a military decision it was incredible. From Cavite the Spaniards would only be able to bring eight shore guns to bear on Dewey's ships instead of the 39 available at Manila. In addition, Montojo was eager to save casualties among his own sailors, preferring to anchor in shallow water so that when his ships sank their crews would be able to reach the shore. It is doubtful if such thoughts ever entered the head of a naval commander on any other occasion in history. Yet Montojo was no coward. He would fight the Americans to save his honour and the honour of his country. He would lose the battle but he would fight with what weapons he had, however feeble.

As dawn broke the white hulls of the Spanish ships stood out sharply against the land. The water of the bay was like a millpond and a slight mist rose above the sea. Some of the Spanish shore batteries now opened fire – as did Montojo's ships – but their marksmanship was poor, with shells falling some miles away from their targets. For 40 minutes the one-sided cannonade continued, with the Americans suffering no damage at all and conserving their own shells until they were well in range. At 5.40 am Dewey spoke quietly to the *Olympia*'s captain: 'You may fire when ready, Gridley', and the flagship opened up with her main armament against the *Reina Cristina*. The Spanish fire continued, wild and inaccurate, and the American ships again suffered no hits. Dewey led his squadron on a course parallel with Montojo's ships, firing broadsides as they went, before turning and closing the range to 5,000 yards. In all, Dewey sailed five times back and forth in parallel with Montojo, each time closing the range slightly until the two squadrons were just 2,000 yards apart. At this latter range the Americans scored hit after hit on the main Spanish ships. Montojo's flagship – the *Reina Cristina* – received the concentrated fire of three American cruisers and was soon reduced to a blazing wreck.

Once the *Reina Cristina* was destroyed the big guns of the American cruisers turned on the rest of the squadron. The wooden cruiser *Castilla* was quickly reduced to a wreck and scuttled by her own crew. Then a curious incident occurred which might have proved serious had the Americans faced first-rate opponents. Dewey was informed by Captain Gridley (incorrectly, as it turned out) that his flagship had just 15 per cent of her ammunition left. Still unaware of how great a victory he had won, the commodore ordered his squadron to withdraw from the vicinity of the Spanish ships. With the bay almost totally obscured by smoke it was proving difficult to know how the battle was going. Three Spanish ships were on fire, but so was the *Boston*, as far as Dewey could tell. Should the American ships run out of ammunition they might easily fall prey to the Spanish shore batteries, even if Montojo's fleet was destroyed. One can imagine Dewey's relief when it was discovered that the misleading message should have read that only 15 per cent of the ammunition had been used so far.

Dewey called his captains aboard the *Olympia* to check on damage to his ships and casualties. The reports were very reassuring. One man (Chief Engineer Randall of the *McCulloch*) had died of a heart attack – possibly as a result of the heat – but no one had succumbed to Spanish fire. The new grey paintwork had been scratched in a few places and the black powder was causing a lot of soot, but the Americans had emerged largely unscathed.

At 11.16 am, after the crews had had their breakfast, the American fleet sailed back into the harbour and resumed the battering of the Spanish ships. There was to be no escape now and Montojo ordered his captains to scuttle their vessels. So shallow was the water that when the *Ulloa* sank, much of her superstructure remained above water and her crew found it easy to swim, wade and scramble ashore.

The victorious Dewey now ordered the Spanish shore batteries to stop firing, otherwise he would bombard the city of Manila. The Spanish governor replied that the batteries would remain silent 'unless it was evident that a disposition of the American ships to bombard the city was being made'. In simple terms the battle was over: now it was time to celebrate. The Americans anchored close to the city of Manila itself and what followed was surreal even for this 'Alice-in-Wonderland' war. Crowds of people gathered along the waterfront, gazing at the American squadron, climbing on the ramparts of the batteries that had been firing only moments before. Appreciating a good audience, the *Olympia*'s band played 'La Paloma' and other Spanish airs to the assembled crowds. But the music proved too much for the poor colonel of artillery who had commanded the batteries, which now served as seats for the concert goers. Feeling himself dishonoured he shot himself through the head. It was a curiously violent conclusion to a beautiful evening.

The American victory at Manila Bay was one of the most one-sided in history. On the Spanish side ten ships were lost, though casualties were light (only 167 men were killed and 224 wounded) – a tribute to the cautious policy of Admiral Montojo. The Americans suffered just seven men slightly wounded and little more than scratches to Dewey's warships. Yet the American marksmanship had been deplorable: of 5,859 shells fired by the American cruisers only 142 scored hits (2.45 per cent). The Spanish shooting was even worse: as few as thirteen hits were registered on Dewey's vessels and more damage was caused to them by the concussion of firing their own 8-inch guns.

On his return home Montojo was court-martialled by the Spanish government in spite of the testimony of an unusual witness for the defence: Commodore Dewey himself, who asserted that the Spanish admiral had fought with great gallantry throughout the battle. Montojo was closer to the truth when he said:

> The inefficiency of the ships composing the small Spanish squadron, the lack of all classes of personnel, especially of gun captains and seaman-gunners, the ineptitude of some of the provisionally engaged engineers, the want of quick-firers . . . and the unprotected nature of the greater part of the Spanish ships, all contributed to make more decided the sacrifice which the squadron offered for its country.

# THE BATTLE OF CORONEL (1914)

Cowardice has been one of the rarest characteristics of naval officers. Unlike land operations, where retreat is almost always a possibility, successful disengagement from an enemy at sea is fraught with difficulties. Until the 16th century naval battles were particularly deadly as retreat was almost never an option for the defeated party. And even in modern times examples of cowardice have been so rare that when they do occur they achieve a rare notoriety. The disgrace of Rear-Admiral Troubridge for failing to engage the German battlecruiser *Goeben* in August 1914 was such a case (see p. 32). Its effect on every serving officer in the Royal Navy was such that each was determined never to let such an accusation be levelled at him. Even where good sense might dictate a more cautious approach, officers felt driven to remove any doubts about their courage by engaging the enemy, whatever the odds. Such was the fate of Admiral Christopher Cradock, a gallant officer of whom no suspicion of cowardice ever existed. And yet, through the incompetence of the Admiralty – and notably the interference of its civilian head, Winston Churchill – Cradock felt himself compelled to seek out and fight a superior German force and go down fighting with his ships. In tackling von Spee's cruisers he knew that he was courting disaster but he felt he had no alternative. He had pressed the Admiralty to reinforce his weak squadron but they had insisted that what he had was enough for the task. To have refused the challenge would, in his mind, have been to lay himself open to the same accusations that were made against Troubridge. With an air of resignation Cradock buried his medals before leaving Port Stanley, in the Falkland Islands, and gave the governor a sealed packet to be sent to the Admiralty 'as soon as my death is confirmed'. He added bitterly, 'I have no intention, after 40 years at sea, of being an unheard victim.' As the governor's ADC later wrote:

> He knew what he was up against and asked for a fast cruiser with big guns to be added to his squadron, for he had nothing very powerful and nothing very fast, but the Admiralty said he'd have to go without. So old Cradock said, 'All right; we'll do without' and he slipped off early one morning, and . . . set out to look for the crack Germans.

The German admiral Graf von Spee (1861–1914), was one of the finest German commanders of the First World War. He honed his squadron into an expert fighting force that proved too strong for Sir Christopher Cradock's flotilla at the battle of Coronel.

The 'crack Germans' were the German China Squadron, commanded by Graf von Spee, one of the most able of the younger generation of German admirals. He relished the roving commission – given him by Tirpitz in 1914 – to strike at British trade and possessions in the vast areas of the Pacific and South Atlantic. His armoured cruisers – *Scharnhorst* and *Gneisenau* – were fast and powerful vessels, able to outfight or outrun anything the British could bring against them, except battlecruisers. Both were noted for their outstanding gunnery, having won the top award in the German navy for the last two years. With the three light cruisers that made up the squadron, the *Scharnhorst* and *Gneisenau* posed a very serious threat to British trade and communications. The British Admiralty's decision to concentrate all the nation's naval strength in the North Sea left many far-flung British outposts vulnerable to German surface raiders. The commander-in-chief,

Admiral Sir John Jellicoe, backed by the First Lord of the Admiralty, Winston Churchill, made it clear that he was unwilling to diminish the Grand Fleet at Scapa Flow by so much as a single Dreadnought battlecruiser, and so Britain was stretched to her limits in countering von Spee. Jellicoe's decision was not popular at the Admiralty and both Prince Louis of Battenburg, the First Sea Lord, and the Chief of War Staff, Sir Doveton Sturdee, were convinced that two battlecruisers should be withdrawn from the North Sea to join the hunt for von Spee. They pointed out to Churchill – vainly as it turned out – that British naval patrols in the South Atlantic consisted of slow and antiquated armoured cruisers or fast, light cruisers, far too weak to face the German raiders. With troop convoys from Australia and New Zealand being held up until suitable protection could be guaranteed, the Admiralty should have made the destruction of the German cruisers top priority.

Much of the blame for this blinkered policy rested with the First Lord of the Admiralty, Winston Churchill. Not content with his political role, Churchill constantly interfered with the work of the naval planners, drafting telegrams, moving ships and poring over maps like a ship's captain. In the words of Richard Hough, 'nothing gave him a greater sense of power and satisfaction than this tactical masterminding from a distance of thousands of miles'. Yet in naval terms Churchill was a mere dilettante and he used his forceful personality to bulldoze his own ideas through against the professional opinions of more experienced if less pugnacious naval experts.

The British commander in the South Atlantic in 1914, Rear-Admiral Sir Christopher Cradock, was a 'fine seaman and leader of men', and a man of great personal courage. But in contrast to von Spee's two fine cruisers, Cradock's armoured cruisers – the *Good Hope* and *Monmouth* – were old and relatively weak vessels, whose main armament of 6-inch guns were located so close to the waterline that they could not be fired in the heavy weather so often prevalent in South Atlantic waters. The total weight of their broadsides – including *Good Hope*'s two 9.2-inch guns, was 2,400 pounds – merely half that of von Spee's ships. And to make matters worse, Cradock's ships were manned almost entirely by reservists – 90 per cent in the case of *Good Hope* – called into action at such short notice that they had not even had time for gunnery practice. Cradock's motley squadron was completed by the fast light cruiser *Glasgow*, a useful but unarmoured vessel, and the 12,000-ton converted liner *Otranto*, suitable only for protecting merchantmen. Churchill's cruellest 'gift' to Cradock was the use of the old pre-Dreadnought battleship *Canopus*, armed with 12-inch guns but in every other respect a useless addition to the squadron in view of its slow maximum speed. For some reason Churchill overestimated the value of *Canopus*, which had been built in 1897 and had been under a 'Care and Maintenance' order since 1913, prior to being scrapped. The First Lord overlooked the fact that though the battleship's guns were of larger calibre than the Germans' main armament, they had a shorter effective range. In addition her reservist crew had had no gunnery experience, and her gunnery officer had never been in a turret before – a poor preparation for facing the gunnery champions of the German fleet. At a maximum of 12 knots her top speed was far too slow for her to be able to bring the Germans to battle unless von Spee wished it. Yet, in spite of these evident drawbacks, Churchill still claimed that the *Canopus* was strong enough to ensure that Cradock would not need the support of the armoured cruiser *Defence*, which alone of the British ships in the Atlantic could be compared to von Spee's.

On 18 October 1914, while Cradock was taking on coal at Port Stanley in the Falklands an engineer's report from *Canopus* said that she would need five days to repair her engines after which, at best, she would only be able to reach 12 knots. Cradock realized that he could only bring von Spee to battle if he abandoned the *Canopus*. He signalled this decision to the Admiralty before setting off up the coast of Chile to search for the Germans. Churchill was alarmed: it had been his intention, he claimed, that the *Canopus* would act as 'a citadel around which all our cruisers in those waters could find absolute security'. But Battenburg should have pointed out to him that this was nonsense. *Canopus* could never get close enough to the Germans to fire her big guns. And Churchill was presumably not intending Cradock to simply skulk around the old battleship without ever attempting to engage von Spee's ships. The First Lord's equation was dangerously flawed. On the other hand there was a ship which would have added immeasurably to Cradock's strength – the *Defence* – and Cradock knew that it would be courting disaster to fight von Spee without her. Yet the Admiralty refused to make her available and as the tragedy moved to its inevitable conclusion, Churchill continued to place all his faith in HMS *Canopus* – the 'citadel' which would make all well in the South Atlantic.

When he received the message from Cradock

which revealed that he was 'going it alone' the First Lord accused the admiral of disobedience. And when the news of Cradock's destruction at the Coronel followed shortly afterwards, Churchill denounced Cradock's stupidity for fighting the Germans without the *Canopus*. In fact, Churchill's misjudgment was monumental. As one of the *Canopus'* officers later commented, if the battleship had been with Cradock when he met the Germans she 'would merely have swelled the casualty list'. As an ironic and poignant postscript to this unfortunate action, on 3 November – two days after the battle of Coronel – the Admiralty decided to reverse their previous decision to refuse Cradock the armoured cruiser *Defence* and ordered her to join him 'with all possible despatch'.

When he heard of Cradock's fate, Vice-Admiral Sir David Beatty – commanding the British battlecruisers at Rosyth – bitterly reflected on where the blame rested:

> Poor old Kit Cradock has gone at Coronel. His death and the loss of the ships and the gallant lives in them can be laid to the door of the incompetency of the Admiralty. They have broken over and over again the first principles of strategy.

Churchill was stung into replying to the criticism that the fault was his and blamed Cradock for failing to concentrate his superior forces. Yet, with Jacky Fisher replacing the feeble Battenburg as First Sea Lord, and the battlecruisers *Invincible* and *Inflexible* being ordered south to destroy von Spee, it was interesting to note how much Churchill changed his tune. His 'citadel' *Canopus* was still at Port Stanley in the Falkland Islands and her captain, H.W. Grant, was now warned 'to avoid being brought to action by a superior force' and that 'if attacked the Admiralty is confident [the] ship will in all circumstances be fought to the last'. It must have come as a shock to Grant to discover that overnight his ship had changed from being an impregnable 'citadel' to being a latter-day Sir Richard Grenville (Grenville in the *Revenge* had single-handedly fought a Spanish fleet off the Azores in 1591). At the last, Churchill, the amateur naval strategist, had remembered that he was first and foremost a politician.

> *'Underwater weapons? I call them underhand, unfair and un-English. They'll never be any use in war and I'll tell you why – I'm going to get the First Lord to announce that we intend to treat all submarines as pirate vessels in wartime. We'll hang their crews.'*
>
> ### The Comptroller of the Admiralty, 1914
>
> The British Admiralty still held to the antiquated notion that war was a kind of international sport in which the Germans should play 'by the rules' – British rules – and send their battle fleet into the North Sea to fight and be destroyed by the British battle fleet in a Trafalgar-like battle.

# THE NAVY AND THE DARDANELLES (1915)

On 31 October 1914, following the attack by the *Goeben* (see p. 32), now under the Turkish flag, on Russian ships in the Black Sea, Britain and France declared war on Turkey. Four days later an Anglo-French squadron carried out a brief ten-minute bombardment on the Dardanelles forts, to test the effects of their naval guns. Although the results were seen as encouraging, the decision to alert the Turks to British intentions has been roundly condemned. Surprise had been lost to no real purpose. The First Lord's decision to order the bombardment was called 'an act of sheer lunacy' by Admiral Bacon and an 'unforgivable error' by Admiral Jellicoe. It was not a good way to start what has been called 'the one strategic idea of the war'.

The Dardanelles Operation was undertaken as a direct response to an appeal from the Russian commander-in-chief, the Grand Duke Nicholas, to relieve

Winston Churchill's plan for a naval attack on the Dardanelles was brilliantly conceived, but the British government failed to give the operation the priority it needed in terms of men, matériel and ships.

pressure on his troops, who were under attack by the Turks in the Caucasus. Ironically, by the time the operation had been planned, the Turks had been driven back and there was no longer any need to help the Russians. But once the wheels had begun to turn the ramshackle Dardanelles operation gathered a momentum of its own. In London the First Sea Lord, Jacky Fisher, supported using pre-Dreadnought battleships to force the Dardanelles and carry the war to Constantinople, hopefully to convince Turkey to make peace. But as usual with Fisher speed was everything: 'Celerity – without it, Failure.' Unfortunately, the British commander in the Mediterranean, to whom would fall the task of implementing the plan, was of a different opinion. Vice-Admiral Sackville H. Carden said, 'I do not think the Dardanelles can be rushed, but they

might be forced by extended operations with a large number of ships.' Carden was not the man to carry out so daring a concept and should have been removed once he had revealed his reservations. It was the same story throughout the whole Gallipoli saga: the best admirals and generals must be kept in the North Sea or in France, whereas anyone would do to command ships or troops against the Turks.

On 13 January Winston Churchill revealed to the cabinet his plans for a naval attack on the Dardanelles, and the idea was welcomed by the politicians present, who had no stomach for the 'slogging match' on the Western Front. The result was that the War Council reached the decision that 'the Admiralty should prepare for a naval expedition in February to bombard and take the Gallipoli Peninsula, with Constantinople as its objective'. But how can a fleet 'take' a peninsula? The example of Admiral Duckworth's failure in 1807 (see p. 26) should have been enough to make people cautious. Without troops to occupy the ground that was won, warship commanders could do no more than sail up and down waving their fists at the enemy. The cabinet decision was a product of muddled thinking and the lack of specialist advice.

The first task for Carden's squadron was to silence the Turkish forts which lined the Dardanelles. Here, Churchill revealed an ignorance of naval affairs forgivable in a civilian with an army background, but unforgivable in a First Lord of the Admiralty with access to any number of technical experts. Inappropriately drawing his lessons from the high-angle howitzers and mortars with which the Germans had silenced the Belgian fortresses, he seemed to imagine that Carden's old battleships would be able to do the same to the Turkish forts. But the naval guns did not have the elevation required, as any naval officer should have been able to tell him. The Third Sea Lord, Admiral Tudor, did tell him that the old pre-Dreadnoughts had a maximum elevation of only 15 degrees and with that sort of flat fire they were never going to approach the accuracy or efficacy of the German Krupp and Skoda mortars. Admiral Dewar warned him,

> The fortress gunner can easily see the ship he is firing at and a great column of water marks the position of his shot, short or over. The fortress gun, on the other hand, merges into the landscape and at long ranges only betrays itself by an occasional flash . . . The sailor has the further disadvantage that the whole of his ship is vulnerable to attack, whereas only a direct hit puts his opponent out of action.

Wise words, but was Churchill listening? A further

danger – unappreciated at the time in spite of the loss of the new battleship *Audacious* – was the threat of mines. What special arrangements would the Admiralty make to clear this deadly and insidious threat? The problem was that Churchill had virtually hypnotized the politicians, who were dazzled by the presentation of the concept without examining the substance, which was very thin. Admiralty experts had expressed reservations but these had been dismissed with *hauteur*.

The German adviser to the Turks, General Liman von Sanders, would have been surprised (or perhaps not?) at the amateurishness of the British preparations. He knew that it was the mines, not the guns, that were the real defenders of the Dardanelles. The guns, in fact, were present primarily to defend the minefields and prevent the British from clearing them at their leisure. The British had got everything the wrong way round.

Meanwhile the Dardanelles Operation – the 'most brilliant strategic operation of the war' – was in the hands of an 'old woman'. Carden was a quite unsuitable choice. He had never even commanded a cruiser squadron and had been made admiral superintendent of Malta in order to 'shelve him'. Knowing this, Jacky Fisher was seriously to blame for not immediately replacing him with a younger commander with a 'bit of go in him'. Carden was a second-rater, if that was not placing him too high. Under Carden was a far more able man, Rear-Admiral de Robeck, as well as the brilliant and impulsive Commodore Roger Keyes. The French had agreed to send a squadron of old battleships, commanded by the gallant and ostentatious Admiral Guépratte.

By the beginning of March the naval operation was ready to start. Carden had eighteen battleships at his disposal, including the 'jewel' of the Grand Fleet, the new and tremendously powerful battleship *Queen Elizabeth*, which had 15-inch guns. In addition, he had the battlecruiser *Inflexible* and the two best pre-Dreadnoughts, *Agamemnon* and *Lord Nelson*. Otherwise, the rest of the ships were expendable, though their crews were clearly not. From the start Carden lacked any kind of drive. On 2 and 3 March he opened the bombardment of the outer forts with just three of his eighteen big ships. For the next three weeks he never used more than a quarter of his ships at any one time. The whole effect was desultory and must have made the Turks wonder why they had been in such awe of the Royal Navy.

On 5 March, though his initial bombardment had failed completely, Carden went on to the next stage. He ordered the suppression of the forts controlling the Narrows. For this the *Queen Elizabeth* was required to use indirect fire with aerial spotting, or with the battleship *Irresistible* inside the straits directing her. Unfortunately, nobody on board the *Queen Elizabeth* took any notice of *Irresistible*'s corrections and so no hits at all were achieved. Nor would the fleet gunnery officers accept the reports of the seaplane pilots who flew from the *Ark Royal*. Churchill later blamed the pilots but the real fault lay with the conservatism of the naval officers, who refused to believe that they needed the new technology provided by aircraft.

Carden meanwhile was under pressure from Roger Keyes to try to sweep the minefields. Keyes' plan was for the old battleship *Canopus* to knock out the Turkish searchlights and then lead seven tiny minesweepers into the minefield under cover of dark. But on the night of 10 March the whole plan went wrong because the *Canopus* just could not knock out the lights. Angrily Keyes remarked, 'We might just as well have been firing at the moon.' The next night they tried again but, according to Keyes: 'The less said about that night the better. To put it briefly, the sweepers turned tail and fled directly they were fired on . . . It did not matter if we lost all seven sweepers, there were 28 more, and the mines had got to be swept . . . we had chucked our hand in and started squealing before we had any [losses].'

As usual Churchill was getting impatient and the effect of having no ground troops was beginning to be felt. The First Lord signalled to Carden, 'Landing parties might destroy the guns of the forts, allowing sweeping operations to clear as much as possible of the minefield.' Exactly. But why mention it now when it was too late to provide the troops necessary?

Meanwhile, Carden was cracking up under the strain of command. On 16 March he broke down and had to resign his command to de Robeck, 'a good sea officer and a fine disciplinarian'. Two days later the first full-scale naval attack was launched to silence the forts at the Narrows. It was one of the decisive days of the entire war, if those taking part had but realized it. The four strongest ships, *Queen Elizabeth*, *Inflexible*, *Agamemnon* and *Lord Nelson* made up the first line abreast, followed by a further fourteen battleships, with cruisers and destroyers behind them. It was the greatest display of naval power ever seen in the Mediterranean, and it was heading for disaster. Although untroubled by the fixed defences, the battleships were peppered by mobile howitzers, though these rarely penetrated the ships' armour. By 2 pm the forts at the Narrows were virtually silenced but now everything went wrong. First the old French battleship *Bouvet* was hit in the

The sinking of the *Irresistible* by a mine during the Allied attempt to breach the Dardanelles defences in April 1915 led to the cancellation of the entire naval operation.

magazine and exploded, sinking with the loss of 640 men. Next, when de Robeck sent the trawlers in to sweep the mines, they simply turned tail and sailed out again. A few minutes later the battlecruiser *Inflexible*, victor of the battle of the Falkland Islands, was hit by a mine and took on a severe list. Before anyone could respond to this disaster, the *Irresistible* hit a mine and drifted towards the shore. These losses were so sudden that de Robeck felt obliged to call off the attack. He assumed that the Turks were floating mines down with the current. In fact, he was wrong. A tiny Turkish steamer had laid a small field of mines at right angles to the main fields and it had been this unexpected obstruction that had struck so decisively. In Keyes' highly charged words, 'It altered the whole course of history.' To add insult to injury, the *Ocean*, which was attempting to tow the *Irresistible*, also hit one of the mines and both ships were lost. With the French ships *Gaulois* and *Suffren* both seriously damaged by gunfire, it had been as bad a day for the Allies as anyone could remember. None of the guns protecting the minefields had been destroyed, nor had the mines been swept. As far as the British were concerned they were back at square one.

But the Turks did not see it this way. They had been firing at the British ships for seven hours with virtually negligible effect. Ships like the *Queen Elizabeth* were impervious to their fire and, with their own ammunition virtually exhausted, they expected to see the British push on towards Constantinople. Surely the Royal Navy could spare a few old battleships to win a war? The First Sea Lord had been prepared to lose twelve battleships to gain a passage through the Straits and was not greatly alarmed by the losses on 18 March. But in Churchill's view, de Robeck had a 'sentimental regard' for the old battleships and hated to see them wasted.

In the meantime, Roger Keyes was planning another attempt to sweep the mines, though the delay that ensued was going to allow the Turks to build up their defences. Within six weeks, according to Enver Pasha, they would have 200 Austrian Skoda howitzers in position. Volunteers to man the minesweeping trawlers had been drawn from the crews of the sunken battleships, while eight destroyers were also fitted to sweep mines. In Keyes' opinion, by 4 April, the fleet was ready for a breakthrough. But de Robeck now dropped his bombshell: in his opinion, the navy could not do the job without substantial army support. As he wrote to Churchill:

I think it will be necessary to take and occupy the Gallipoli Peninsula by land forces before it will be possible for first-rate ships, capable of dealing with the *Goeben*, to be certain of getting through.

Churchill was shocked:

Why turn and change at this fateful hour and impose upon the Army an ordeal of incalculable severity? An attack by the Army if it failed would commit us irrevocably in a way no naval attack could have done.

The eventual failures of the Dardanelles Operation and the subsequent Gallipoli campaign have been blamed on Winston Churchill. Accusations of every kind have been levelled at him, notably for interfering in naval affairs when he knew nothing of them. However, in his defence it must be said that the strategic concept on which the operation was based was clearly beyond the intellects of some of his critics. The navy, for example, came out of the whole matter badly. Ships' commanders had not shown the old virtues, embodied in men like Keyes, of making the impossible possible. The risks taken by Nelson at Aboukir Bay or Copenhagen were as great as if not greater than those facing de Robeck in the Straits. Men of the right calibre would have got the job done. The standard of leadership during the Dardanelles operation was quite deplorable and reflects badly on the 'senior service'. If the war could have been won in the east, where were Beatty or Jellicoe to win it? And where were the Dreadnoughts for which the public purse had gaped for a dozen years? These were the questions that should have been asked, not why did untrained trawler captains and fishermen – brave enough to face the fiercest of the elements – fail to sweep mines and panic at their unaccustomed exposure to gunfire? As one observer has said, 'The fishermen had been asked to do the Navy's job, and had no more succeeded than if the Navy had been sent to catch fish off Iceland.' Why had the Admiralty planned an operation without giving enough thought to the vital question of minesweeping? What Keyes tried to do in late March – too late as it proved – was what should have been done before the expedition was sent. If the mines had been swept on 18 March then the battleships, headed by the *Queen Elizabeth*, would have reached Constantinople, and against her the *Goeben,* for all her reputation, would have been no more than an *hors d'oeuvre.*

But it was easier to blame the meddler, First Lord of the Admiralty Winston Churchill – the man who conceived the only brilliant strategy of the entire war and was sacked for it.

# THE BATTLE OF THE DOGGER BANK (1915)

If the world of John Buchan's Richard Hannay may seem very far away now, in 1914 it was very real. Spies, codes and secret weapons were the stuff of intelligence work and before the war had even been under way for two months the British – fortuitously – had achieved an important intelligence victory over Germany. The capture of the German cruiser *Magdeburg* by the Russians in August had revealed an undreamed-of treasure: the German naval code books. Showing a splendid spirit of cooperation the Russians delivered this book to the British Admiralty by the hands of Captain Kredoff and Commander Smirnoff, who arrived at Scapa Flow on the British cruiser *Theseus* on 10 October 1914. Within three days the code book was in the possession of the First Lord of the Admiralty, Winston Churchill. This 'coup' was followed by an extraordinary gift from the sea: a chest of German secret documents dredged up by a British trawler off the Dutch coast. This included all that the British needed to complete their mastery of the German codes. From now on any wireless signal made by the Germans could be deciphered by naval intelligence in the famous Room 40. It was a heaven-sent opportunity, but what use would the British Admiralty make of it?

The German High Seas Fleet commander, Admiral von Ingenohl, followed a policy of attempting to trap isolated divisions of the Grand Fleet – notably Admiral Beatty's battlecruisers – in order to reduce the numerical advantage enjoyed by the British. This led to a series of 'tip-and-run' raids on the east coast of Britain, during which the German battlecruisers bombarded coastal towns in the hope that they would draw their British pursuers onto minefields or into the waiting clutches of von Ingenohl's battleships. Several times this plan nearly worked and it certainly frustrated the British public, who demanded to know 'Where was the Navy?' After one damaging raid on King's Lynn, Yarmouth and Sheringham the Queen Mother, Alexandra, demanded that Lord Fisher provide 'rockets with spikes and hooks to defend our Norfolk coast' against Zeppelins.

On 15 December 1914, thanks to Room 40, the

Admiral Beatty was regarded as a second Nelson for his
courageous and dashing approach. But at the Dogger Bank
and at Jutland he failed to make the most of his opportunity
to destroy the German battlecruisers.

Admiralty had clear advance warning that the Germans
were planning a major sortie into the North Sea. The
German battlecruisers, commanded by Admiral Hipper, were planning to bombard the coastal towns of
Scarborough, Hartlepool and Whitby, but this time the
British battlecruiser squadron under Admiral Beatty,
with the 2nd Battle Squadron of six fast Dreadnought
battleships under Vice-Admiral Warrender, were expecting them. The First Lord of the Admiralty, Winston
Churchill, could scarcely conceal his excitement, 'To
have this tremendous prize . . . actually within our
claws.' But the opportunity was lost through the
bungling of Beatty's flag lieutenant, Ralph Seymour.
At about 11.00 am the two forces were rushing towards
each other, with the Germans blithely ignorant of the
trap they were entering, but then bad weather intervened, reducing visibility to a mile. One of Beatty's
light cruiser screen, the *Southampton*, commanded by

Commodore Goodenough, sighted an enemy light
cruiser which was acting as advanced lookout for the
German battlecruisers. Two British cruisers, *Southampton* and *Birmingham*, immediately engaged the enemy
and Goodenough summoned up the *Falmouth* and
*Nottingham* to support him. But Beatty wanted the
latter two cruisers to remain in their scouting positions
as he thought Goodenough quite strong enough to deal
with the German screening cruisers. He therefore
signalled by searchlight to *Nottingham*, 'Light cruisers –
resume your position for look-out. Take station ahead
five miles.' Beatty only meant the signal to apply to the
*Nottingham* and *Falmouth*, but failed to mention them
by name. When the *Nottingham* received the signal she
passed it on to Goodenough, who assumed it applied
to all of his light cruisers. As a result he broke off action
and resumed his screening position. Hipper, warned of
the British presence by his own light cruisers, was able
to avoid the jaws of the British trap.

Beatty was furious and demanded Goodenough's
dismissal but he was blaming the wrong man. It had
been his misleading signal – easily misinterpreted – that
had led to the failure of the operation. It was not just
a 'technical error' as has been suggested, but a breakdown in communication between the commander and
Goodenough caused by an intermediary – Flag Lieutenant Seymour – who was unable to interpret his
admiral's wishes clearly enough. That Beatty knew this
in his heart of hearts is clear from a comment he later
made to a friend about Seymour: 'He lost three battles
for me.' If Beatty knew this and did nothing about it,
then the blame is his.

This 'near miss' acted as a kind of curtain raiser to the
main event, the first meeting of the rival battlecruiser
fleets at the battle of the Dogger Bank on 24 January,
1915. The formula was the same as for the earlier
abortive operation, with Beatty leading out five of his
battlecruisers from Rosyth: *Lion* (flagship), *Tiger*, *Princess Royal*, *New Zealand* and *Indomitable*. A notable
absentee was his best gunnery ship, the *Queen Mary*,
which was in dock. Her absence was to have an
important effect on the outcome of the battle. The
German battlecruisers, again under Hipper, were in the
formation *Seydlitz* (flagship), *Moltke*, *Derfflinger*, *Blücher*.
The latter, it should be noted, was more of an armoured
cruiser than a true battlecruiser and not really strong
enough to stand in the line of battle. It had been a
mistake to bring her, particularly as her maximum
speed of 23 knots determined the speed of the entire
squadron.

At full speed, 27 knots, Beatty's ships overhauled the

Germans, except for *Indomitable* which lagged rather badly. Both squadrons opened fire but in the smoke the Germans seemed to be concentrating their fire on the first ship in the British line, Beatty's *Lion*. Beatty – through Seymour – now made the first of his rather confusing signals: 'Engage the corresponding ships in the enemy's line.' He intended each of his ships to fire at their opposites: *Lion* against *Seydlitz*; *Tiger* against *Moltke*; *Princess Royal* against *Derfflinger*; *New Zealand* against *Blücher*. But there were five British ships to four German and this prompted Captain Pelly – in Beatty's words 'a little bit of the nervous excited type' – to count from the back, assuming that the *Indomitable* was to fight the *Blücher*, while everybody moved up one, leaving *Lion* with no obvious target except to join him in firing at the *Seydlitz*. The result of this error was that nobody fired at the *Moltke* at all, leaving her free to concentrate on Beatty's flagship. To make matters worse, Pelly confused his salvoes with those of the *Lion* and thought he was scoring hits. In fact, the *Tiger's* shooting was quite deplorable in spite of her being the only ship present with director firing.

Partly as a result of Pelly's error the Germans were battering the *Lion*, knocking out two of her dynamos, ripping off her armour and flooding her. So serious was this latter hit that the port engine had to be stopped, causing her to fall out of line, two miles off the fighting. In the meantime the *Indomitable* had reached the scene and was ordered by Beatty to finish off the battered *Blücher*. At this moment Beatty had a sudden bout of 'periscopitis'. He personally claimed to have seen a submarine although in fact there were none near. He signalled to his squadron to turn 8 points to starboard, making the chasing ships – *Tiger*, *Princess Royal* and *New Zealand* – cut across the wake of the German battlecruisers, now with a free run to home. It was a bad moment for Beatty. How could a submarine threatening the *Lion* have any effect on his other ships, flying after the Germans at 27 knots? But this was only the first of two errors which were to lose Beatty the chance to destroy the Germans.

As the *Lion* fell further behind, Beatty realized that he could no longer control the fighting from his flagship. But with no electricity for his searchlight or wireless he would have to signal his intentions by flag. Confusion set in. He ordered Seymour to raise 'Attack the rear of the enemy' but the signal 'Course N.E.' was still flying and Admiral Moore, now leading the squadron, read the extraordinary signal – 'Attack the rear of the enemy heading N.E.' This could only mean the crippled *Blücher*. The result was that the three British

battlecruisers called off the chase and returned to finish off the stricken German vessel, which was soon surrounded by four British Dreadnoughts, pounding her to pieces. Beatty was beside himself with anger and raised the signal 'Keep near the enemy' which did not help either, just making everyone close in to point-blank range on the wretched *Blücher*.

Beatty called up a destroyer and shifted his flag to the *Princess Royal*, before continuing the chase. But it was far too late now: the Germans had escaped, leaving the *Blücher* fighting to the last against overwhelming firepower. Suffering over 70 hits from heavy shells she finally rolled over and sank – a poor return for the golden opportunity that Beatty had missed. In fact, apart from the loss of an armoured cruiser, the Germans made one significant gain from the battle. Hipper's flagship, the *Seydlitz*, had been hit by a 13.5-inch shell from the *Lion*, which had penetrated her armour and caused a serious fire in the ammunition chambers below two of her turrets. Only the prompt action of one of her officers, who with his bare hands turned a red hot wheel to flood the magazines, prevented an explosion of the kind which occurred three times in British battlecruisers at Jutland. The methodical Germans learned from their narrow escape and introduced anti-flash arrangements into all their capital ships. The British would have to learn the hard way.

The battle of the Dogger Bank had been a clear, if qualified, British victory. The enemy had fled, leaving behind the *Blücher* to be sunk by the British at their leisure (see pp. 55 and 57). British casualties had been just 50 killed and wounded, against German losses of well over a thousand. The *Lion* had been badly damaged but so had the *Seydlitz*. However, the British were far from happy with the performance of their ships. With the slower *New Zealand* and *Indomitable* hardly in the battle to begin with, and with *Tiger* virtually non-existent through her appalling gunnery, it was left to the *Lion* and *Princess Royal* to take on three modern German battlecruisers. This was disconcerting, yet had the crack *Queen Mary* been present it is doubtful if the *Seydlitz* would have escaped, damaged as she was.

Fisher was furious and looked for scalps. He regarded the decision to break off the chase after the retreating Germans as unjustifiable whatever signals were flying. Rear-Admiral Moore in the *New Zealand* was made to take the blame for not ignoring Beatty's signals, and lost his command. As for Captain Pelly of the *Tiger*, he was, in Fisher's words, 'a poltroon' fit only to be in charge of a barracks. As Fisher burst out, 'Any fool can obey orders.' In defence of the *Tiger's* marksmanship – just one hit out of 355 shells fired – it must be observed that she was a new ship, with a poor crew made up of many deserters, and had never fired her big guns at a moving target. It seems harsh to expect her to replace the Grand Fleet's champion gunnery ship, the *Queen Mary*.

The battle had been a catalogue of errors by both sides, yet the biggest errors had been made by the British. To add to that, the shooting of the battlecruisers had been so poor that Sir John Jellicoe, commander-in-chief of the Grand Fleet, insisted that Beatty devote more attention to it. Fisher got his blood sacrifice when he sacked the gunnery officer of the *Tiger*.

---

*'Their guns are good, calibrations too close, gunlaying excellent, but the projectile no good, and I am sure we can stand a lot of it.'*

**Admiral Beatty speaking after the battle of the Dogger Bank, 1915**

This disastrous assessment of the fighting at the battle of the Dogger Bank overlooked the fact that Beatty's own flagship, the *Lion*, had almost succumbed to a flash fire in the magazine. The Germans learned of this danger when a similar thing happened aboard Hipper's flagship, the *Seydlitz*. British complacency of this kind condemned three British battlecruisers to destruction at Jutland a year later in 1916.

---

# THE BATTLE OF THE DENMARK STRAIT (1941)

The action between the *Hood* and the *Bismarck* is probably the most famous single ship encounter in naval history. Yet so much legend and romance surround the battle that it is frequently forgotten that the *Bismarck* fired just five salvoes at the great British battlecruiser, while the *Hood* spent its time firing at the heavy cruiser *Prinz Eugen* by mistake. And it was the *Prinz Eugen* that first set fire to the British flagship. In fact, so much went wrong from the British point of view during – and even before – the engagement, that what followed can only be regarded as a total mismatch, a terrible error on the part of the Admiralty which was to cost 1,400 British lives.

News that the *Bismarck* had broken out in company with the heavy cruiser *Prinz Eugen* on 21 May 1941 placed the British Admiralty in a difficult position. In the first place, they could not be certain of the German battleship's mission, whether she was aiming to attack British bases in Iceland or – more likely – to attack the Atlantic convoy routes. Equally difficult was the task of allocating British resources in sufficient strength to combat the German leviathan. No single British battleship was a match for the *Bismarck* – the *Rodney* or *Nelson* had heavier guns and could have withstood a lot of punishment, but they were slow, ungainly and unlikely to gain any advantage in a slugging-match, which the *Bismarck* could break off at her own choosing. The *King George V* was a better bet, and yet she would need considerable help, probably from the *Rodney*. Nothing else would do. The old 'R' class battleships would have been simply murdered, while the three British battlecruisers – *Hood*, *Repulse* and *Renown* – were out of their class. Even the *Hood*, which most closely resembled the *Bismarck* in size and armament, was deficient in one vital area: armour. Against the *Bismarck*'s massive and modern Wotan armour-plating, the *Hood*'s protection was ridiculously puny. One had only to remember that *Hood* had been designed as a battlecruiser, as an extension of the 'Splendid Cats' which formed the 'eyes' of the Grand Fleet in the First World War. She was fast, sleek and beautiful. She had powerful claws but she was also terribly vulnerable. As Brassey had said in 1908, the bigger the battlecruisers became the sooner someone would forget their real purpose and expect them to trade blows with a battleship. That day came – with predictable results – on 24 May 1941.

Sir Donald Tovey, commander-in-chief of the Home Fleet, tried to 'field' two possible routes for the *Bismarck*, north and south of Iceland. In the Denmark Strait, north of Iceland, he allocated the County-class cruisers *Suffolk* and *Norfolk* to shadow the German raiders if they should come that way, while between Iceland and the Faeroes the cruisers *Arethusa*, *Manchester* and *Birmingham* would keep watch. He ordered Vice-Admiral Lancelot Holland in the *Hood*, together with the new battleship *Prince of Wales*, to cover the Denmark Strait, while he with the *King George V* and the *Rodney* would cover the southern route.

Tovey had few good cards in his hand yet he should have known that Holland's group was just not strong enough to take on the *Bismarck*. The *Hood*'s defects were known to one and all. She was probably the best-loved ship in the whole navy – one of the most famous in Britain's history – yet her fame rested on factors which would not help her against a modern, state-of-the-art battleship. In her world trip between the wars she was welcomed everywhere as a work of art (see p. 55) – something more than just steel and grey paint, a living thing. The Mayor of San Francisco had been so taken with her he had said, 'We surrender our city to you; we capitulate.' Her decks never ran with the blood of her crew savaged in battle; sand and brine rarely found their way across her pristine surfaces – more the fashionable footwear of ladies at receptions and celebrations. Her gangways echoed with the sounds of excited children and her admiral's quarters with the small talk of distinguished guests at cocktail parties. The *Hood* became more than a warship; she became an ambassador of all that was best in Britain, a living symbol of the nation. But she also became less than a warship – a representative of past glories, of past patterns of warfare, with a fragile beauty that was no match for the harsh school of modern warfare. Her weakness was known and yet her complete reconstruction was put off again and again until with the outbreak of war in 1939, it was too late. In January 1941 the decision was taken to equip the battlecruiser with one of Professor Lindemann's latest gadgets, UP rocket launchers to fire parachute and cable rockets against low-flying aircraft. The rockets sprayed aerial mines in

The launching of the *Bismarck* in 1939. By 1941 the age of the battleship was over, and none of them, however strong, could long survive the threat from naval airpower. On her first foray into the Atlantic, the *Bismarck* was as certain to face destruction at the hands of British aircraft as Force Z was later to succumb to Japanese air power off Singapore (see p. 68).

the path of the aircraft. The trouble was not just that UP did not work but that it involved piling up crates of explosive warheads on deck, where they could be ignited by gunfire. The *Hood* received a battery on top of her 'B' turret, one on either side of her forward funnel and one each side of the boat deck. This all added to the ship's vulnerability, notably to falling shells fired from long range. And with deck armour of just 2.5 inches she would be fatally vulnerable to a long-range encounter with a battleship.

By 1941 the *Hood* was quite unsuited to exposure against modern battleships. Why this was forgotten at such a crucial moment is difficult to understand. In a sense *Hood* was a disaster waiting to happen. And pairing her with the *Prince of Wales* was an act of professional insanity. The *Prince of Wales* was just four months old and had experienced more than her fair share of teething troubles. In fact, she was already regarded as an unlucky ship, having run aground shortly after leaving her fitting-out at Liverpool and having had to steam to Rosyth with two of her screws lashed to her upper deck. While at Rosyth her gunners had fired their pom-poms by mistake and had injured a dockyard worker, while two of her crew had suffered nasty falls. But her main problem was with her quadruple turrets. Captain Leach had assured Tovey that his ship was fully operational, yet when it joined the *Hood* it still had civilian contractors aboard trying to get her defective guns working. She was just not up to facing a battleship like the *Bismarck* which was at the peak of fighting efficiency. Thus when Admiral Holland set out to look for the *Bismarck* it was with a totally unrealistic appreciation of his own strength. Rather than locating the German squadron and shadowing it until stronger forces were available, Holland was determined to go straight into action. This attitude was misguided and irresponsible. Nor can Tovey escape blame in not stressing the importance of shielding the *Hood* from the *Bismarck*'s fire as far as possible. If the battlecruiser possessed any virtue it was in attack; defensively she had only her speed to rely on. The *Prince of Wales* was the better defensive ship and therefore should have been prepared to take upon herself much of the German fire. This would suggest that a separate approach by the two ships acting independently would have been recommendable, inevitably dividing the German fire. But Holland apparently dismissed this option and even took the lead from the *Prince of Wales* so that he was bound to attract the first German salvoes, the very thing that *Hood* had most to fear – long-range, plunging fire onto inadequately armoured deck surfaces.

Unknown to the Germans the two British ships were closing on them at a combined speed of more than 55 miles an hour. Radio silence prevailed aboard the British vessels and there was an expectant air of excitement. Like Beatty at Jutland in 1916, Holland seemed to be driving his 'Cat' as if she was a fast car, losing his tactical senses in the excitement of the moment. He spread out his four destroyers, trying to widen his chances of locating the Germans, but sadly ensuring that none of them would be able to participate in the coming engagement. At 4.30 am on 24 May, with visibility improving, Holland ordered Captain Leach to launch the *Prince of Wales'* Walrus seaplane. True to form the plane could not take off as its fuel had been contaminated by sea water.

And then came the first sighting at 5.35 am – two warships, apparently identical in outline. It was the *Bismarck* and the *Prinz Eugen*, but which was which? Surely the battleship would be leading, or so Holland assumed, but he was wrong. The German Admiral Lutjens had, only hours before, asked the *Prinz Eugen* to take the lead, after a brief engagement with the shadowing British cruisers, *Norfolk* and *Suffolk*. Holland left himself no time for reflection and made the signal to the *Prince of Wales*, 'Enemy in sight. Am engaging.' The die was cast and neither Tovey in the *King George V* nor First Sea Lord Dudley Pound in Whitehall could do anything to stop him. For some reason, never adequately explained, the previously 'cool-headed Lancelot Holland' had become wild and impetuous in contact with the enemy. As someone who knew Holland well later wrote, 'I just can't understand the tactics of the *Hood* action.'

Holland's plan seems to have been to concentrate the fire of the two British ships on the *Bismarck*, while the two shadowing cruisers took care of the *Prinz Eugen*. He therefore signalled to Leach, 'Stand by to open fire. Target left-hand ship.' But this was a disastrous mistake. He was calling for concentrated fire at the *Prinz Eugen*, leaving the *Bismarck* free to wreak havoc with her 15-inch guns. To add to this Holland was also allowing the enemy to 'cross his T' – the aim of naval commanders throughout history – so that the Germans would be able to fire all their guns at the approaching British ships, which could only reply with their forward turrets. This was a calculated gamble to close the range and was partly inspired by the fact that *Hood*'s vertical armour was far more likely to resist the German heavy shells at short range than her horizontal armour would resist the long-range plunging shells. But the reduction of *Hood* to just four 15-inch guns and

*Prince of Wales* to six 14-inch effectively halved British firepower at the opening of the engagement. Clearly an approach separately from either beam would have been less risky. It was then that the jinx aboard the *Prince of Wales* appeared again. One of her forward turrets became inoperable and the battleship was soon reduced to just three-gun salvoes.

The gunnery officer of the *Prince of Wales* immediately noticed that the *Hood* had incorrectly identified the German ships and was firing at the *Prinz Eugen*. Thus the most powerful battleship of its time was matching its full main armament against just three of Leach's 14-inch guns. The British were soon to be punished. The first salvoes from the *Prince of Wales* were shifted to the *Bismarck* without consulting Admiral Holland, but they were woefully inaccurate – nearly a thousand yards from the target, due to the inoperability of her range-finders in heavy spray. Ironically it was the *Prinz Eugen* which struck first in this battle of the titans. She hit the *Hood* with an 8-inch shell near one of her funnels and ignited spare ammunition for her 4-inch guns and the exposed crates of UP rockets. At once a large fire broke out, not threatening to the ship, but fierce enough to illuminate the scene in the strange half-light of the northern morning.

Holland had taken a calculated risk in providing the 'T' for the Germans to cross but he may have felt that he had just got away with it. After four salvoes from the *Bismarck*, it was now time for the two British ships to turn to port and bring their rear turrets into action. At 19,000 yards he gave the order to turn just as the fifth salvo from the *Bismarck* headed towards the *Hood*. It was as if history was repeating itself. *Queen Mary*, *Indefatigable* and *Invincible* had all been exposed at Jutland to a fleet action for which they were not designed. And now the *Hood*, greatest of her breed, was to follow them. There was a stupendous explosion, then the great battlecruiser dissolved in flames, broke in half and sank. Her entire crew of 1,419 died with her, except just three men. The *Hood* was the victim of an insane mismatch which flew in the face of every lesson learned at sea since the battle of the Dogger Bank in 1915. The *Hood*'s destruction had been built into her by her architects and by her constructors, John Brown. Even as the welders and riveters fitted her armour plating in 1918 it was already inadequate.

The *Hood* had been badly handled by her impetuous commander, who seems to have given little thought to the likely consequences of matching her against the steel colossus of the *Bismarck*. Even worse than taking on the challenge, he had first reduced her firepower by

half, allowed the enemy to concentrate all their fire on her and then mistakenly fired on her escorting cruiser instead of the *Bismarck* herself. It had been a series of tragic errors of judgment. The Admiralty later spoke of the *Hood* perishing from a single 'unlucky' shell. There was no luck in it. She was bound to expect some damage in a battle with the *Bismarck* and almost any shell on her decks might have proved fatal.

The death of the *Hood* was subject to two special investigations. The fire amongst the ammunition and UP rockets – dramatic as it was – did not contribute to the death of the ship. Nor did she perish, as is so often claimed, by an explosive flash in a gun-turret penetrating a magazine. The strongest likelihood is that the fifth salvo from the *Bismarck* penetrated the deck armour near one of her turrets, igniting the 4-inch magazine and then the 15-inch magazine. It would not have been difficult for the four 15-inch German shells to pass through the 2-inch upper deck, the 3-inch main deck and finally the 2-inch lower deck, when plunging at a steep angle at long range. To prevent this, Holland had tried to shorten the range. Yet if the *Hood* was so vulnerable that her commander had to take such chances to overcome a gross deficiency in her defences, she should never have been used against so strong an opponent in the first place.

What followed was an anticlimax. Even the hunt for the *Bismarck*, one of the most exciting naval chases in history, seemed almost unimportant after *Hood*'s immolation. The loss of the flagship in such a way must have been a terrible shock for Captain Leach of the *Prince of Wales*, and he now found himself facing the full fury of the German fire. Yet in spite of the fact that her after quadruple turret jammed completely and she was hit repeatedly, the *Prince of Wales* did manage to land three hits on the *Bismarck*, one of which caused her to seep oil and ship water. Ironically, it was this hit which was finally to seal the fate of the German battleship.

The sudden death of Admiral Holland meant that the *Prince of Wales* now came under the command of Rear-Admiral Wake-Walker, in the cruiser *Norfolk*. The pressing question was, should the damaged British battleship renew the action with the *Bismarck*? Wake-Walker was clear in his own mind:

> I had seen her [the *Prince of Wales*] forced out of action after ten minutes' engagement, at the end of which her salvoes were falling short and had a very large spread indeed. As a result of the action she was short of one gun and her bridge was wrecked. She was a brand-new ship, with new turrets in which mechanical breakdowns had occurred and were to be expected, apart from the

damage, and she had had a bare minimum for working up. I had been unable to observe any hits for certain on the *Bismarck* and her shooting had given striking proof of its efficiency, To put it in a nutshell, I did not and do not consider that in her then state of efficiency the *Prince of Wales* was a match for the *Bismarck*.

Wake-Walker was clear in his mind, yet at the Admiralty in London the loss of the *Hood* seems to have caused at least two people – Pound and Churchill – to lose their heads. Pound was furious with Wake-Walker and encouraged by the deputy chief of naval operations, Tom Phillips, he tried to prod him into resuming the action. But as Wake-Walker was quite aware, to put the *Prince of Wales* back in the ring after she had thrown in the towel would be murder. Pound was relentless, trying to bully Wake-Walker into doing something he knew to be wrong. Even after the successful conclusion of the entire operation Pound had not forgiven him. On his return to Scapa Flow, Tovey was contacted by Pound with the idea that Wake-Walker and Captain Leach of the *Prince of Wales*

should be court-martialled for not re-engaging the *Bismarck*. Tovey angrily defended the actions of his subordinates even when Pound said that he would order a court-martial, and the commander-in-chief said that he was prepared to resign if necessary and act as prisoner's friend in court. Churchill then intervened and told Pound to 'leave it'.

Once the *Prince of Wales* limped out of the struggle against the *Bismarck*, the chase was taken up by more appropriate adversaries. Eventually, it was the aerial power of the Fleet Air Arm and the big guns of the Home Fleet battleships – *King George V* and *Rodney* – that finally put an end to the *Bismarck*. Even then the Admiralty had a final opportunity to demonstrate its capacity to misunderstand, misinterpret and mislead. Before the final battle took place, Tovey had indicated that the flagship *King George V* was running low on fuel. This prompted Churchill to send the following operational signal:

> We cannot visualise the situation from your signals. *Bismarck* must be sunk at all costs and if to do this it is

The *Bismarck* fires at the *Hood* in the early hours of an Arctic morning. It took her five salvoes to sink the great British battlecruiser.

necessary for *King George V* to remain on the scene she must do so even if it subsequently means towing *King George V*.

This ridiculous signal was the occasion for a good deal of laughter after the operation had come to a successful conclusion, but at the time it caused intense anger. It was so remarkably ignorant of what was possible. For an admiral to 'run out of fuel' in the battle area, leaving himself an easy prey for U-boats, was unthinkable. And to suggest that towing was an option simply meant presenting the Luftwaffe or any passing U-boat skipper with two targets instead of one. To sink the *Bismarck* was important but to lose half the Home Fleet in the process was criminal folly. The performance of the Admiralty during the *Bismarck* saga had been understandably coloured by the shock of losing the *Hood*. Yet, despite her beautiful lines, she was a symbol of bad planning. She had been a product of an old man's fancy and it was wrong for the shades of Jacky Fisher to impose themselves on a second world conflict. Against the strongest naval threat that Germany could offer Britain opposed the halt and the lame. It was a shameful failure in the higher direction of the war.

## EXERCISE 'TIGER' (1944)

In their preparations for the D-Day landings in Normandy on 6 June 1944 the Americans carried out exercises at Slapton Sands in Devon. But during one of these exercises things went so wrong that four times as many American lives were lost as were lost to enemy fire at Utah Beach on D-Day itself. For over 40 years the American authorities chose to draw a veil over the events at Slapton Sands. The series of shocking blunders, by both American and British personnel, might have damaged Anglo-American relations at a crucial stage of the war.

The American troops stationed near Torbay in Devon included many inexperienced soldiers who seemed to regard the war as one big game. Even their officers – many 'fat, grey and oldish' – failed to convince them of the dangers that lay ahead. As a result the decision was taken – by Eisenhower himself – to make exercises tougher and more realistic by using live ammunition. But no one bothered to tell the men that

their ammunition was live and the results were all too predictable. Careless and relaxed on what they thought were just exercises, the American troops were horrified to find that soldiers were dying all around them. It was against this background of tragedy and botched staff work that the early exercises, codenamed 'Duck' and 'Beaver', took place, and the date for the final exercise – 'Tiger' – drew near.

The main purpose of Exercise 'Tiger' was to embark troops in the Torbay–Plymouth area, take them to sea and then disembark them with naval and air support at Slapton Sands. But the one part of the 'real thing' that the Americans had not allowed for was the presence of an active enemy. German E-boats – fast motor-torpedo boats – were a regular threat in the area and it was routine for the Royal Navy to keep a watch on the French port of Cherbourg, from where they were known to operate. But the level of protection that was provided for Exercise 'Tiger' was hopelessly inadequate.

Exercise 'Tiger' began on the evening of 26 April, when troops embarked on their landing ships – LSTs – and headed out to sea across Lyme Bay. It was known that E-boats were operating in that area and so the Royal Navy placed an extra patrol across the bay. The first landings, by the 101st Airborne Division, passed off without incident. But the second invasion group, from the US 4th Division, was less fortunate. This second convoy suffered from just about every mishap that could have occurred. The Royal Navy had assigned as escorts for the convoy just two vessels, the corvette HMS *Azalea* and the old destroyer HMS *Scimitar*, a survivor from the First World War. These two ships would have had their work cut out to match the speed of modern E-boats in any case, but as fate would have it the *Scimitar* suffered some slight damage in a collision with an American vessel and went into dock for repairs. This blunder was to cost the lives of nearly 1,000 American servicemen.

The mistakes proliferated. Because of a typing error the American landing ships were operating on a different radio frequency from HMS *Azalea*, as well as British navy headquarters on shore. As a result, when German E-boats were spotted after midnight on 28 April only the *Azalea* got the message, and its commander – assuming that the American vessels had picked up the same message – made no effort to inform them.

The first sign of trouble was an outbreak of firing at about 1.30 am on 28 April and the American naval crews went to action stations. They were about to be attacked by a flotilla of nine German E-boats based at Cherbourg, under the command of Lieutenant Günther Rabe. Rabe could not believe his luck; in front of him was a line of American LSTs, strung out invitingly and without adequate protection. It was an opportunity of a lifetime.

What happened next is very confusing, pieced together as it has had to be from the reports of hundreds of men, under fire at sea and in pitch darkness. When the firing began most of the soldiers thought it was just another element in the 'toughening up' process that had been a feature of the build-up to D-Day. But as the torpedoes began to strike and as men were thrown into the cold and oily sea, it soon became obvious that this was the real thing. The sea was bitterly cold and many of the soldiers became unconscious from shock when they hit the water or numbed so they died from exposure.

In the space of a few minutes, just after 2 am explosions rent the night as LSTs 507, 289 and 531 were hit by torpedoes. So fast were the German vessels that no precise sighting could be made and LST 496 strafed the decks of LST 511 by mistake, killing and wounding some of the men aboard. The night was illuminated by lines of yellow, blue and white tracer, and explosions erupting all around, and red flames coursing across the sea, now thoroughly covered in oil. Inadequate training added a new horror to this dreadful night: the lifebelts actually drowned the men who tried to use them. Each soldier in the convoy had been equipped with a lifebelt which would be inflated if either of two carbon dioxide capsules were punctured. But the men had not been shown how to wear them correctly and as a result they often put them round their waists instead of under their armpits. As a result, when the men were in the water the lifebelt made them top heavy and forced their heads back under water. It was clear from bodies found later that many men had been drowned in this way.

In the darkness the LSTs were entirely on their own. But where was their escort? During this confused phase in the fighting the LSTs received no support from HMS *Azalea* at all, and the commanders did not know whether to stay together or scatter and try to make their way back to port. LST 499 radioed a distress message, to the effect that the convoy had been attacked by submarines but, although the message was received, there was no chance that help could reach them in time. Meanwhile, the Germans had returned to Cherbourg, having suffered no losses themselves and having completely wrecked their target convoy, sink-ing two LSTs and killing in the vicinity of 1,000 American soldiers.

Exercise 'Tiger' had been both a fiasco and a tragedy. But who was to blame? The hunt for scapegoats began. On the British side there was quite a case to answer. The Royal Navy had been responsible for escorting Convoy T-4 with just the *Azalea* and the *Scimitar* and to allow the latter to go into Plymouth dockyard for repairs was a terrible mistake. The Admiralty was forced to admit that the *Scimitar* was perfectly sea-worthy in the calm sea conditions which prevailed during the night of 27/28 April, and therefore should not have been allowed to forgo her duty. In any case, why had a replacement not been made available? Apparently news of *Scimitar*'s docking had not reached naval headquarters at Plymouth until 11 pm on 27 April. There had been a number of British destroyers in the vicinity that night, including HMS *Onslow* and HMS *Saladin*, but neither had been close enough to cover the convoy in the event of a German attack. In any case, the corvette *Azalea* had had instructions that she was not to engage the enemy but to 'close the coast', curious instructions in the context of what happened. Nevertheless, she was acting under the orders of American Rear-Admiral D.P. Moon, who was the operational commander for 'Tiger', and he chose not to change her orders in spite of having already received warnings of E-boat action that night. When the German attack took place the convoy was some 15 miles to the west of Portland Bill and *Azalea* confined her activity to escorting the six undamaged LSTs towards the shore, before returning to escort the damaged LST 289 along the coast to Dartmouth. By this time there was nothing that she could have done to help LSTs 507 and 531, which had both gone down.

What is inexplicable is how the operation was allowed to take place in the full knowledge that there was a serious E-boat threat in the area and that the Germans were actually at sea on the night of 27/28 April. Rear Admiral Moon interviewed the commander of HMS *Azalea*, Lieutenant Commander Geddes, the day after the disaster. Moon asked Geddes what were his reactions to seeing his fellow escort *Scimitar* leaving station and going into Plymouth for repairs. Geddes replied that he assumed that everything was in order and that some arrangement had been made by *Scimitar*'s commander for a replacement. In the event of an attack, he explained, there was very little that his corvette could have done from her position to intercept the intruders. What is inexplicable is the fact that throughout the operation there was no radio communication between *Azalea* and the LSTs because they were operating on different wavelengths. For some reason Geddes chose not to bring his own radio wavelength into conformity with the American vessels.

Moon also interviewed Lieutenant Commander Shee, the officer commanding the *Scimitar*. He asked him about the extent of the damage to his vessel and was told that the *Scimitar* had suffered a hole 'about two feet wide and two feet long . . . about 12 feet above the water line'. According to Shee this would not have even reduced his top speed in good weather. Moon asked Shee why he had not sent him a dispatch about the damage and was told, 'I didn't consider it serious enough . . . and as I was returning to Plymouth I made the signal as a routine signal to inform them of the damage.'

There was no villain, or villainy, to account for the disaster which struck Exercise 'Tiger'. It was human frailty – the small errors of many people – which combined to make simple mistakes appalling in their consequences. Moon reported his findings to Admiral Leatham at Plymouth and these were passed on to the naval commander of the Western Task Force, Admiral Kirk. But there was no remedy for the fact that 946 American lives had been lost in an unnecessary disaster.

While one group of military men was trying to uncover the reasons for the 'Tiger' fiasco, another group was charged with the opposite task: to cover up as far as humanly possible this botched example of Anglo-American cooperation. It was difficult for anyone to look positively on the events of 27/28 April. So poor had combined operations been between the British and the Americans that if the news had broken that nearly 1,000 American soldiers had been drowned in a fiasco, Anglo-American relations could have been harmed on the brink of the most important Allied operation of the war. Details of 'Tiger' had to be kept hidden – the dead buried secretly, the wounded whisked away to Wales beyond any possibility of them talking to their fellow GIs.

# THE BATTLE OF LEYTE GULF (1944)

It may seem incredible to reduce a battle as vast and as complex as Leyte Gulf to a study of the actions of two commanders – one American and one Japanese – yet each was responsible for errors which might have affected not just the outcome of a single battle but the progress of the entire war in the Pacific. On the American side the aptly named 'Bull' Halsey saw the matador's cloak being brandished by Admiral Ozawa and charged at it without a thought for his orders or for the potentially dangerous situation he was leaving behind him. For the Japanese, Admiral Kurita, suffering from dengue fever and the after-effects of being rescued from the sea, found himself in the gap left by Halsey's charge north, with an American landing force entirely at his mercy. In the end, Halsey's blunder was not punished, because Kurita failed to take advantage of it. The Japanese lost the battle and most of their remaining naval strength. Leyte Gulf had been a saga of blunders and the Japanese suffered by making more of them than the Americans.

By 1944, as defeat in the Pacific War came closer, the Japanese began to retreat into a world of make-believe, a mood which seemed to affect everyone from the emperor down. The Japanese could not face the possibility that the Americans might penetrate what they considered the 'essential sea area' around Japan and so they simply tried to wish the Americans away. Perhaps another *Kamikaze* wind would save them as it had in the 13th century by dispersing the great fleet of Mongol ruler Kublai Khan. This flight from reality meant that the Japanese propaganda services lost all self-control and continually boasted of spectacular victories and enormous American losses. This was all very well to maintain public morale but if the army and navy leaders began to believe their own lies then the country was doomed. To an extent this is what happened. In the Formosa battles, prior to Leyte Gulf, it was said that the Imperial Navy had destroyed '60 per cent of America's effective naval strength', sinking over 500,000 tons of shipping and killing an estimated 26,000 American naval personnel. Emperor Hirohito joined in the fun by announcing that 53 US ships had been sunk, including sixteen aircraft carriers. Day by day the total increased. Soon the Japanese 'victory' off Formosa was claimed to be as great and crushing as Admiral Togo's victory over the Russians at Tsushima in 1905. But none of this was true. Admiral Halsey's 3rd Fleet had suffered damage to just one carrier and two cruisers, with no sinkings at all.

Even senior Japanese planners were subject to wild swings of emotion, from near hysteria at the 'destruction of Halsey's fleet' to deep depression when they took a more objective view of America's progress

American Admiral 'Bull' Halsey allowed himself to be lured away from the landing areas at Leyte Gulf by Admiral Ozawa. Only the incompetence of the Japanese Vice-Admiral Kurita prevented a major American defeat.

towards the home islands of Japan. At such times her leaders knew that should the Americans sever communications between Japan and her southern conquests, by retaking the Philippines, then the war would be lost. With this in mind the plan entitled *Sho I* was prepared. *Sho I* was little short of a *kamikaze* action by the entire Japanese navy. Accepting the probability of defeat and the destruction of her fleet, Japan's commander-in-chief, Admiral Toyoda, hoped to delay a successful American invasion of the Philippines by up to a year, during which time it might be possible for Japan to rebuild her shattered economy. But he was not optimistic of its success. His orders to Admiral Kurita were simple: 'Hit the American transports, break up the invasion, and sink as many ships as you can.' To give Kurita time and space to act, Admiral Ozawa – possibly Japan's most able commander – was given the near-suicidal job of luring Halsey away from Leyte; few of his ships were expected to survive. This kind of fatalism – with its willingness to waste ships and their commanders – was a far cry from the Western way of warfare.

The *Sho* plan needed a lot of luck and the advantage of surprise. But America's knowledge of Japanese codes and her domination of the skies meant *Sho I* had no chance of achieving anything significant without the Americans knowing about it. Intercepted reports enabled Admiral Nimitz at Honolulu to counter any Japanese manoeuvre. In any case, *Sho I* was far too complex, involving four separate task forces cooperating over thousands of miles of ocean, in the face of enemy air superiority. There were too many loose ends which might, and did, unravel.

The main Japanese strike force of five battleships commanded by Vice-Admiral Kurita left North Borneo on 22 October to strike the invasion beaches at Leyte from the north, supported by Vice-Admiral Nishimura's Task Force C and Vice-Admiral Shima's small Task Force D, which sailed from the Inland Sea of Japan. Shima's job was to pass through the Suriago Strait between Leyte and Mindanao and catch Admiral Kincaid's 7th Fleet in a pincers movement. Knowing that Kincaid would be supported by Halsey's 3rd Fleet the Japanese planned to lure Halsey away to the north by sending Vice-Admiral Ozawa with one heavy carrier, three light carriers and two hybrid battleship/carriers as a decoy or bait for the American 3rd Fleet. If everything went according to plan – a big 'if' – and if Halsey took the 'bait', then Kurita and Nishimura ought to have the opportunity to mop up the invasion fleet at Leyte.

The Americans had ensured command of the skies during the invasion of Leyte so that when MacArthur's landings began on 20 October they were untroubled by Japanese planes. By midnight on that day 132,000 men were ashore with 200,000 tons of supplies and equipment. Already *Sho I* was too late to catch the loaded transports and troop ships before they disgorged their cargoes on the beaches. But the invasion sites were still vulnerable and would provide tempting targets for Kurita, with nearly 500 landing craft and hundreds of transports and supply vessels of all kinds crammed together on the beaches.

On 23 October, Kurita's fleet was sighted by two American submarines near Palwan island. Kurita's anti-submarine precautions were so negligent at this stage that the Americans were able to punish him for it, torpedoing three cruisers – including Kurita's flagship, *Atago*. Being dumped into the sea while suffering from dengue fever was not a pleasant experience for a man of Kurita's age. Rescued by a destroyer and taken to *Yamato* to recover, he must have felt that he had a personal score now to settle with the Americans. But how much the shock of his experiences affected his later performance we can only guess.

The next morning – on entering the Sibuyan Sea – Kurita's task force came under massed air attack. His new flagship, *Yamato,* was shaken by two bomb hits and took aboard 2,000 tons of water, causing her to list temporarily. With the skies filled with American planes Kurita must have wondered where his air cover was. Toyoda had ordered the air commander on Luzon to use all his aircraft to protect Kurita's fleet but instead he had launched his 200 land-based planes against Halsey's American carriers. Although he managed to sink the light carrier *Princeton* Toyoda paid a heavy price by losing virtually his whole air fleet, leaving Kurita unprotected. With only their anti-aircraft guns available, Kurita's ships suffered hits from the swarms of American planes. The battleship *Musashi* – previously considered unsinkable – was struck by nineteen torpedoes and seventeen bombs and sank with almost all her crew. Yet as night fell Kurita, though crippled, still had a powerful force of four battleships, six heavy cruisers, two light cruisers and ten destroyers. The Japanese admiral may have been feeling depressed, but he was about to have two pieces of amazing luck. Pilots the world over are optimistic. From hundreds or even thousands of feet – and under constant anti-aircraft fire – it is difficult to be certain of the damage inflicted on ships, zig-zagging across a smoke-shrouded ocean. Near misses can seem to be fatal hits. When the reports

American light cruisers under fire from Admiral Kurita's battleships at Leyte Gulf, Kurita broke off his action without inflicting severe casualties on the Americans.

of the air attacks on Kurita reached Halsey they convinced him that the Japanese commander had suffered such heavy losses that he was no longer a threat. But Halsey was wrong: Kurita's fleet was mostly intact and was still heading for San Bernardino Strait. At the same time, Halsey received the first report of Ozawa's fleet approaching from the north.

Halsey must have known that Ozawa's force was only a decoy; just a part of the immense US force would have been enough to drive Ozawa away. Yet, in the full knowledge that the Japanese wanted him to chase Ozawa with his whole fleet, and without absolute certainty that Kurita no longer posed a threat to the landings at Leyte, Halsey ordered his entire fleet to turn north. His battleship commander, Vice-Admiral Willis Lee, did suggest that he be allowed to remain behind at San Bernardino in case Kurita did arrive. But Halsey said 'No', he wanted his battleships with him. 'Bull' Halsey was looking for the 'big kill' and he knew that Ozawa presented him with the chance of a lifetime. If he waited for Kurita – who might never come – he would lose his chance of destroying Ozawa. Halsey now allowed his aggression to get the better of him and made a decision which could have led to the worst American defeat of the war. To make matters worse he did not even inform Admiral Kincaid that he was about to abandon him, nor did he tell Nimitz. Messages sent

to Pearl Harbor were titled 'for information' as if there was nothing that the commander-in-chief need know or could do about it if he did know. Kincaid only learned of what Halsey was doing by monitoring 3rd Fleet's communications. In this way Kincaid made a misleading discovery – the existence of a phantom 'Task Force 34'.

When Lee discussed with Halsey the possibility of his remaining behind in case Kurita should break though, Halsey had tinkered with the idea of creating a task force of battleships and carriers, to be known as Task Force 34. This was what Kincaid had heard and it misled him into thinking that Halsey had already set it up to protect Kincaid's ships while he went north to pursue Ozawa. Nimitz, not surprisingly, had reached the same conclusion and so neither he nor Kincaid was unduly worried. After all, nobody in their right mind would simply sail off in pursuit of a decoy, leaving the invasion beaches open to enemy attack. Or would they?

Meanwhile, Kurita had emerged unscathed from the San Bernardino Strait and found that the expected American covering force had gone. Instead, as he hurried south towards the unprotected invasion beaches he ran into resistance from an unexpected and unlikely source. Rear-Admiral Thomas Sprague with eighteen escort carriers – affectionately called 'Woolworth carriers' – now found himself between Kurita and the success of his mission. At 6.46 am an escort carrier from Sprague's group – nicknamed Taffy 3 – made a sighting of hostile ships approaching from the north-west. Sprague was astonished. Where was Halsey? How had the Japanese slipped past him? Kurita made his first sighting at about the same time and soon realized that he had a group of unprotected carriers at his mercy. Sprague was now facing four Japanese battleships, including the world's biggest, *Yamato*, with nine 18-inch guns. He did what he could by getting his planes (Hellcats, Wildcats and Avengers) into the air and soon had the Japanese zigzagging to avoid the American torpedo attacks. But without dive bombers Sprague could do little more than delay the inevitable. He sent out SOS requests to Halsey, but the 'Bull' was by now some 300 miles away.

Yet now that he had his prey within his grasp Kurita seemed to lose his head. Perhaps the stress of the campaign so far – his own rescue from the sea, his fever, the loss of the *Musashi* – caught up with him. His handling of his ships in the next few hours was atrocious. Instead of forming a battle line for his heavy ships he issued the crazy order 'General attack', which sent every Japanese ship off on its own, pursuing its own target and out of his control. Faced with total extinction Sprague sent his destroyers into action, firing torpedoes at the approaching behemoth – Kurita's *Yamato* – until the shells from the battleships slammed into the destroyers 'like a puppy dog being smacked by a truck'. The American destroyer captains displayed great gallantry in the face of overwhelming odds. First the *Johnston* was sunk by 14-inch shells and then the *Hoel* went down in a welter of over 40 heavy shells. The escort carrier *Gambier Bay* was sunk by four Japanese cruisers but then two of these 'assassins' were in turn sent to the bottom by the carrier's planes.

Uncertainty seemed to plague Kurita's every move. He was torn between destroying the carriers or turning towards the invasion beaches at Leyte. Panic seems to have been close to the surface in the Japanese ships that day. Reports of false air attacks were common and information came in that Halsey's fleet had been sighted heading south – another false alarm. At 12.36, torn between irreconcilable targets, Kurita just seemed to give up, and headed back towards San Bernardino Straits and safety. It had been a deplorable display by the Japanese commander. As one American wit observed from the bridge of an escort carrier, 'Goddammit, boys, they're getting away.'

Far to the north Halsey had made contact with Ozawa and was preparing to destroy the decoy. There was little the Japanese admiral could do, as most of his planes had been lost already. For ten hours Halsey's planes pounded Ozawa's ships, sinking all four carriers – *Zuikaku*, *Chitose*, *Chiyoda* and *Zuiho* – though failing to finish the hybrid battleship-carriers, *Ise* and *Hyuga*. But if Halsey was enjoying this one-sided fight, he was not amused to receive the startling news that Kurita had slipped in behind him and was loose in the vicinity of Leyte island. Kincaid's calls for assistance forced Halsey to detach a carrier group – even though these ships could not reach Kincaid at best for four hours! At 10.00 a message from Nimitz arrived which must have spoiled Halsey's day. The commander-in-chief was intrigued to know where Task Force 34 was, if there was such a force. Nimitz ordered Halsey to detach Lee and his six battleships to return to the aid of Kincaid. Halsey felt torn. He was hoping still to finish off the hybrid battleships which was why he had brought Lee in the first place. Yet the disgrace that would fall on his head if a disaster occurred to 7th Fleet or MacArthur's invasion force would far outweigh the glory of two more Japanese 'scalps'. Even so, it took Halsey a full hour to decide that his nation's interests came before his own. After all, he claimed, it was too late for Lee to reach Kincaid to be of much assistance. Kurita must have succeeded or failed by now, and if the latter the credit would be Kincaid's. Halsey was unrepentant and said later that he had regretted the decision to detach Lee as it enabled the *Ise* and *Hyuga* to escape.

Halsey was a fighting admiral and it is not difficult to guess how he felt at this moment. Yet his superior officer, Admiral Nimitz, had given him an order and he should have obeyed it at once. Halsey was in danger of playing 'war games' with the lives of thousands of his compatriots who looked to him for protection, as well as the national interest. His behaviour was more in keeping with the stereotyped view that the Japanese had of Americans – of ill-disciplined and 'gung-ho' gun-slingers, devoid of the martial virtues valued by military nations such as the Germans and Japanese. As Samuel Morrison has pointed out, had Halsey detached Lee when he was first informed of Kurita's presence, and had Lee sailed south at full speed, he would have been able to bring Kurita to battle during the night of 25/26 October when, with the advantage of his radar-guided guns, he could have achieved a total victory over the main Japanese task force. It is doubtful if Nimitz ever fully forgave Halsey's petulant and selfish display.